Healing is healing..

and Healing is Possible ♡

Kim Barthel

Conversations With a Rattlesnake

Library and Archives Canada Cataloguing in Publication

Fleury, Theo, 1968-, author
    Conversations with a rattlesnake : raw and honest reflections on healing
and trauma / Theo Fleury, Kim Barthel.

Includes bibliographical references.
Issued in print and electronic formats.
ISBN 978-1-77141-071-7 (bound).--ISBN 978-1-77141-077-9 (html)

    1. Fleury, Theo 1968- --Mental health. 2. Psychic trauma. 3. Child
abuse. 4. Substance abuse. 5. Adult child sexual abuse victims--Canada--
Biography. 6. Hockey players--Canada--Biography. I. Barthel, Kim,
1962-, author II. Title.

GV848.5.F56A3 2014   796.962092   C2014-905885-3
                                                     C2014-905886-1

Conversations With a Rattlesnake

Raw and Honest Reflections on Healing and Trauma

Theo Fleury and Kim Barthel

Book Cover Design: Marla Thompson
Typeset: Greg Salisbury
Portrait Photographers: Hélène Cyr Photography;
Perry Thompson Photography
Editorial Team: Julie Salisbury, Nina Shoroplova, and Bob Spensley

DISCLAIMER: This book is a guide intended to offer information on how to heal from trauma. It is not intended in any way to replace other professional health care or mental health advice, but to support it. Readers of this publication agree that neither the authors nor their publisher will be held responsible or liable for damages that may be alleged or result directly or indirectly from the reading of this publication.

MIX
Paper from
responsible sources
FSC® C016245

Printed in Canada

Dedication

This book is dedicated to those who have found their voices, to those who are still searching for their courage, and to those who are in helping roles, listening with compassion.

We all carry some level of pain, and, to varying degrees, we are all trying to make a difference in other people's lives.

So this book is dedicated to everyone. We're all in this together.

Lyrics from the song "Walk With Thousands" by Theo Fleury and Phil Deschambault.

Gettin' rid of all our shame
Let's lift our heads and never bow them again
Courage through and through

We are no longer just a face in the crowd
We've found our voice and will sing it loud
Change and victory too

Let's stick our neck out
Let's make a lot of noise
Let them hear us shout so they can't avoid

Let them understand
All we wanna do
Is let the daylight in
So let the daylight in

Our greatest wish for this book is that it serves as an empowerment tool for people looking to have healing conversations of their own.

Here's your opportunity to join the greatest team in the history of the world—the one that is bringing awareness to the subject of relationship trauma.

Theo and Kim

Testimonials

"Though sexual abuse & the trauma it creates are the impetuses behind these healing conversations, Theo's candidness & Kim's attunement & subsequent responses reveal truths helpful to all who have ever faced suffering in their lives ... in other words, all of us. Rattlesnake venom, when harvested with skillful hands, makes for powerful medicine. This book is powerful medicine."
Dorion Dellabough, Psychotherapist

"What my dad's doing with Kim to help people makes me really proud. Maybe I should tell him."
Beaux Fleury, Theo's seventeen-year-old son

"Mindful relationships are at the core of what we humans desperately need to learn. As a teacher of therapists, Kim explains complex concepts with grace and compassion, enabling the reader to tune into the intricacies of healing and its role in the evolution of the human spirit. As the conversation between Kim & Theo ensues, it unravels the honest and safe connection between two individuals who have set out on a mission to give people back to themselves. The science of connection couldn't be explained better than this as the conversation takes the reader through the mind boggling and humbling brain phenomena of human relationships. A must-read for everyone in the business of helping others grow and learn, which practically is each and every one of us."
Manoj Pathnapuram, Speech and Language Pathologist and Trainer in Singapore

"Kim and Theo achieve a depth to their conversation that removes the labels of victim, offender, addict, and discovers an understanding of the human condition that must be heard by criminal justice, advocacy groups, and anyone struggling to heal."
Dr. Don Castaldi, Forensic Psychologist

"I could not put this book down! I felt like I was enjoying a lively conversation with Theo and Kim. This book is a Canadian 'Eat, Pray, Love,' complete with stories of hockey and Tim Hortons, woven together with honesty, compassion, and solid science. Theo and Kim explain the complex science behind attachment theory, maternal depression, infant mental health, and brain development in a riveting storytelling style. They share information that every parent and future parent on earth should know. We all need to understand the profound negative effects of early life trauma on later life. You might discover you need this book to start your own healing. Theo and Kim have given us a gift, explaining science and helping approaches through storytelling and conversation and showing how we can grow and heal together."
Dr. Nicole Letourneau, RN, PhD, FCAHS

"*Conversations With a Rattlesnake* is a tour de force. With Kim Barthel's incredible experience, vast therapeutic knowledge, and Sherlock Holmes-esque intuition, she's able to assess, understand, and explain complex biopsychosocial dynamics in moments. For this level of personal discussion with Theo Fleury to be made public—it's a game changer."
Tara Bishop, Executive Director of Footholds Therapy Center

"Kim and Theo's conversation provides the reader with a unique opportunity to see the inner workings of a therapeutic relationship. Whether you are a therapist, in therapy, or a fan of Theo's, this book is a must-read. The vulnerability and courage shown by each author allow the reader to see the magic of a safe relationship. I am joining the conversation!"
Eugene Hayduk, Social Worker, BSW, RSW

"When I first met Theo in a smoky Calgary bar in 2004, he was a disgraced and drunk yet endearing hockey player with a chip on his shoulder. Ten years later, Theoren is a proud, sophisticated, and caring man, with nothing to prove and love to give. Until Theoren truly got sober and addressed his demons, he lived every day of his life with something to prove; that he was big enough, that he was smart enough, that he was tough enough, that he could drink more, use more, bed more, laugh more, just be more and better than the guy across from him. Over the years, he has peeled the onion of his emotions and root causes, enabling Theoren to demonstrate a gentle disposition of confidence and understanding. His capacity to care for and understand his friends, family, and strangers has allowed him to feel compassion for others without compromising his masculinity. Theoren Fleury listens when you speak to him and his responses are not canned or opportunities for him to be bigger, better, funnier, or brasher. He responds according to the true direction of his heart and his mind, both of which are of infinite proportions. Theoren Fleury was a magnificent and world-class hockey player, but in witnessing his personal growth, it is an understatement to suggest that he is an even more impressive man than he ever was a hockey player. Theoren's spiritual growth is a map and model for those who want to discover who they truly are … as people, not what the world expects them to be. The transformation is nearly complete and I couldn't be more proud of him."
Steve Parsons, Theo's best friend

"*Conversations With a Rattlesnake* is a deeply touching and insightful dialogue between two genuine (authentic) human beings. As the process unfolds, each learns and receives therapeutic gifts from the other. As a therapist, I treasure the mutually honest exchange between Kim and Theo. It's encouraging to witness them walking the walk through these important topics, but it's also fun to watch their playfulness; never a dull moment!"
Marie McKenzie, Occupational Therapist, Physiotherapist, and Neurotoxicology Researcher

"Theo and Kim inspire us to believe that abuse is not our fault, that we can survive, and that we can teach the world how to protect children. This epidemic can be stopped."
Irmie Nickel, MA, BOT, OT, Executive Director, Aulneau Renewal Centre

Acknowledgements

The process for writing this book was a little uncommon. The content was compiled from a series of conversations that occurred between the two of us over two years, but it's structured as if we are having the discussion in one session today. Some of it is word-for-word from what was recorded at the time, and some of it is melded together from scribbled notes and memories from a thousand-plus conversations along the way.

What was pretty incredible about pulling this book together is that everyone who directly helped out really did get personally involved. Everyone got triggered in their own ways—not just Theo by any stretch—and a heck of a lot of personal growth occurred for a whole series of now-interconnected friends. Just from having basic conversations around these not-often-talked-about concepts, our close friends were naturally hooked, and became highly motivated themselves to be more self-aware. As a long series of excellent conversations ensued, our support networks naturally grew, and continue to expand!

The people supporting the mission of creating *Conversations With a Rattlesnake* are many; thank you, all. But the ones we both want to acknowledge especially—whether their thoughts, energy, and commitment were subtle or overt—are Julie Salisbury our publisher; Nina Shoroplova our editor; the staff at Influence Publishing; and a whole slew of our friends, family, and colleagues: Dawn, Amber and Robert in Calgary, Alberta; Colin and Dave in Victoria, British Columbia; Jason and Erika in Copenhagen; Manoj in Singapore; Tara and Don in Nanaimo, British Columbia; Irmie and Eugene in Winnipeg, Manitoba; and Miss Marie in Atlanta, Georgia.

We would also like to extend our heartfelt gratitude to Bob Spensley. Without his own passion for helping relationships to flourish, and his personal commitment to our collective cause, this book might just be a series of really cool ideas, still waiting to be shared in print.

And, of course, thank you to Josh, Lista, Beaux, Tatym, and Skylah whose understanding of the immensity of this subject allowed them to have amazing patience throughout.

Lastly, thanks to the literally thousands of people we've met and talked with about trauma and healing (and everything in between). You are our inspiration.

Theo and Kim

Contents

Foreword

I have a new hero, Don Cherry told a nationwide TV audience back in the 1990s. "His name is Theoren Fleury." The iconic hockey commentator was lauding the future Calgary Flames captain's on-ice achievements as the smallest yet one of the most dynamic, spontaneously inventive, aggressive, and talented players in the National Hockey League. With this book, Fleury, Stanley Cup winner and Olympic gold medalist, has exceeded anything he ever accomplished in the rink. *Conversations With a Rattlesnake*, written—or, one should say, spoken—with his therapist and friend Kim Barthel, documents and embodies nothing less than Theo Fleury's co-creation of himself as a conscious human being.

His story is well-known. Sexually abused for years by his junior hockey coach, Theo scaled the heights of NHL stardom, all the while living in a haze of addictions from alcohol to cocaine, from sex and food to gambling. Let go by the Calgary team he had led with flare, guts, and ability, and playing for seven million dollars a year in New York, he later confessed, "When I left the rink, I didn't know who I was." Glen Sather, his manager in the Big Apple, told him he would no longer have Fleury on the team even if he worked for free. One day, exhausted from drugs and desperate living, Fleury fell flat on his face on the ice.

His public acknowledgement of his abuse and the trial of his tormentor may be seen as the triumphant end of a painful journey but, as *Conversations With a Rattlesnake* reveals, it proved to be only another stage. His calvary was far from over. He had a lifetime of self-loathing, rage, and shame to resolve and, too, the guilt to expiate for the hurt he had caused others, including the mothers of three of his children and his children themselves. "I don't even know how many people's feelings I may have hurt," he confesses, a rueful admission familiar to all of us who have been caught up in cycles of addiction and narcissism.

In this book we get to travel with not the public Fleury, but the private one. The journey, it has been pointed out, is the longest one we ever embark on: the distance from our heart to our head. What makes that short trip such an agonizing marathon for many of us is, as Fleury and Barthel so engagingly show, childhood suffering and the defenses we erect to avoid feeling the pain. "The pain, the pain, the pain," Theo once said, calling cocaine and vodka his "magic elixir."

"You don't have any tools; you don't have any patience or ability to tolerate the discomfort of feeling anything," he recalls. Or, as my own mantra has it, "The first question is, always, not why the addiction, but why the pain."

Conversations With a Rattlesnake earns its subtitle, *Raw and Honest Reflections on Healing and Trauma*. Based partly on workshops Fleury and Barthel have conducted together, the book is in the form of an intentional conversation between two people exploring the themes of suffering and shame, healing and redemption. Although at times it feels they are a little too self-consciously conducting a seminar, as if with one eye to an unseen audience, Fleury and Barthel achieve their aim of sharing not only what they have learned, but also how they have learned it. What they teach goes beyond Fleury's personal transformation. Illuminated by Kim Barthel's insights and research and by Theo's own humorously self-deprecating and keen awareness, the discussion ranges over the field of trauma and recovery, therapy and human development. For professional and layperson alike their exchange is refreshing and interesting throughout.

The greatest loss incurred by childhood trauma is the loss of what we may call positive self-regard, the ability to view oneself clearly and with empathy. When he looks at himself, the traumatized person sees someone unworthy, weak, and even deserving of his suffering. Not like other human beings. Alone.

In the case of all abused children, that isolation precedes the abuse and is, in fact, what enables it to happen. Theo's coach could recognize in the boy the vulnerability that comes from the absence of supportive adult relationships in the family of origin. Theo wanted more than the attainment of his major league ambitions—he needed someone's approval; as much as he hated the acts forced upon him, he longed to be wanted. We all substitute the wanting of others when we cannot want ourselves and many, like young Theo, pay a heavy price. And, Theo, as is the case with most abused children, had no one to tell.

The essential teaching is how Kim attends to Theo as no one ever did in his childhood, with what she calls "relentless positivity." Theo, in turn, hones his capacity to attend to himself with compassion and curiosity. She refuses to confuse him with his thoughts, behaviours, emotional reactions, or with his aggression.

"Your face and your story were a tragic but not uncommon example of the way the layers of pain fold upon each other within our lives' stories. I think your veil of rage was a form of protection for you, a strategy you initially used to keep others away from your vulnerability," she tells him. Hockey and toughness may have been Fleury's refuge and salvation, but all his success served also to help him hide from himself. "The days of being only tough are over," he says, with relief.

Prompted by Kim's gentle guidance, it is with obvious delight that Theo keeps discovering that he is not alone with his dysfunctional patterns or his anguish. It is a revelation to him when, liberated by his own example, others share publicly not only what was perpetrated upon them but, on occasion, even that they themselves have perpetrated. He learns, as we learn with him reading this book, that we all share the same boat. "Hurt people hurt people," our conversationalists are fond of quoting.

For all his past suffering and ongoing challenges, Fleury refuses to see himself as a victim. "A victim is stuck," is among his many pithy observations. "I think of the word 'victim' as shaming. I'm sick of feeling ashamed and I have no tolerance for it. It holds people back."

Nor does he pretend to be beyond his problems. "I'm only a thousand times better than when I was thinking of killing myself," he reports with mock arrogance. "I know it's ongoing work over a lifetime and never complete." Or, as Barthel says, "It's impossible to erase the memory of trauma; it's how you deal with it that matters." And that is the most vivid lesson in this book—intimate conversation, mutual confessional, rich therapeutic manual, primer on childhood—it is the present that matters. We cannot change the past but, with insight, courage, and self-empathy we can take responsibility for the present.

And the co-creation of Theoren Fleury's newly emerged consciousness of which he is determined to make a gift to the world? This is where *Conversations With a Rattlesnake* reaches its spiritual core. Eventually we all have to come in from the dreadful isolation and cold that trauma and loss and the arising of the egoic, narcissistic mind impose on us. None of us can do it by ourselves. Here, Kim Barthel is Theo's able collaborator; he acknowledges many others along the way from previous therapists to friends, strangers, and AA-sponsors. And ultimately, a power greater than any of us, the God of his understanding, which others may call Reality or Truth. "I used to regulate myself with my addictions or by playing hockey," he says, "but now I think I need relationship with a universal being to help me with this." He finds solace and strength in traditional First Nations teachings, practices, and rituals.

Looking back at his adolescence Fleury has at times wistfully imagined that the person he calls Big Theo could have come and, taking Little Theo by the hand, led him out of the dark terror of abuse into the protective light. With this book, Big Theo has shown up.

Gabor Maté, MD

Author, *In The Realm of Hungry Ghosts: Close Encounters With Addiction*

Prologue

Theo Fleury is a former NHL hockey player who is a living legend both on and off the ice. His Stanley Cup, Olympic gold, and outstanding sense of teamwork were contradicted by erratic behaviour, wild substance abuse, and broken relationships. His disclosure of childhood sexual abuse by his coach, brought to light in *Playing With Fire*, propelled him to the spotlight of advocacy with the intention of waking people up to the reality that sexual abuse happens and it causes a lot of pain.[i]

In *Conversations With a Rattlesnake*, Theo Fleury and renowned therapist Kim Barthel team up and delve into the core of Theo's on-going personal issues in a refreshingly informed and compassionate way. They are honest and clear about the dynamics within his trauma and recovery, so that others can learn from them. For these powerful and sensitive topics, which affect millions of people from all walks of life, a textbook just wouldn't cut it. So that more readers are able to digest and connect with the information, it's told as a series of engaging conversations, like you'd have with your most trusted friend over the kitchen table, only this friend is a much-loved therapist who uses everyday language and isn't perfect herself. The stories essentially use Theo's life as a candid example, but you are invited to be present and mindful about your own journey as you get triggered along the way. Their conversations are held in the spirit of emotional safety—a key to maintaining trust in any relationship—and are designed to be helpful to you for your own reflections.

What does a rattlesnake have to do with Theo? Snakes are often thought of as symbols of our inner demons and our potential to do wicked things to ourselves and others. But the snake is also a symbol of transformation and initiation. What other animal can literally shed its skin and start afresh, again and again?

Theo-as-rattlesnake is appropriate to consider in another way too.

It was in a desert near Santa Fe, New Mexico—where rattlesnakes live—where Theo threw away the suicidal handgun that had been in his mouth and rattling away against his teeth. Out of long-carried pain and self-inflicted loneliness, masked by cocaine and vodka, he'd been as close that day as anyone comes to taking his own life. Instead, he chose to live. Through this book, ten years after having hit rock bottom, Theo is not only actively getting the help he needs, he is doing everything he can to share his learning with others who can relate to surviving childhood trauma.

The term "Conversations With a Rattlesnake" alludes to the idea of talking in a safe therapeutic context with someone who cares about you, while consciously reflecting on everything (shadow side included) that makes you who you are and who you want to be. If you could really shed your skin, what would you choose next for yourself?

This is Theo's opportunity and process. And all of ours.

If a rattler in this very moment is choosing to slither over the gun that Theo tossed away out in that lonely desert … well, maybe there's a line in a country song yet to be sung about that. Life *absolutely* goes on.

1

Unexpected Allies

"There aren't no straight lines on my highway."
Theo Fleury and The Death Valley Rebels,
from "As the Story Goes"ⁱⁱ

I can't remember the first time I told my abuse story. I was probably fuckin' wasted. That says a lot about how I coped really. I needed to be piss drunk to share my feelings. Being drunk was the only time it was safe to "feel." Nobody suspected that I was holdin' onto secrets. I had set myself up to look really good on the outside. Lookin' like I had it all, money, fame ... but on the inside, I was basically dying. You're only as sick as your secrets, as the AA folks know well.ⁱⁱⁱ Man, I was sick.

Just a few years ago, I couldn't even sit in a chair for ten minutes without feeling like I was jumping out of my skin. Even after *Playing With Fire* came out, I was constantly anxious, in some ways even more so. What had kept my secrets in place all those years was caring too much about what others thought of me. I didn't want to look weak. I learned to bury my feelings. "Suck it up"; that's what I had learned, as if it was my only option. I know that tough love was meant to keep me on the straight and narrow, but hearing "suck it up" just made me feel guilty, and for what I don't know. I now see how damaging this way of dealing with my feelings was to my healing process.

The first time I shared my sexual abuse story publicly was at a speaking engagement in Strathmore, Alberta, even before there was any idea of writing *Playing With Fire*. That was my first public speaking gig where hockey wasn't the topic. It was a fundraiser for a women's shelter. Back when our family was running a cement company, the guy who worked in the business next door came over looking for a celebrity speaker. So I said, "Sure, I'll give it a shot."

The focus of the fundraiser was to support women who'd experienced physical abuse. There were more than five hundred people in the room for this event. Even the media was present. I thought to myself, "I can relate to these women, so I might as well talk about that." It wasn't a written speech or a planned talk; the disclosure just came out of me, rolled right out of my mouth. My wife Jenn was in the room watching my talk and she was so proud of me for finally saying something. There was a lot of emotion all around and for some unknown reason, for which I'm thankful, the media kept it quiet at the time. Very classy of them. The audience even gave me a standing ovation. I remember feeling drained, emotional, and tired. I had to go home right after and recover.

I had only revealed my sexual abuse to a few people before writing *Playing With Fire*. Most people really didn't know. But, once the story was public, nobody seemed surprised. It was as if they were just waiting for me to say that I was "one of the boys." What often shocked people about me was my behaviour, the places I went, the things I did, and the people I hung out with. But no one seemed to stop and really wonder *why* I acted the way that I did. What was going on underneath the surface was something I was dealing with (actually not dealing with), all by myself.

Yeah, I'd told my story to therapists at the drug and alcohol treatment centres where I was mandated to go. Some very well-intentioned therapists tried to help me to tie together the reasons for my behaviour. To face myself. But it was so early in the process I couldn't really put together any of the pieces yet. Although the painful layers of the onion began to peel off, it left me feeling like I had been sliced open with a razor blade. My pain medications—abusing drugs, alcohol, gambling, sex, and food—were taken away from me cold turkey. Going to forced therapy was like taking a freezing cold shower with no warmth afterwards. All of a sudden I was left raw and the pain I was used to numbing out was still there.

For those who don't know, it takes a long time to find new ways to cope with that pain underneath addiction. You're so used to not being able to identify feelings; whether you are happy, sad, mad, or scared; it was all the same—uncomfortable. All you know is that, "There's some kind of feeling here and I need to make it go away." You don't have any tools; you don't have any patience or ability to tolerate the discomfort of feeling anything.

The people I was hanging out with outside the rink didn't help my healing process much. You just don't sit in a room when you're completely fuckin' wasted and say, "Guess what, man. I am really sad." Those kinds of conversations didn't happen, those kinds of relationships didn't happen. I couldn't trust anybody, least of all men. I would rather be alone. No one was ever really close as a guy friend, other than my best friend Chuck who died way too soon. But even we didn't talk much about the hard stuff. He knew, but that was just stuff we chose not to talk about.

I can see in hindsight that when I was having problems in

the past, there were a lot of people trying to help. But at the time, that didn't make it any easier. People like Al Coates, the General Manager of the Calgary Flames, came to me several times and said, "Hey, I care more about you as a person than I do as a hockey player. How can I help you?"

We still talk and I appreciate his care. But back then I was still a relatively high-functioning guy, at least compared to the gong show of what came next in New York and Chicago, and obviously I just wasn't interested in getting help. I was a selfish, self-centred asshole.

You know what? I don't want to be that guy anymore. Any way I look at it, and I've now looked at it upside down and sideways, being the way I was did not help me.

Even after *Playing With Fire* came out and I started to talk about my experiences in public, I was a mess inside. I knew I wanted to get better, but I just didn't know where to start. Or, importantly, I didn't know who I could trust. I'd go around the country telling people my experiences (to prevent abuse from happening to others), but my anger didn't decrease and my personal relationships were stuck in dysfunction.

A few bright lights had come on for me since I'd stopped drinking and using drugs. I will forever be grateful for my relationship with Grandma Ruth Shield Woman, who remains a constant source of nurturance and wisdom for me. She's from the Siksika Nation near Calgary, and she helped me understand I'm part of something bigger and that I have an important role to play in helping others. Some of my family members have also been supportive in different ways, but I still essentially felt alone with my demons, or snakes, as the story goes.

You know how people say that when the student is ready the

teacher appears? Well, the day I met this Kim Barthel therapist woman in May 2012 at the Aulneau Renewal Centre in Winnipeg was like a bloody thunderbolt of brilliance went off and I haven't looked back.

I've since called her the "Wayne Gretzky of Therapy," and I'm really thankful for the time and dedication and care that she's put into helping me figure myself out. The one key aha moment from that first day that I'll never forget is when Kim put into words that it wasn't my fault. She said it in a way that I could really hear it for the first time. It was like that scene in *Good Will Hunting* between Robin Williams and Matt Damon: "It's not your fault, it's not your fault, it's not your fault …" But she explained why it wasn't my fault and, my God, that made such a difference. I came out of that first workshop in Winnipeg so pumped. Hell, I was ready to put on my skates and play so well I could have helped the Flames win the Stanley Cup that year! Well, maybe not; I am getting a little bit older. But you know what I'm talking about! (*smiling*)

Kim: I remember that day. The first thing you said to me when you walked up to me after my presentation was, "Hey, you, you just changed my life and you're gonna work with me for the rest of yours." I was kind of stunned. I remember standing there with my husband Bob, both of us with our mouths open, thinking, "What just happened?"

Theo: It was amazing. It was like you were explaining me inside and out, and I didn't feel threatened by any of it. One hell of a liberating combination. I guess we should never underestimate the potential for finding help when we least expect it.

Kim: Thanks. And what you have is such a wealth of challenging issues and an equal willingness to work on them. That's rare, you know.

Theo: Making up for lost time. You know, other people have *got* to hear this information. We've got to share it with the world!

Kim: Hmm! (*considering what such a non-traditional approach would look like*) When I first saw the book *Playing With Fire*—I passed by it in airport bookstores all across Canada—I was struck by the hideous face on the cover. It was like it was glaring at me. I didn't pick it up right away, because your face was so angry. But it was the sadness in your eyes that hit me most, reminding me that people are complex and not only as they seem on the surface.

Theo: I am tired of that face representing my identity to the world. I also hate the image that was portrayed of me in the HBO documentary that is still being played over and over.[iv] That's old news and doesn't come close to showing my reality today.

Kim: When I finally got the courage to read *Playing With Fire*, every aspect of your story made sense to me. As a therapist, I've been dedicating my life to trying to understand why people do what they do. "There is Always a Reason for the Behaviour" is the name of a workshop I've offered for years to therapists dealing with complex special needs, and I firmly believe the concept applies to all of us. I've always tried to figure out what lies beneath the surface of destructive actions, when people hurt themselves and others. I find it fascinating that we sometimes make decisions, mostly unconsciously, that seem to eat away at the core of our human spirit. Why do we do these things? Your face and your story were tragic but not uncommon examples of the way the layers of pain fold upon each other within our lives' stories. I think your veil of rage was a form of protection for you, a strategy you initially used to keep others away from your vulnerability.

Theo: You know it. But what made you decide that you would be willing to work with me?

Kim: When I met you in person, I was struck by your relative warmth and openness in comparison to what I was expecting. I saw your vulnerability and also your motivation. I didn't see a person who'd been sexually abused; I saw a survivor with a hell of a lot of resilience.

Theo: That's a nice way to say it.

Kim: You are adamant that you don't want to be called "a victim." Why?

Theo: A victim is someone who is stuck.

Kim: And it's a label.

Theo: A label that doesn't help the person wearing it. I think of the word "victim" as shaming. I'm sick of feeling ashamed and I have no tolerance for it. It holds people back.

Kim: You realize you're all about trying to move forward; I think that's where we relate to each other the most.

Theo: The foundation of what you and I instantly realized together is that so many people are hurting, people everywhere, no matter their income or social status or age or culture or gender; it's like some of us humans are just stuck on a treadmill of suffering.

Kim: We go on reinforcing the same dysfunctional patterns and making the same kinds of scratch-your-head choices over and over, and then numbing ourselves with a variety of methods (not only booze and drugs) when our pain comes to the surface.

Theo: The ray of light that came through that first day is that maybe together we could help these people to consciously choose to get off the treadmill that's not serving them. If we worked together you could introduce some cutting-edge information about the science of trauma and healing, just like you were doing that day, but even expanded, and I'd just be everyone's guinea pig as I work to get healthier. Seeing as my life was already out there for all to read about, I thought this is a great way to rewire my own brain and commit to my own healing.

Kim: The premise is that by using your life story and personal progress, others could see it as an example for reflection on their own lives. We got really excited about the idea that we could actually help people re-evaluate their own commonly held beliefs and patterns, and without judgment!

Theo: At dinner that first day we had a great talk, also with your husband Bob and my former manager Carey, about "How is it that people actually get better? What is the real sincere key to having deep insights about how we are and how we want to be? And what ultimately provides the motivation for wanting to change?"

Kim: It's surprisingly simple, isn't it? It's talking with trusted friends. That's what ultimately helps people feel better. Therapy can help, reading books can help, time certainly can help, but our closest friends and safe relationships are what it comes down to.

Theo: So since talking with friends is really it—how about we try to get people to elevate these kinds of conversations with a bit more information and some examples of courage, maybe, if that's what people see in me dealing with my crap. I'd be more than happy if people would learn from my mistakes.

Kim: What your ongoing story describes is a possibility for change. It even gives me hope.

Theo: I'd love the world to change overnight, but we both know that's not going to happen. As Grandma Ruth reminded me, change begins with one person at a time.

Kim: I know you like to think big and achieve miracles, but when you plant seeds, you never know where those seeds and seeds from those seeds will grow. Reaching one person's heart is a miracle and when change happens there can be a ripple effect. We never know who they'll talk to, and how far that influence will reach. You know what teachers remind each other at breaks on really hard days? That even if twenty-nine out of thirty kids aren't listening, all it takes is one of them to open their mind for it all to be more than worthwhile. And sometimes, it's not the one they think it'll be. Sometimes, that's the miracle.

Theo: As I say, "Never quit before the miracle."

Kim: Reminds me of a life-changing lesson I learned in Rankin Inlet, Nunavut. I lived up there for a couple years when I first met Bob, and I helped develop mental health and special needs services for kids. There was this one teenage boy who was known to be dangerous, who had also been traumatized as a young child. He would come into my office and sit looking at his feet with his hood pulled over his head and would say nothing for hours at a time.

At night, I would go home and tell Bob that this kid was my biggest failure. He wouldn't talk to me, I couldn't do therapy, I felt useless. Bob would say, "Whoever that kid is, if you expect him to talk, he'll be out of your office so fast, and then he will be your greatest failure. Just keep him safe and wait."

So, I stopped having any expectations of him ever talking to me. Still, I brought him cookies, wrote him notes, and sometimes, had what seemed like short one-way conversations with myself, hoping that I was making any kind of a connection, but never really knowing.

When we left the North (which is an amazing part of Canada

by the way) I worried about this guy, wondering what would become of him.

Several years later, I bumped into him in the airport in Winnipeg. I was very excited to see him again. But I knew that if I got too exuberant in my emotions, that would turn him away, so I coolly said, "Hey," without any animation.

He said, "Hey you, Blondie. Want you to know something. You stopped me from killing myself every day for two years. And I carry you with me in my head every day."

Theo: Sometimes we are making a difference even when we don't think we are.

Kim: I'm so humbled by that experience. And it reminds me to be more tuned in to small acts of kindness, I guess, that might make a big difference.

Theo: Small is good, anything that works is good. Don't underestimate small. Hey, I remember what I asked you at that first dinner. You'd made up some questions for the panel discussion at that Winnipeg conference, and I thought they were very reflective, self-reflective. I think I just asked if you had more of those questions in your head.

Kim: It's endless. We can grow until we stop breathing.

Theo: So we agreed that you'd try to teach me everything you knew and I'd try to share everything I'd never really wanted to, for the greater good. And that was how it started.

Kim: Discussions were fast and furious in the weeks and months that followed, no question. We were each working our regular jobs more than full-time (me mostly training therapists and you on the speaking circuit), but what we were doing was fascinating and, in truth, your progress was extraordinary. You are a very quick learner. You've been extremely motivated to learn as much as you can on everything to do with understanding yourself and how you can change your own life for the better. You ever see *Red Green* on TV?

Theo: Yep. He says, "Keep your stick on the ice." Good advice. (*laughing*)

Kim: I was thinking of the men's prayer at the end of the show, something like (*in a deep voice*) "I'm a man, but I can change, if I have to, I guess." It's so typical. How many people out there relate to that? All of us? You, though, you are really choosing to change. That's so cool.

Theo: I think I have to. Maybe Red and I aren't so different.

Kim: Wow.

Theo: Right away I had some aha moments that made me just want to learn more.

Kim: I love it when that personal lightbulb goes on from insights, with full brightness. My own or others'. That's why a lot of people get into teaching and want to become therapists for that matter. It feels amazing to help.

Theo: The reason we're writing this book is just to extend this helping. The key concepts you talk about will all be discussed. The amount of tools in my toolbox, the information, and strategies to deal with my stuff; it's all gotta be shared.

Kim: It's been about two years since we started, and I'd say your conscious choices to be more mindful are increasing still. But you know what, it's helping others learn what you're learning that's our biggest joy and mission today.

Theo: Let me be the first to say that I've got a long way to go and I am still making mistakes. If anyone thinks I'm all perfect now, they're crazy. I'm only a thousand times better than when I was thinking of killing myself. Not all the way. I know it's ongoing work over a lifetime and never complete.

Kim: And you're fine with that?

Theo: Absolutely. Hey, this healing stuff is addictive. If it's not serving me to do cocaine, I might as well do something that feels as good and is good for me.

Kim: You're pretty smart.

Theo: Genius! (*laughing*) But you know, aside from all this healing stuff, we couldn't be more different.

Kim: You used to play hockey, right?

Theo: I know, I know. You can't stand to watch it. Aren't you Canadian?

Kim: Back in the day, I had a boyfriend who was really good at it, and I overdosed on spectating. Swore I'd never do it again. It really pisses my husband off, because one of his greatest joys is helping the Montreal Canadiens by encouraging them through the TV set. I just refuse to stay in the room when any game's on TV.

Theo: (*laughing*) I understand Bob made you sit in a bar once in Davidson, Saskatchewan, to watch a playoff game, so I requested a photo as proof.

Kim: I was a fish out of water in there. So weird. I think I could make a long list of how your life as described in *Playing With Fire* was nothing like mine: I don't drink, I've never seen drugs, I've never even had a cigarette, never slept with a prostitute (*laughing*), although I worked as a therapist with a bunch of them. I can't even count well enough to play cards; I hate country and western music …

Theo: Ouch, that last one hurt. (*smiling*)

Kim: I'm trying to like country music. There is this one song I like. "As the Story Go-o-oes, as the story go-o-oes … I'm sleeping on couches I no longer own." Do you know that one? (*smiling knowingly*) When you opened for Johnny Reid at the Stampede, Bob and I belted it out in a taxi on the way there, and the Indian taxi driver said it sounded pretty catchy!

Theo: He has good taste.

Kim: Speaking of Indian taxi drivers, I was teaching in Hyderabad, India last year and the driver (a bright man studying to be a doctor) asked me, "What do you do for a living Ma'am?" I said I teach about trauma and abuse, and he said he just finished reading a great book from Canada that his brother-in-law had sent him. He reached beside him and held up a copy of your ugly face! (*laughing*) I just about peed.

Theo: See, we never know where our messages end up.

Kim: True. So plant seeds, and trust in the universe that the right person will get what they need at the right time.

Theo: Just thought of another thing that made us different at the beginning. You talked about sensitive topics all day long and, until recently, I'd been really good at avoiding those as much as possible.

Kim: (*smiling*) So, is there anything we have in common?

Theo: I know the answer to that. We both know what it's like to be hurt, and we both want to help people. That's all that matters. It's probably a good thing that you don't care about my hockey stuff, 'cause for a lot of people it's been a distraction. I like that you see me as a person, no more, no less.

Kim: We don't fit the traditional client/therapist roles anymore; we're more like friends who bring totally different experiences and skill sets to the same worktable. You know there's endless work to do in this field.

Theo: It would be crazy not to share our collective knowledge and reflections at this point. I know that if others could talk about this stuff it would help release their burdens too.

2

It's Not My Fault

"I am real, I am me, and I am free."
From the Song, "I Am Who I Am"
Theo Fleury and the Death Valley Rebels

Theo: My life will never be the same. Sitting around my kitchen table in Calgary listening to you talk about the science of relationships changed my life. That's when I came to realize that my sexual abuse wasn't the only cause of my pain. "It's not your fault" sunk in.

Kim: (*smiling*) That was a huge shift for you, wasn't it? You'd walked around for years blaming the abuse (and internally blaming yourself) for everything that had gone wrong in your life. And you were understandably angry and focused on that abuse.

Theo: Damn right. Before then I didn't have the tools to begin to see it any other way. I was absolutely stuck there. Look at me in that HBO documentary! How unwell I was! For something like thirty years, I was stuck there. I know some people who are stuck a lot longer.

Kim: When you say they're stuck, what are they stuck in?

Theo: Pain. Emotional pain.

Kim: That emotional pain, at its essence, is shame. Shame is the intensely painful feeling we have when we believe that we are inherently flawed and therefore unworthy of love and belonging. Shame is felt in the body, and it's like feeling the whole of our being is rotten and undeserving.

Theo: I think I'm confusing feelings of shame and guilt. What's the difference?

Kim: Guilt is different than shame. With guilt, the behaviour is bad; with shame, it feels like you as a person are bad. Guilt is "I did something bad"; shame is "I am bad." Shame is a destructive force and it doesn't help anyone. Guilt can be a moral compass and can actually be helpful in modifying behaviour. This difference is profound in understanding how to talk about what we're feeling.

Theo: Hmm. (*rubbing his forehead*)

Kim: What specifically was it that I said that opened you up to thinking about it in a broader way, that your issues were more than just about your sexual abuse?

Theo: It's when you talked about relationships between babies and their parents. About how they matter so much. You said those earliest relationships set up the patterns for how we all cope with challenges and stress for the rest of our lives. I know I had a chaotic upbringing, but I had no idea that it would influence how I cope with stress, even as an adult. My mom was always crying and depressed, and my dad was a raging alcoholic most of the time. There is no doubt this information is critical to me understanding myself.

Kim: It is important throughout all of this conversation about parents not to blame them. They also didn't have the tools at the time to be different or to recognize the effect they might have had upon you as a child.

Theo: They loved me as much as they could. That's how I think about it.

Kim: And remember, no parent in the whole world is perfect (*smiling*), not even if they're therapists and teach this stuff all day long!

Theo: I want to hear more about how we're affected by early relationships.

Kim: Well, what researchers have learned in the past decade of brain science is that how parents interact with their children affects how their baby's brain will grow. For a baby, the way a sensitive parent attunes to them directly stimulates the love chemicals in their brain. Psychologist Anita Remig calls this tuning in between a parent and baby "gleaming and beaming."[v] When parents and babies are emotionally connected, both their brains light up like Christmas tree lightbulbs with mutual enjoyment.

Theo: Is this what happens to adults when they first fall in love?

Kim: Um, there are some similarities. For a baby, each experience of gleaming and beaming repeatedly activates the brain circuits, helping to grow the brain. For adults, these brain circuits are generally already there and they get reactivated each time we feel love. We are hardwired for love and connection.

Theo: Sounds awesome. But what does gleaming and beaming even look like?

Kim: The classic picture of gleaming and beaming is when the parent and the child are looking at each other, mimicking each other, paying attention to one another. It's as if nothing else in the world matters in that moment for either of them. It's that magical connection that comes from loving caregiving where parent and baby can emotionally "feel" each other. As if the parent is inside the child's mind. This allows the child to feel "seen" and understood, helping them to develop a sense of who they are in the eyes of someone who cares about them.

Theo: I can imagine that is what unconditional love is like. Where someone loves you no matter what you do. Not sure I have ever had that experience.

Kim: I think we all have moments of that feeling, because even the lady in the grocery store can gleam and beam with us. No matter who we do this with, loving feelings are the result of a chemical known as oxytocin that's produced inside our brain. (Oxytocin is way better than OxyContin—OxyContin is a pharmaceutical opiate, highly damaging to the brain; the two are not to be confused.) When a baby is loved, nurtured, and soothed by a parent, the dance between them releases this hormone oxytocin that activates and grows new brain connections for babies.

Theo: I'd like some of that!

Kim: What is even more cool is that repeated hits of natural oxytocin, from gleaming and beaming with a baby, helps develop the baby's right prefrontal cortex, which is the senior executive of their thinking brain, and is also the part of the brain that regulates all their emotions.

Theo: You're saying healthy relationships make us smarter?

Kim: Absolutely, that is what is being proven in science today. Relationships matter. The brain grows optimally under conditions of comfort and emotional safety.

Theo: What stops parents from tuning in to their babies?

Kim: When a parent has a history of trauma, depression, addiction, or when they live in constant danger, they are preoccupied with their own survival. This is completely understandable. But what happens is that the nurturance they are able to give their baby is very different in quality. The parent cannot be as sensitive to the needs of their child because they have to prioritize themselves. When a mom is depressed or anxious, she will have difficulty putting her mind in the mind of her child, because her own feelings are so consuming. It is not her fault, but it happens nonetheless.

Theo: My mom was depressed and anxious even when she was a teenager. By the time I came along, she was chronically depressed. I guess my mom didn't have much energy to gleam and beam with me.

Kim: It's hard to hear some of this information, isn't it? I remember you had such a strong reaction to the videos of moms and babies that I show at conferences.[vi]

Theo: The one that showed what healthy and fucked up early relationships look like is really hard for me to watch. I can feel the differences between the happiness of the baby with the nurturing parent and the loneliness of the baby who felt insecure with their emotionally unavailable parent. I feel a bit sick inside watching those videos, 'cause I know which baby I was.

Kim: That is an example of having what's called "an implicit memory" triggered within you, something you can't recall happening in concrete terms, because you were so young. But it's something you can remember feeling in your body. Implicit memory is known as our unconscious memory; it's the stuff we remember without recalling any details.

Theo: I felt sad. It just dawned on me how much I'd missed out on.

Kim: A lot of people get triggered by watching those videos. Canada is actually a leader in the field of research about the effects of maternal depression on developing babies. An example is some of the work done by Dr. Nicole Letourneau at the University of Calgary, which is and will be helpful in appreciating the importance of a mother's mental health.[vii]

Theo: Does this apply to any caregiver, or just moms?

Kim: Pretty well right from birth, infants can read the facial expressions and body language of their caregivers, no matter who they are. The feelings that the caregivers experience are written all over their faces. The baby internalizes and personalizes all of these nonverbal cues within a small fraction of a second.[viii] This nonverbal information that the baby absorbs turns on particular cells known as "mirror neurons" in the baby's brain. Mirror neurons give us shared experiences. The mirror neurons in the baby's brain essentially copy the state of their parents' brains. Depressed parents' brains create depressed babies' brains.

Theo: Ouch.

Kim: There's another part to this. According to neuroscientist Lane Strathearn, when a securely attached parent looks at their baby, they get a loving oxytocin "hit" regardless of whether the baby is happy or agitated.[ix] When emotionally unavailable parents— like moms who are depressed—look at their babies, research says they only get an oxytocin, loving hit when the baby is smiling and happy. What is even more astonishing is that the emotionally unavailable moms in this study experienced disgust every time their baby was upset and crying.

Theo: Was my mom's depression an example of what you're talking about?

Kim: Having compassion for your mom, depression and anxiety were a form of suffering for her. But if you'd be crying as a baby, and you'd look up to see the face of someone who isn't happy with you, that would be additionally stressful to your system. And when babies look at a disgusted face, they will shut down whatever emotions they are feeling. The baby experiences this kind of rupture with their parent as shame. When we experience shame, we shut down.[x] There is a lot of emerging research studying these relationship dynamics and their effects on our behaviour.

Theo: Shit. Would you call what I experienced a neglectful upbringing?

Kim: I don't think any parent intends to neglect their child. But when a parent is unavailable for whatever reason, the child feels abandoned, rejected, and unlovable. This becomes encoded deeply in their unconscious implicit memory and doesn't give the baby much experience of being valued and understood. These feelings of abandonment can shadow all future relationships.

Theo: I'm coming to internalize that my core issues are abandonment, rejection, and feeling unlovable. Are you telling me that I must have first felt these as an infant? 'Cause if you are, that explains a lot.

Kim: Sure. All of us experience abandonment, rejection, and low self-worth to some extent during our lives. And yes, all of us had our first experiences with these feelings as infants. Remember, an infant can't make sense of things and can't say to themselves, "Oh, my parents are having a bad day." An infant can't help but personalize whatever they experience. There are actually brain cells around the heart that can feel the rupture of disconnection in a relationship.[xi] Isn't that amazing? Our heart has its own brain.

Theo: I thought my brain was in my ass. (*smiling like a troublemaker*)

Kim: (*laughing*) What it means is that when we're feeling like our hearts are breaking emotionally, our physical hearts are feeling something.

Theo: I hate that heartbreak feeling.

Kim: For an infant, they would likely feel their first heartbreak when they don't get the connection they need with their parent. And that is where developmental trauma can begin. Babies have no way of knowing that they aren't the cause of their parents' distress. So it's most likely that the first time any of us felt ashamed was in early infancy, feeling that it must have been our fault whenever our parents seemed unhappy.

Theo: This explains every intimate relationship I have ever had. All of my emotional triggers that cause me to explode are related to feeling abandoned or rejected. Huh! This understanding will help me to forgive myself a little for my reactions.

Kim: Bringing these experiences to our consciousness allows us to become aware of our feelings before we jump into reactivity and hurt other people's feelings. Great way to help prevent future explosions. This is an example of how understanding yourself can change your behaviour and stabilize your current relationships.

Theo: How can I learn more from my childhood if I can't remember most of it?

Kim: There are two kinds of memory. One is called "explicit memory," which is recall. When you remember what you ate for dinner, your times tables, and how to spell your name, that is recall memory, and it's stored in nice neat file drawers in your brain. But the part of you that remembers those things doesn't start developing until you are about three years old. You don't have recall memory for early infancy.

Theo: I think my first memories are from when I was around five. Going to the rink for my first hockey practice.

Kim: So in your explicit memory you've always been a hockey player. Neat. There is another kind of remembering that we've already mentioned—implicit memory—and it's available in your brain right from birth, and probably even before birth. It's the emotional memory for all your experiences and is predominantly encoded on the right side of your brain. Your implicit memory continues to store new emotional memories for the rest of your life, influencing much of how you think and act.

Theo: Explicit memory is remembering what colour dress a beautiful lady wore, and implicit memory is remembering how it felt to look at it. Our implicit memory is often stronger, right?

Kim: Yes, and faster! At the beginning of our lives, it's all about implicit memory. Many brain scientists are now calling the first several months after birth the "fourth trimester," because so much brain growth unfolds at that time. A big part of a young infant's environment is the relationship between them and their parents; they rely on them for absolutely everything. The emotional connection between them is hardwired into the brain as a part of their implicit memory.

Theo: Holy shit! That is profound. How we act and think is actually driven by these early events that we can't even recall?

Kim: When your mom was stressed or unavailable, then her stress became your stress. As a baby, of course, you couldn't make sense of it. When there was a lot of chaos around you as an infant, that is what your brain encoded, with the result that what you implicitly remember about relationships will be the feeling of chaos.

Theo: All my intimate relationships were filled with chaos—monumental ups and downs. This must have felt familiar and, therefore, safe in that way, right? Do we always seek what's familiar, even when it's not good for us?

Kim: Do we not all still eat Tim Hortons doughnuts? Yes, the familiar is often preferred to the unknown, regardless of the outcome. You knew that answer.

Theo: Of course, I knew that answer. (*with a slight cockiness*)

Kim: You probably want to know if the vigilance and anxiety in the baby who's often stressed always persist, even into adulthood.

Theo: Do they?

Kim: They don't have to, but they certainly can. It depends how much healthy soothing and comfort they get along the way. What's important to note is that implicit memories (triggering both positive and negative feelings) operate in the background of our reactions to everything, every day, even now as adults.

I remember one time you and I were in Edmonton getting ready to give a presentation at the Legislative Assembly about trauma and healing. We were sitting in the lobby of a hotel waiting for another colleague, and you had your back to the door. I was facing the lobby, watching all the people coming toward us and walking by to get to the elevator. Although they were walking right in our direction, people who were calm and relaxed remained unnoticed by you. But you would turn your head and orient your eyes to every single person who was agitated, irritated, or angry. Before this happened, I used to think you were simply distractible. But at that moment, it became clear that what you are is vigilant and intuitively gifted in orienting to danger. I believe your implicit memory of threat is still operating in the background of your consciousness.

Theo: Another lightbulb moment!

All my teachers said I had ADD.[xii] I certainly couldn't sit still in school, so I always believed them. Now, I can see what I have is a gift! The hyperawareness of threat probably kept me more alert on the ice, come to think of it. I always was able to know which players were the threats and which ones I could walk over.

Kim: Who were the real competitors?

Theo: The guys on the other teams who I most respected for their killer instinct were Adam Foote, Claude Lemieux, Tie Domi, Chris Chelios, Scott Stevens, Chris Pronger, Mark Messier, and every single player on the Edmonton Oilers.

Kim: I've heard of Mark Messier. He's bald, right?

Theo: Ya, and he eats chips. (*laughing*) I think my early implicit memories must have made me a better player to have been able to deal with all those characters.

Kim: It probably helped keep you alive!

Theo: Another implicit memory I have is this one: One time as part of a mandatory therapy session, years ago, I did something called "EMDR" for trauma.[xiii] It's a way that apparently helps to change how we feel about disturbing implicit memories and it was pretty cool. It helped me to remember an incident when we lived in Williams Lake, British Columbia. I must have been about two years old. I "remembered" a whole bunch of chaos. My dad had drunk himself into a fucking oblivion; he was close to dying, he'd drunk so much. I remembered the ambulance coming to pick him up. Ironically, I repeated the exact same scenario when Beaux was two years old. You learn what you see and you repeat what you learn. If you don't deal with the trauma you've suffered, the patterns will repeat themselves and manifest in many different ways.

Kim: That's an intense situation for a little kid, both for you and for Beaux. Many times, these types of implicit memories result in reactions that don't make sense, even years later. When an implicit memory gets activated, it "triggers" us to respond with strong emotions. The behavioural responses to these triggered unconscious emotions are often regrettable.

Theo: I've had lots of experience with those regrettable behaviours. Your body is so much on automatic pilot that you don't even realize that you've been triggered. It is definitely unconscious, unprocessed stuff.

Kim: Negative triggers can come from implicit memories of early developmental trauma, such as chaos, neglect, abuse ... All infants develop ways to interact with their caregivers to ensure their survival. These are called "attachment strategies."

Theo: It felt like there was a lot of chaos at our house.

Kim: I think you likely adapted to chaos very early in life. Infants have to learn to read their caregivers in order to know how to communicate their needs. These back and forth interactions between babies and their parents are the earliest implicit memories we have. These initial threads of human connection directly influence how we interact with people as we grow.

Theo: And these attachment patterns that we develop as babies, they stay with us even when we're adults?

Kim: (*nodding*) Although we can always learn new strategies as we mature, the infant ones act like a default program in a computer. They are the easiest files to open when we are stressed. We revert back to those early patterns reactively without thinking.

Theo: When I get stressed, and I don't understand why I am doing what I am doing, is this an example of me going back to my early attachment pattern?

Kim: Yeah. The reason Attachment Theory exists is to explain how these behaviours unfold. There are different types of parents out there, and kids develop protective strategies from the earliest ages so they can cope as well as they can. There are three attachment styles that babies adopt so that they can get their needs met by their parents. Even though these strategies develop in infancy, they stay with us over our lifetime.

Theo: Interesting! (*leaning forward*)

Kim: These attachment styles, originally named by Dr. Mary Ainsworth, are known as Types A, B, and C. Type B children are securely attached; they are comfortable to be left alone for brief periods of time, but they are always happy to see their parents return. Securely attached kids are comfortable in their own skin.

Theo: I saw what that looked like on those videos and I definitely can't relate to that

Kim: Not many of us truly can. Most of us are insecurely attached to some degree and use the A or C strategies.

Theo: How does insecure attachment play out?

Kim: It depends most on what the parents are like. When parents are unpredictable and inconsistent—rushing to console their kids one minute then leaving them alone for hours the next—their kids tend to develop the Type C strategy response. These kids become reactive. They get upset when they are left alone even for a moment, and are not easily consoled when their parents do come back. Type C kids demand connection, wind themselves up, and create a lot of drama, and they are often resentful. When their parents do return, it's as if these kids want them to pay for leaving them in the first place.

Theo: I like that video you show of Stewie from *Family Guy* standing at the edge of his mom's bed repeatedly saying, "Mom, mom, mom, mommy, mommy, mommy, Lois, Lois, Lois," until she explodes with frustration. Once he has Lois's attention, Stewie feels satisfied. He says, "Hi," giggles, and runs out of the room; he never wanted anything from her other than attention. He's an attention-seeking C, isn't he?

Kim: He certainly is. At that moment he's the poster child for the Cs. But the term "Attention seeking" has such a negative sound to it. I prefer to call it "connection seeking." Connection is about validation and self-worth, which are necessary! Cs feel very stressed when they are not feeling connected.

Theo: So what would a parent do with a kid like Stewie who goes around creating drama? I wouldn't know what to do in that case.

Kim: It's a challenge. These kids alternate between demanding their parents attend to them and then pushing them away. It's very confusing for a parent. The solution to make things easier for reactive kids—Cs—is to be more consistent as parents.

Theo: That hits a chord for me, as I have definitely not been consistent as a parent.

Kim: It's never too late to change. That's why I think it's helpful to understand this stuff.

Theo: And these patterns are still a part of us when we're adults? Thinking about it, I have a lot of Cs in my life.

Kim: Yes, the patterns we develop as children do stay with us.

Theo: And what do these C kids look like when they grow up, if they don't learn any self-awareness?

Kim: As adults, these reactive individuals often maintain the desperation for connection and believe that their needs will never be met. They tend to become more self-absorbed than others. Ironically, their exaggerated neediness for attention—connection—may push others away and thus create the self-fulfilling outcome of the rejection that they dread.

Theo: I have been in relationship with a number of them. It is so hard to remember in the moment that their aggressive behaviour really means, "Come here. I need you."

Kim: That is the crux of the matter for the connection-seeking C. They learn that the only way to get what they need is to demand it or it will never happen. And remember, Cs don't bottle up their emotions; at least we know what they're thinking.

Theo: I can be reactive too. Does that mean I am a connection seeker?

Kim: That is such a good question, because there are different motivations for being reactive. Cs react to demand closeness, whereas I think you react from the position of the A, which is all about keeping people distant. We have to understand the intent of the behaviour to know which strategy is being used.

Theo: So tell me about the A's!

Kim: (*thinking*) Labels suck. The A, B, and C strategies are not like boxes that we fit into. We can move between strategies dependent on the relationship we're in. Some kids behave like As to their moms and Cs to their dads, as an example. Are you okay with calling them A, B, and C in this case?

Theo: Sure, I get what you're saying, and I understand these patterns aren't set in stone.

Kim: That makes me feel better when we talk about these terms. Back to avoidant A strategy kids. They are the opposite of the Cs. Type A children develop an avoidant response to parents who were consistently unavailable emotionally, dismissive, or constantly critical. From feeling neglected, these kids learn that they actually feel safer when there is less contact with their parents. Type A kids avoid connection simply because it's too painful to hope for it and experience more rejection.

Theo: Well, I can feel that one in my chest.

Kim: Hearing you say that, I can feel it in my chest too.

Theo: So what did my A attachment strategy look like?

Kim: What I know of your childhood from your stories is that your mom experienced significant depression and your dad was unpredictable whenever he was at home.

Theo: That sums it up.

Kim: Well, the primary caregiver is the one who is around the most when you are growing up. And when that caregiver is emotionally unavailable, the child will naturally become preoccupied with that person's feelings.

Theo: My parents were just scraping by and there was a lot of cause for stress, most of it caused by my dad's alcoholism.

Kim: I'm glad you recognize they were trying their best. That's all you were doing too. By avoiding connection and keeping emotional distance, it would have felt like the safest way for you to cope. As a result, both kids and adults with this strategy feel anxiety whenever a relationship gets too close, because connection has never felt safe for them.

Theo: Ooph! (*big exhale*) This avoidant strategy you describe was and is definitely my coping pattern. I spent the least amount of time at home as possible. Home was not a fun place to be, because my mom was always so anxious and confrontational. I've never really seen her smile a lot. I've often been in relationships with women who were a lot like my mother.

Kim: That's really common, Theo. Remember we often seek the familiar. If not for us, at least it's good news for Freud. He would be pleased with himself that there seems to be something to his theories!

Theo: I heard Freud was making up his theories when he was doing lines of cocaine.

In any case, when my mother was anxious or antagonistic, I would take off from home and not return until I knew that I wouldn't have to deal with her anymore. So in my relationships, when the women in my life became confrontational (wanting to fucking fight), I would leave, go out, get shit-faced, come home at three, four, five in the morning, and hope we wouldn't talk about it the next day. I wanted to avoid confrontation.

Kim: Hmm. We avoid confrontation, often because we feel guilty about what we do.

Theo: Sometimes. But sometimes I really just needed time to myself. The woman in my life at the time, whoever she was, never seemed to tolerate that need. My need for space would trigger them with their own shit. It could well be that my need for space made them feel abandoned, unlovable, or rejected themselves. But think about it: I never had any time to myself. I was always part of a team. I just didn't have any time alone.

Kim: You've just given a perfect example here of Type A avoidant thinking. If you were a connection-seeking C, you wouldn't want "space" or ask for time alone. For some people, A's especially, being smothered is as tough to deal with as being neglected.

Theo: I just got something! Ultimately, what bothers me about my mom is the same thing I don't like about myself.

Kim: And what is the mirror there? How are you alike?

Theo: We're both codependents.

Kim: What do you mean by that?

Theo: As I understand it from Alcoholics Anonymous, a codependent person is someone who is controlled or manipulated by an addict. My mom was codependent on my dad. I was codependent on both of them. And then I also had a lot of my own family become codependent on me. Codependents are often family members of alcoholics. They grow up with the mindset that their own happiness depends on someone else's happiness, which is pretty sad.

Kim: That's how I understand it too, and you just directly linked codependency with the avoidant A strategy! There is an overlap. To avoid closeness, A's can adopt a superficial people-pleasing version of the strategy, and it can look and feel just like enabling. When someone is codependent, they focus on the needs of the other first, which means they put a lower priority on their own needs. There's always a reason for the behaviour, and the reason codependent people enable addictive behaviour is either to protect themselves from confrontation or out of fear that their non-compliance will end the relationship.

Theo: There is a group called Al-Anon that is completely designed to help support friends and families of alcoholics, and a big part of what they talk about is how to set boundaries and stop enabling. They all come to realize that by doing whatever the addict wants them to do isn't in anybody's best interests.

Kim: This is all rational, but as a kid it's about survival. When kids are preoccupied with their parents' needs, it's understandable how enabling patterns emerge.

Theo: Stuff you think is just "normal" is much more complicated, eh? When we're young, we all think whatever is going on in our life is normal. If my dad came home with a six-pack, drank it right away and went out looking for another one, that was normal. That is what every dad does. Right? Nobody ever said, "This isn't normal."

It was only when he showed up at the rink drunk when everybody else could see him that I realized that wasn't typical for other families. If I couldn't regulate my dad before he got home, there would be a fucking argument and I'd see more trauma. "Just go in the house, Dad, and go to sleep."

Other times, I used to wait up at night for him to come home so I'd see what kind of shape he'd be in. Was there gonna be another argument? Would I have to put on my referee jersey again? I had to become the adult in the house.

Kim: There is a clear example of you having to be the parent to your dad. You had to take care of him in order for you to feel safe. This kind of experience leaves a child feeling insecure, anxious, and always on alert.

Theo: I was definitely preoccupied with my dad's unpredictability. You know, instead of this book being called *Conversations With a Rattlesnake*, it could just as easily have been called "Conversations About Feeling Abandoned" or "Conversations About Not Being Good Enough" or "Conversations About Not Feeling Lovable." That's what it comes down to.

Kim: It's true. At the core of all of us is the need for love and acceptance.

Theo: All the women in my life ultimately abandoned me and this is what I was most afraid of and what I experienced with my mother.

Kim: The very things we fear the most keep happening, until we stop fearing them.

Theo: That's a good line.

I know that I want to change this cycle going forward.

Kim: (*nodding with assurance*) In the face of their anxiety, avoidant kids "suck up" their negative emotions and put on a happy face. The intention is to cheer up others; it's a form of people pleasing. It is hard to tell when something is bothering these kids though, as they rarely let people see that they're upset until they explode. Attachment theorists Pat Crittenden and Andrea Landini call this superficial happiness a "false positive emotion."[xiv] It's not true happiness, but forced positivity with the intention of keeping others happy.

Theo: It sounds exhausting. In my most intimate relationships, whenever there was conflict, my natural instinct was to bolt out the door; avoid conflict. But where did I think I was going? I was terrified by the concept of abandonment and would do anything to avoid it. I would regularly hold in my feelings in order to keep the peace. Once I stopped drinking, I couldn't suppress my feelings anymore. Once I couldn't suck it up, I threw it up. All over everyone. I stopped being so obedient. Without drinking, I didn't have a coping mechanism anymore. I would fucking explode if I didn't say what was on my mind. I became much more reactive and that's when my feelings seemed to be the most out of control.

Kim: When people who have avoided their negative feelings all their life begin to stop suppressing them, they blow up easily. Their emotions are close to the surface. It isn't until they learn to sit with the discomfort of their feelings that they become comfortable in their own skin. It's hard work.

Theo: Do A strategies often marry C strategies?

Kim: It is the most common pairing.

Theo: I think divorce rates are so high because two people who are traumatized often unconsciously pick each other as mates. What happens throughout the whole relationship is they trigger each other, over and over. And when they get sick of being triggered, they just end the relationship. They don't have the skills to make it work. Communication breaks down, intimacy breaks down. It is much easier to leave than to sit with your emotional shit and try to learn from it.

Kim: That seems true, but if you don't learn in one relationship, the unhealthy patterns will just follow you to the next one. Healthy relationships involve more than love; they take a lot of skill. When you don't have the tools, it is much harder.

Theo: All my partners had to do was threaten to leave me and I'd forget how to think straight. My heart would race and my stomach would cramp.

Kim: Ach. (*pained look*) Do you ever remember the avoidant A strategy showing up in your hockey career?

Theo: Fuck, yeah. I think the hockey world reinforced my "suck it up" tendency. I had to comply and hold in my feelings in order to play the game. Mostly, my sad feelings. I know my angry feelings came out on the ice, where it was often appropriate as an outlet. But abandonment wasn't much of a factor, because I felt connected and appreciated almost all the time. I'm really thankful for hockey and the relative stability it gave me. In hindsight, I appreciate it even more.

Kim: I agree. Someone could definitely write a good book on the therapeutic value of playing hockey. Or team sports of any nature. I am definitely beginning to appreciate hockey, at least from that perspective!

Theo: You're learning. (*smiling*)

Kim: I hope I always will be.

Hey, does it make sense to you that the A strategy people have the   greatest risk for developing anxiety disorders and serious mental illnesses? It's because they can become so shut down. This shutdown strategy is also highly connected to immune disorders; like Crohn's disease, for example. Laurence Heller, a trauma psychologist, says that when we are chronically subjected to a lot of stress that builds up, our immune and digestive systems get in trouble and become vulnerable to disease.[xv]

Theo: I'd heard that my Crohn's was linked to stress, but I didn't know that it was connected to the way I deal with my feelings and relationships.

Kim: That's where stress comes from. Many avoidant A's work hard at pleasing others, not to connect, but to feel good enough. Children and later adults who compulsively please others may perpetuate this pattern in relationships with all kinds of other people. Those who become highly compliant, especially to those in positions of authority, may become vulnerable to exploitation.

Theo: My God, that explains my abuse situation right there. Giving up my power to authority in order to feel safe. How bloody ironic! My strategy was an attempt to keep me emotionally safe by complying, and it actually led me to the 180° exact opposite of safety.

Kim: It's not your fault. These attachment strategies are understandable in infant contexts, but as your experience shows, they outlive their usefulness as we get older, and then they interfere with healthy relationships later on.

Theo: Yep. I am seeing this now.

Kim: Teenagers who use the people-pleasing A strategy can become promiscuous, both socially and sexually. They may have superficial relationships with lots of people, which avoids any depth of intimacy that true emotional relationships might bring them. Intimacy is very scary as it increases the odds of potential rejection. There is some truth to what Bob tells our eighteen-year-old daughter, "When you open yourself up to love, you open yourself up to pain." To prevent this vulnerability, many avoidant A's become totally self-reliant, where they avoid relationships altogether. This certainly isn't the goal either.

Theo: I guess the trick is to balance it. (*pausing*) You know what it makes me think? The whole time I have been on this earth, I have been trying to get better. The people who have been in my life have been helping me do that. You learn from interaction with everyone, even the challenging people. There's no such thing as coincidence. It's a part of your master plan and those lessons will be put in front of you until you get them. And because you are usually with someone who is just as traumatized as you are, it's difficult to have a relationship that is healthy. Life is about acquiring information to figure out "you," not anybody else—"you."

Kim: As adults, when this avoidant pattern persists as your only strategy, it creates what Dr. Pat Crittenden calls an "externally assembled adult self," in which the individual's entire personality relies on the opinions of others. They equate praise with self-worth, and criticism with self-hatred. Their self-esteem is fragile.

Theo: I can relate to that. A thousand great things can happen in one day, and I will get stuck pausing about the one crappy thing. Although I don't want others' opinions to matter, they do.

Kim: It's easy to fall into that hole.

Theo: All of this tells me I never really had a chance. It wasn't my fault that I cope the way that I do. I can now see how all this unfolded. But because I recognize it, now at least I have a clue about what I need to work on.

Kim: You were always doing the best you could with what you had. To protect ourselves, we adapt to survive.

Theo: Which is what we are all doing. If you are abused, the experience seems to further reinforce feelings of abandonment, feeling unlovable, and feeling not good enough. That is what abuse hardwires in us. The thread between my parent stuff, my abuse stuff, and my relationship stuff is all part of the same story underneath. No wonder I have often been in relationships with people who were also emotionally abusive. It just reinforced the same story over and over.

Kim: Many A's often cope with abuse by becoming increasingly self-reliant and separate from their uncomfortable feelings, often through addiction.

Theo: I was so self-reliant and shut off, especially when I was drinking. When the abuse stopped, I began abusing myself. Self-reliance keeps us lonely. Usually, we unconsciously choose people who are emotionally unavailable and the cycle repeats itself. Therein lies the inner conflict.

So as I'm trying to become less of an A, do you think I'll turn into more of a C? Come to think of it, I was such a shit disturber at school. I'm sure my teachers would have thought of me as a C.

Kim: The connection-seeking strategy may show up in a predominantly avoidant A child when they start to feel safe enough to first try out a different approach. It is important to remember that these strategies are not "bad"; they are about coping.

Theo: Do you think if you'd write a note about that to my old teachers, maybe they'd forgive me? (*laughing*)

Kim: (*grinning*) I just thought of something important. As we understand ourselves more and heal, it's not about taking away the strategies we do have. It's about adding new ones. This gives us more flexibility in how we respond to everyday interactions. But as we are learning, it is natural to go from one extreme to the other and settle somewhere in the middle. While the A's are preoccupied with others, and the Cs are preoccupied with themselves, I guess the goal is to be able to be mindful of both other and self at the same time.

Theo: I would really like to add more tools to my strategy toolkit so that my kids have a better me as a parent. 'Cause I believe my coping strategies affect them. It would be good if our kids didn't need the extremes of either of these strategies to feel okay.

Kim: For sure.

Theo: I know I'm always talking about parents and sometimes you mention "caregivers." Can anyone mess you up when you're really little?

Kim: Yes and everyone can help regulate you, too. Meaning "calm you down" or "bring you up" as you need. Sometimes, it's not the biological parents who take care of the children. I work with a lot of foster parents, adoptive parents, group home workers, teachers, and people who are giving care but aren't the ones who conceived the child. Attachment relationships form with anyone who takes care of a child. So it's true—I switch between those terms. I could also interchange moms and dads more often in my descriptions. My husband was a single dad for the first three years of our daughter's life before I met him. I know first-hand there are absolutely amazing dads who take care of babies too. I think I say "mom" so much because of the numbers of moms in that role, but I don't mean to exclude anyone at all.

Theo: All of this stuff blows my mind. I always thought I was the way I was because of my genetics. This information about brain development and parenting helps me to appreciate the complexity of why I do what I do. But even though this stuff helps me understand myself, it is important not to look for excuses. I could say, "My parents fucked me up, so I am just going to be a fuckup for the rest of my life." But at the end of the day that doesn't work for me. I want to be better than that. I hope that my kids—when they think about me—come to the same place that I am at today with my parents.

Kim: That is beautiful.

Theo: (*audibly sighing with relief*) It truly isn't my fault; in fact, no one is at fault really. As you say over and over, "We're all doing the best we can with what we have." Let's get rid of the shame and think about today. What can I do today? I am an adult and I make my own choices. And I have to live with the good and the bad of those choices, which says "I am human." This is humbling. This helps me to be less angry. People have been living in my head rent-free, and I'm just now beginning to realize I'm actually the fucking landlord. Time to clean house.

3

Healing Conversations

"People are hungry for messages of hope and life.
What are you broadcasting?"
Morgan Brittany

Kim: I think at some level we all want to clean house, live life more fully.

Theo: But how? And what's the easiest way to start?

Kim: Talking. Safe, open, and vulnerable conversation is such an undervalued force for positive change. The thoughts we have, the words we use, and the relationships we say them in are what shape our brain, for better or for worse.

Theo: Understanding my early infant patterns of coping opens the door for more comfortable conversation about my sexual abuse.

Kim: Why is that?

Theo: Because the shame is so much less, knowing it wasn't my fault. Before that, the shame was blocking me, continuing to interfere with any progress I thought I might be making. It wasn't just that information though; it was finding the right person to talk with.

Kim: We can have all the conversations we want with ourselves, but it's not the same, is it? We understand ourselves better when we hear ourselves talk out loud; it helps us to process our thoughts.

Theo: Even though I could talk about my sexual abuse publicly, it didn't immediately change my dysfunction.

Kim: Do you find it interesting that you initially found it easier to talk about your trauma to thousands of people rather than intimately with one person?

Theo: When I first told my story on stage, it was a one-way conversation and there was a safe distance in that. Over the past two years, this has really transformed. Eh! (*smiling*)

Kim: That's for sure. But the healing process has to start somewhere, and everyone's journey is so individual. I bet there aren't too many people who will find their healing path through writing a book and talking on stage with a friend.

Theo: You're right. It's the safe relationship between us that's making this change possible for me. It's suffering in silence that is exactly what we're trying to prevent for others. I mean, it would be fuckin' awesome if we could eradicate trauma and sexual abuse from the planet, but what we're up against is the biggest epidemic known to man. The most recent study I saw about the stats was in the *Canadian Medical Association Journal* that says 32 percent of the adults in Canada have experienced child abuse, which includes physical abuse, sexual abuse, and/or exposure to domestic violence. It also says that child abuse has really strong associations with mental conditions.[xvi]

One in three! That is an epidemic. Almost twelve million people in our country alone. Given the world's population of seven billion, if the percentage is the same—and we know not everyone's reporting it—a third of us means over 2.3 billion people are faced with having to deal with this stuff that they didn't ask for. This shit doesn't go away overnight, and we're not so naive as to hope otherwise.

Kim: Those stats remind us we really aren't alone. The change starts by having healthy conversations with whomever we trust, so we can at least begin to lighten our load.

Theo: This is pretty obvious, but it's important not to just go up to a random stranger and disclose your personal story; that wouldn't be helpful. What we're talking about is sensitive stuff. It needs to be handled with a lot of care.

Kim: We all know how telling our story to the wrong person can often make our pain worse.

Theo: That probably explains why we bury it for as long as we do. We're worried about what people will do with the information. Or if the story gets out, that other people could get hurt.

Kim: And sometimes, people don't have the energy to engage in their own healing.

Theo: I know I had a lot of difficulty opening up to the therapists I was ordered to see. I just wasn't ready. And I gotta say that I wish some of those therapists would learn how to get clients to feel safe and open up more. (*as if talking to a regular therapist*) You may have these ethical boundaries but listen, if you don't tell me anything about yourself in a session, I'm not revealing anything to you.

Kim: You know why therapists don't open up about their personal stuff though, right? They are worried about transference and countertransference and being unprofessional.

Theo: What are transference and countertransference exactly?

Kim: It's about the projecting of our personal stuff back and forth, which could confuse or compromise the therapeutic results for the client. These projections can be sneaky, like if one of them reminded the other of someone else from their past there could be triggers that would limit either of them being objective. Or the biggest taboo in therapy—like in the movie *The Prince of Tides*—when the therapist and client fall in love.

Theo: I get that. And I held myself back well from really liking one of my therapists in New York. (*thinking*) But on the other end of that, there would be no benefits at all if clients don't feel safe enough to open up.

Kim: Good thing we don't have to worry about that because we aren't in a professional client/therapist relationship; we're friends.

Theo: Right, we're friends and we're colleagues, and we've talked more in the past two years than any client/therapist team would ever do. I recognize that this is not traditional therapy. It's sharing a common mission to learn as much as we can and share it.

Kim: But I get what you're saying. Before you open up, you need to feel safe. And in order for that to happen, you need to have some kind of relationship with the person you're talking with. Totally fair. My belief is that skilled and mindful therapists are very tuned in and could benefit from the insights of whatever comes up between them and the client, and that those could be used as an opportunity for growth.

Theo: When someone is vulnerable with me, I am more likely to be vulnerable with them.

Kim: Maybe because the stuff we talk about is so sensitive, I definitely bring my therapy knowledge to all of our interactions. Good therapists, like secure attachment figures, need to uniquely modify the way they interact with every client to best suit their client's unique version of attachment strategies. Not every client would want or even feel comfortable with their therapist being vulnerable. What makes a person feel safe is the feeling of being cared for, seen, and understood. That is what I think you perceive when you are speaking about vulnerability.

Theo: Ah, maybe you're right. I am using the word "vulnerability," but I think what I really mean is authentic. A person who is present, open, and interested. If they aren't that, it's not worth connecting. When they are that, there is a lot to talk about.

Kim: There is still some level of stigma about going to see a therapist, isn't there? Many people feel it's a weakness to admit they need help, especially men. And many therapists have the reputation of being either fluffy, condescending, or crazy themselves.

Theo: Some people don't seek help because they are living in denial, like the river in Egypt. (*joking*)

Kim: A lot of people don't think they need any help. But as Bob always says, "We're all special needs in different ways." We certainly do all have our hang-ups, issues, and quirks. What I personally believe is that we could all benefit from more insight.

Theo: If you truly believe the responsibility for your problems lies one hundred percent with other people, that is a sure sign of needing help.

Kim: There are also other people who know they are hurting, but sincerely don't believe there's anything that will make them feel better.

Theo: That is sad. You are ultimately the only person who is in charge of how you feel and you are the only person who can change how you feel.

Kim: Now you're starting to sound like a therapist. What I'd add is that healing is actually a natural process, and negative thoughts only serve to stand in its way.

Theo: And I'm learning there really are some people out there who know how to listen, when to keep secrets, and really do care.

Kim: Yes. There really are people out there that we can trust. So much of this stuff is about relationship.

Theo: Yeah, that's what I'm figuring out.

Kim: In healing from trauma, it's not as much what happened to you, but how you deal with it that has the most impact on how you cope. I used to work with a veteran on Vancouver Island who had just returned from Afghanistan. He told me that he believed he would be better when he no longer remembered his trauma. And I said, "And then, you'll be dead." It's impossible to erase the memory of trauma; it's how you deal with it that matters.

Theo: That makes a lot of sense. In my case, a huge motivation was I didn't want my kids to repeat my dysfunctional coping strategies themselves. That is still a huge motivator for me.

Kim: And when your healing happens, it doesn't just make *you* feel better, but everyone else around you feels better too.

Theo: I've got a good line for an ad: "Even if your healing doesn't make you lose weight, you're guaranteed to feel lighter." (*grinning*)

Kim: So right. But safety—as you say—is critical for this process.

Theo: You're talking about safety in the context of relationship, right? Not seatbelts and helmets?

Kim: Exactly. Boundaries, honesty, vulnerability, compassion, and a sense of ease create the foundations for safety in a relationship, whether it's therapeutic or otherwise. This is often the challenge for someone with something to reveal: who to tell, and how to tell it so that they don't end up feeling more alone. You have to be discerning in who you choose to share yourself vulnerably with.

Theo: I just know with my intuition when a person is safe and when they are not. I can read it in their eyes. Interestingly, I see a lot more people around now who are safe than I used to.

Kim: We're actually like the babies who read their parents' faces. The amygdala (the emotional centre in our brain) makes a very quick judgment of who is safe and who is not. We are born with a great deal of relational knowing. Implicitly, we read faces, interpret body language, and listen to tones of voice for survival cues. Laurence Heller says we just inherently feel a sense of heartfelt expansion in our body when we're in an authentic person-to-person connection, and that we can also feel it viscerally—as distress throughout our body—when the connection with that person fails.[xvii]

Theo: Cool.

Kim: Psychology researchers took a group of babies who could crawl and placed them on a Plexiglas platform three feet off the ground. These babies were anxiously able to appreciate that they were up high. Each baby was placed at one end of the plank with the parent located at the opposite end. The researchers discovered that if the parent smiled and nodded at the baby, he would crawl effortlessly across the Plexiglas plate toward his parent. But when the parent showed fear or no expression at all, that baby would not move.[xviii] We rely so much on these types of social clues to keep us safe.

Theo: Hmm. My mom would have expressed fear for sure. So I wouldn't have moved? What does that say?

Kim: You would have taken the "go" cues from other people for other things. But you may have spent some time as an infant not quite knowing what was safe and what wasn't.

Theo: That explains a lot.

Kim: One time, I was in an elevator in the Empire State Building. There were eight of us in there. Somewhere half way up, the elevator stopped suddenly. It seemed like we all instantly went into fear. You could feel the tension immediately. I wondered how long we would be in there, if I'd ever get out before I had to pee, or worse. Tuning in to the others, I noticed that one guy in the group looked relaxed and unaffected. We all noticed him; he just looked like he knew something the rest of us didn't. He noticed that we noticed his demeanour and he commented, "Yeah, yeah; the elevator stops like this all the time." We all exhaled together and then, as if on cue, the elevator started working again. Nonverbal communication is loaded with information and we affect each other with more than just our words.

Theo: Words clarify impressions though.

Kim: Of course. But sometimes the words we say and the nonverbal cues we give off don't send the same message. It's what I call "when the inside and the outside don't match." It's typical for example, in emotionally absent parents who say, "I love you," when they're playing Candy Crush on their iPad; then they're not connected to the words. If we want to know the truth about how people are feeling, it's the nonverbal cues that are worth paying more attention to.

Theo: Some of us don't want to know the negative stuff others are feeling.

Kim: True, but it works the other way as well. Sometimes we say something negative, but our body language is telling a totally opposite story, like when someone says no but nods yes. Trust the nod over the words.

Theo: Why are some people not so good at reading these cues?

Kim: Well, there are a couple of reasons. Remember we talked about how the brain adapts? If you live in conditions of threat, you will begin to see danger where danger does not exist. Research tells us that some individuals will develop the skill of reading fear in other people's faces faster, but they may also misinterpret neutral faces as dangerous ones.[xix]

Theo: This would be good in a war zone, but not so good when you're at home with your wife and kids. That could get you into a lot of trouble, couldn't it? This is kind of like veterans who come back from war and suffer from post-traumatic stress. They're super-vigilant like me, right?

Kim: Yes. I believe what you have in common with some war veterans is that you both learned to keep yourself safe by reading danger. The challenge is to retrain your brain for the appropriate interpretation of these cues.

Theo: That must be really hard for the vets.

Kim: It's common among people who have experienced abuse as well. Once I had a teenage client tell me, "I hate your face." Needless to say, I thought that was offensive, but have been trained over the years to consider the source before reacting. I asked, "What is it that you don't like about my face?"

He said "You have a crease between your eyes; you're judgmental, angry."

I said, "My wrinkles are always there; they're part of my forehead. Even though I am judgmental sometimes, I wasn't thinking judgmentally just now."

I asked him if I'd sounded angry or if I'd said something threatening.

He said, "No. Oh, shit! I see that kind of face in lots of people and I want to smash it ..."

He understood then that he'd been reading people wrongly. This experience explained many of his aggressive outbursts. He had been labelled with a conduct disorder, but at the root of it, his amygdala was just overreactive; he had an instinctive fight response. He'd truly been thinking he was in real danger when he wasn't. Sometimes, this kind of awareness can help to mellow people naturally, without drugs.

Theo: I think I am very good at reading faces and danger; but I frequently attracted danger over and over. Why would that be?

Kim: "Danger" would give you an adrenaline hit! What I know about you is the minute you are bored you lose focus and attention. Adrenaline temporarily sharpens your attention. You can become addicted to adrenaline. In a sense, you like danger. At least, your brain seems to like it.

Theo: I've decided I don't want danger anymore in my relationships, though. It's tiring. How do I change that?

Kim: That isn't a quick fix. It's like changing all addictive patterns. We have to slow down our responses and think before we act, or do what we can to get the adrenaline from another source. Bungee jump every morning or something!

Theo: I'm afraid of heights, but I get your point. Kim, are you addicted to adrenaline?

Kim: Working with challenging behaviours actually gives me an adrenaline hit. (*smiling*)

Theo: Happy to enable you with your addiction! (*laughing*)

Kim: In order to change the brain's perception of danger, you have to experience more safety.

Theo: I don't think I'm alone in equating the concept of safety with boredom.

Kim: Then we need to rethink how you define safety. Not as something dull; but as something empowering and exciting; because if you're feeling emotionally safe, you can tackle just about anything with sincere confidence, rather than being motivated by fear.

Theo: Huh. (*nodding*) I like that. So how do we begin to experience safety in conversations?

Kim: Find someone you trust. They are the ones who are tuned in to what you are saying and not thinking only about themselves while they are listening to you. They are present to you without an agenda.

Theo: That seems rare, but the right thing to look for.

Kim: I could make a list of the number of people I've been in long conversations with who never once asked me anything about myself.

Theo: Maybe you're too giving? I practise this skill of asking with you, making sure I don't just talk about myself. Truth is we should all be caring about the people we care about.

Kim: I think that for many people who feel safe with someone, they finally have a place where they can talk and just dump their stuff, especially self-contained people who start opening up. They can forget to check in with the other person. It is natural and I do it to my friend Marie fairly regularly. I love her for listening.

Theo: Ultimately, I think the listener has to be able to hold the space for the other person. This is what makes the difference. The more strength and safety you are holding for the other person, the more they're going to reveal to you.

Kim: (*smiling*) You are talking about "holding space"! That's therapy-speak. Very different from "fucking shit" language.

Theo: Yeah, yeah. I think that it is important that listeners don't feel like they have to "fix" the person telling the story. There is healing in just sharing.

Kim: The way we're talking about it, the definition of healing isn't curing; it's coming to terms with what is.

Theo: It's finding a way to live with your demons.

Kim: One conversation that will forever stand out in my mind as an example of "holding space" occurred at one of our "Conversations With a Rattlesnake" forums. This particular conversation occurred at the very last minute of the day. A man was sitting way at the back of the room squirming in his chair, almost ready to explode; anyone could tell he had something he just had to say. He forcibly raised his hand and bolted onto his feet, and began to speak from his heart. He shifted his weight rapidly side to side while he began to let go of a million pounds of shame. He declared, in a room full of survivors, "I was abused and I became a violent offender. I've never felt as safe as I do in this moment to say this."

I remember how you grabbed my hand in shock and how the tears came to both our eyes in wonder—how could this possibly be happening in a room full of people who'd been sharing their experiences of abuse? We marvelled at his courage and thanked him for his willingness to share such a difficult part of himself. He visibly transformed in front of our eyes. His shoulders relaxed, his hands opened, and he smiled. The entire room was calm and held the space for this man to speak his truth.

Theo: That was also a transformational moment for me. It changed my thinking, taking in that conversation. It was the first time I saw the suffering of an offender and the cycle of abuse. My initial reaction was, "Fuck him," but you, Kim, held the space for me, which helped me to shift from a reactive response to compassion. You helped me totally change my whole way of thinking about being in the victim position. I had held on so tightly to my position of wanting justice against the offender that I was locked into my anger. That experience in that room transformed me. When a survivor can hold the space for an offender, it's like a spiritual shift. We were able to model compassion through example. No one got up and left, everyone was riveted, and they understood his dilemma. We all felt the shame and pain of his secret.

Kim: When you can see something good in every person, you reflect that back to them when you are listening. I think it is easiest to "hold the space" when you feel comfortable in your own skin. It is easier to encourage others when you are drawing from your own confidence, the knowing that another person is not taking anything away from you.

Theo: When I am not feeling confident or comfortable, I think I often come across as arrogant.

Kim: Good insight on your part. Whenever we have strong, unforgiving opinions about right and wrong, this closes our channels of communication. It reduces the safety in our conversation. Susan Gillis Chapman, a meditation writer, describes the phenomenon of arrogance as toxic, creating an illusion of superiority that masks the real vulnerability underneath.[xx] Arrogance creates separation in relationship.

Theo: I'm more and more convinced that vulnerability is the key to connection. It is often what people try to avoid. But vulnerability is power. I used to be terrified of showing my vulnerability, and now I see it as a gift and a strength. And women love it.

Kim: My goodness. But I bet there's some truth to that! Vulnerability is still hard for me sometimes. When I encounter mean and hurtful comments, they trigger me into feeling like a bad girl. Not good enough. I'm not comfortable showing that to everybody in the moment.

Theo: Which is crazy, because you know you are more than good enough.

Kim: Implicit memory stuff is not logical. I think the reason I work so hard at everything is to feel good enough.

Theo: Is that your family of origin stuff?

Kim: Undeniably. When I perceive a comment that was intended to be hurtful—"perceive" is the operative word—I always wish that I had the right thing to say in that moment. But the best response typically requires vulnerability. For example, "I feel hurt by what I just heard. Did you mean it to be hurtful or could you say it in a way that I could hear it better?" If they say they actually meant to hurt me on purpose, I'd be surprised, because no one wants to own their meanness. Hurt people hurt people; it's about not personalizing it. But when I am feeling defensive I can't think properly. And if I were upset, I'd have obviously resonated with something that they'd said. Between my husband and me, we have an acknowledged knowing; if one of us is ever defensive, it's because the other one is right.

Theo: And I often feel defensive …

Kim: My fall-back script in those challenging moments when I can't think of anything else to say is to respond with something like, "This is hard for me." Moving into that space of vulnerability empowers me and helps me to honour myself. That's how I create my own safety in the middle of a tough conversation, and it buys me some time to think.

Theo: Another thing that helps me to keep a conversation safe is to stop comparing myself to others. If I have to compare myself to anyone else to make myself feel better, then I am sick. I find I'm healthier when I don't care so much about what other people think.

Kim: Comparisons, which I can be guilty of making, are rooted in insecurity and contempt. When I think, "I wish I were as beautiful as her," I'm showing my insecurity and contempt for myself. It's self-deprecating. It's also important not to compare the person you're talking with to anyone else. At best, that's a distraction; at worst, you are making huge judgments. We have to know that the person we are talking with can feel and see these judgments in the conversation.

Theo: I know that sometimes I get triggered in the middle of a conversation and can project my own shit on the other person. I don't always know in the moment when I am projecting, but sometimes I reflect on it afterwards. This mindfulness stuff is new to me. I was wired and trained to react; slowing down and thinking are things I am still working on.

Kim: We all project our own stuff on others every day. It is virtually impossible not to "project" at least some of the time. Projections mostly happen when we defend ourselves against unpleasant feelings by denying their existence in ourselves and instead attributing them to others. For example, a person who is rude may constantly accuse other people of being rude. There's a great quote by Anaïs Nin: "We don't see things as they are. We see things as we are." I love that honesty about our own biases.

Theo: These are the things that seep in when a conversation goes sideways. I guess it helps to pay attention to your feelings when you are talking.

Kim: Always. (*smiling*) Remember we've talked about Don Miguel Ruiz, the Toltec Spiritual teacher?

Theo: I do, the Mexican guy who wrote a book called *The Four Agreements*.[xxi] Like the Ten Commandments, but shorter. (*smiling*)

Kim: Right. His second agreement is "Don't take anything personally" and his rationale for this is that nothing other people do is because of you. Everything they do is a projection of their own reality. Which means everything we do is a projection of our own reality.

Theo: So that totally jives with what Anaïs Nin is saying, that we see things as we are …

Kim: I just saw his son has got a new book coming out this fall, and it's got a rattlesnake on the cover! It's called *My Good Friend the Rattlesnake*.[xxii] How cool is that?

Theo: Rattlesnakes are the symbol of transformation, after all. (*smiling*) Maybe I'll have to read that one.

Kim: Yes. And in order to have these transformations, it takes mindfulness. Paying attention to our thoughts and feelings helps us to become aware of when out-of-sync moments are happening in conversations. And that awareness is what can bring the conversation back into the safety zone.

Theo: I guess arrogance, put-downs, or projections can trigger others to relive their painful implicit memories. When I can separate myself from the other person's stuff, I am present and not affected by their experience.

Kim: That's it. It's about not taking it personally.

Theo: When you've been traumatized, I think those triggers are really close to the surface.

Kim: They are. For some people remembering and talking about a trauma is like reliving the experience all over again. It can re-traumatize them. It can actually reactivate the pain circuit in the brain. Re-traumatizing yourself is counterproductive. Worst case, you relive what was arguably the most horrible experience of your life and then someone who doesn't care about you either dismisses it or blabs about it to other people. We all need to be mindful, as listeners and friends, that storytelling is critical for the teller.

Theo: When I first went on the speaking circuit and told my abuse story over and over, I think I was re-traumatizing myself.

Kim: I think you were, too.

Theo: How can you tell when someone is being re-traumatized in a conversation?

Kim: They may start to disappear; their eyes can look empty and lost; they may lose their train of thought; they may stop talking in the middle of a sentence. They check out.

Theo: Is that what you call "dissociation"? When I went to the treatment centres, they used that word a lot to describe what you're talking about.

Kim: Yes. I remember the scene from your HBO *Playing With Fire* documentary when you were in Santa Fe, driving up and down a street in the middle of the desert looking for your old house where you'd considered suicide. I watched the distress in your face when you couldn't even find it. Lapses in memory like that often happen to people who are dissociating. It was hard to watch.

Theo: Why does that happen?

Kim: In that example, you were triggered by where you were and the memory it was connected to. We associate places with emotions. A lot of bad things happened for you in Santa Fe; so, it's no wonder you had difficulty retrieving your memories clearly.

Theo: I just felt stupid watching that scene. (*looking away*)

Kim: I'm so sorry you had that experience. Dissociation is nothing to be ashamed of.

Theo: Watching that whole documentary was traumatizing for me.

Kim: That person on the video is very different from the person I know now.

Dissociation is natural though, and happens as a result of a stress response. It's a floating, absent feeling. It can last a long time, especially if you were traumatized as an infant, when you didn't have the option to fight or run away. Checking out would have been the only strategy you had in your earliest days. This is one reason why early infant trauma is often linked to mental illness in later adulthood.

Theo: I have no idea if I dissociated as an infant; but I know that I did during the times I was sexually abused.

Kim: Did you see the movie *Precious*? Parts of it were very disturbing to watch. What stands out in relation to the topic of dissociation is how she'd retreat into a fantasy world about being an MTV video singer every time she was being sexually assaulted by her father.

Theo: By the time I watched that movie, I was already feeling a bit better about myself. I'm sure if I'd seen it earlier, it would have been more of a trigger for me.

Kim: I know I dissociated during parts of watching that movie. Some people dissociate so much that their personality and memories begin to fragment. Fragmented individuals cannot find a way to tell a clear story about their own lives.

Theo: When I was full on in my addiction, I was definitely fragmented. I couldn't access any memories or string together a timeline.

Kim: When people reach the limits of their terror, their survival brain throws the circuit breaker on their mind, and they check out. They no longer feel sensations in their body. If you check out repeatedly, then over time, you will lose the awareness of how your body feels.

Theo: I can describe it best like having been on Novocain at the dentist. You feel kind of numb.

Kim: In therapy, people who frequently dissociate as a part of their experience find the question, "What do you feel in your body?" very anxiety-producing and frustrating.

Theo: I hate that fucking question. I have no idea how I feel in my body. I also hate massages, the feeling disgusts me. I don't like it when someone unfamiliar touches me. What is healthy touch? Even though in my mind I know massage is healthy, I am so used to checking out that I can't discern that it is healthy touching. 'Cause when you're on the massage table, you're face down and you can't see anything, right? It would be even more challenging if the masseur was male. If I was having a massage like that, I would feel intense anxiety and then immediately check out. It's about trust.

Kim: Learning to feel safe in your body helps you to keep your emotions regulated. This is especially important for healthy sexuality. When you begin to dissociate or check out, it is helpful to look at your surroundings, listen for sounds, feel the arms of the chair, or sit forward with the weight on your feet. These sensations will quickly bring you back into the present moment.

Theo: I still have trouble being in a hotel room by myself. An uncomfortable queasy feeling. I was abused in a dark room. I didn't have the tools to end it. The big Theo might have walked in and taken the little Theo out of the dark. I don't need some stranger to help me soothe myself. For many years, I couldn't sleep.

Kim: (*softly*) Do you realize how fragmented the words you just said were? The sentences were very disjointed. That was a great example of having difficulty talking about something that was traumatizing.

Theo: (*sighing*) Thanks for helping me to understand. While I was being sexually abused, I felt frozen as if I couldn't move. If someone would have offered me a million dollars to have been able to stand up in those moments, I still couldn't have done it. I hate that, but I really couldn't.

Kim: (*looking with compassion*) When you were frozen like that, that was your brain protecting you. The "freeze" response happens when you have no other options. When you are totally in terror, even the most basic fight-or-flight responses don't work. When you are that afraid, there is a lot of high energy screaming in the sympathetic branch of the autonomic nervous system. "Freeze" is like in the movies when someone is hanging off a cliff and someone else says, "Just give me your hand," and they legitimately can't even reach out. They are immobilized by fear.

Theo: I wish someone would have taken me out of those dark rooms. Fight and flight came pretty naturally to me in other circumstances, but not that one.

Kim: This all happens so fast, without consciousness. These fight-or-flight or freeze responses happen automatically. Instead of calling it the autonomic nervous system, a lot of people call it the "automatic" nervous system, because it happens so automatically.

Theo: I guess I must have used my sympathetic nervous system all the time when I was playing hockey.

Kim: I think you are right. The chemistry of the sympathetic nervous system is adrenaline. You are an adrenaline junky, remember? Having this jacked up response on all the time is like living in constant fear.

Theo: Uh huh. (*nodding*)

Kim: The sympathetic—don't know why it's called that as it's not very sympathetic to our bodies—nervous system was never designed to be turned on all the time. Its job is to fire up briefly, to give us enough adrenaline to either fight our enemies or run to save our lives. One of my heroes in the neuroscience field is Dr. Robert Sapolsky. He wrote a great book about stress called *Why Zebras Don't Get Ulcers*.[xxiii]

Theo: I guess I never thought about animals even having ulcers.

Kim: When a zebra is chased by a lion on a savannah and it survives, it doesn't lie down on the grass immobilized. After being chased, the zebra shakes its body all over like a wet dog and in so doing, gets rid of all the stressful chemicals. Then it goes back to eating its grass, and carries on with doing all the regular zebra things.

Theo: Humans don't do that, do they? We get immobilized, and then we get ulcers.

Kim: We definitely haven't learned to shake it off. It's not really socially appropriate for us to walk around and shake our bodies in the bank when we feel stressed.

Theo: (*laughing*) I can just imagine people walking around shaking. Should we?

Kim: We know that moving our bodies releases stress hormones, so maybe it would help us.

Theo: (*shaking like a wet dog and laughing*) I'm going to consciously try and do this shake thing twice a day when I brush my teeth.

Kim: (*smiling*) I'm sure Rob Sapolsky would have a good laugh at that! (*thinking*) I wonder if he actively shakes after stressful moments, knowing what he knows? In his *National Geographic* documentary, *Stress: Portrait of a Killer* (I quote him a lot in my lectures), Rob says "No zebra on earth would understand why we have the same chemical stress responses as when we think about taxes, mortality, the ozone layer, and public speaking as they do when they're running from the lion to save their lives."[xxiv]

Theo: (*looking serious*) Didn't you know, Kim, in between periods, we'd go into the dressing room and do a "team shake." It really helped to prepare us for the next period.

Kim: Bullshit! You're making fun of me. What I think really happened during games is that your coaches purposefully activated your sympathetic nervous systems by pushing you to achieve.

Theo: That's how they got the best out of us: by yelling at us and challenging the way we'd do things. There was never any praise. It was that tough love era in hockey that I grew up in. The expectation was that I was going to go out there and play well every night. Actually, I put more expectations on myself than any of my coaches did, so part of it was on me. But when you are hungry, angry, lonely, and tired, your sensitivity to the criticism is heightened.

Kim: Hmm, those conditions would make you more susceptible to fight-or-flight responses, which would work in your team's favour.

Theo: Freeze responses obviously wouldn't help anyone in hockey.

Kim: No, they wouldn't. What's interesting about freezing in response to stress is that the terror branches (sympathetic) and the calming branches (parasympathetic) of our stress manager (autonomic nervous system) are both fully on-line at the same time. It's like having the gas pedal pressed firmly to the floor and slamming on the brakes at the same time. So when the engine is revving at high speed but the brakes are fully engaged, the car is stuck at a standstill, frozen. The immobility is both terrifying and exhausting.

Theo: I've been frozen many times, but never on the ice; only in relationships. I used to leave my body every time Graham James would rape me. I was absolutely frozen, paralyzed, and that was the reaction my assaulter was looking for. Compliance. That immobilized fear. I wonder, does the assaulter know you are checking out?

Kim: (*looking empathetically*) Sad part is I don't know if they'd care. That is one of the tragedies of abuse.

Theo: I can see how the dissociation was helpful in the moment; it allowed me to not go insane, I guess. But in the long term, it probably wasn't good for me, right? So many people ask, "Why didn't you just leave?" I couldn't; I was fucking paralyzed.

Kim: (*with sadness*) Yup. I am sorry this is a hard conversation. I don't want it to be re-traumatizing for you. I want you to know I am watching you closely right now and you look present and comfortable enough, signalling me that you are safely able to continue.

Theo: I'm okay.

Kim: New science is beginning to explain what is happening right here in this conversation. When a trauma story is told in the presence of a calm and caring person, the brain re-experiences the stress of the trauma in a new way, combining an old channel of distress together with a new state of care and connection. This experience rewires implicit and explicit memories together differently. By dialling down the intensity of the trauma response, the brain is learning that the old experience doesn't feel as horrific as it was previously perceived.

Theo: There are a lot of layers to the onion that need to be peeled off. And that takes lots of safe and nurturing conversations to happen. I want people to understand what the abuser is really like, though; so it's okay to keep going.

Kim: (*exhaling*) I think that an abusive person is unable to truly care about the other, as it would be horrific for them to connect to their actions if they did. It's hard to imagine that if an abuser were able to put his or her mind in the mind of the other, he or she would still engage in causing such hurt. But I know enough as a therapist to know there are a lot of highly disturbed people in the world. I don't like to think of them as inherently evil though. However we define them and their actions, which will vary according to our personal frames of reference, I definitely think the general population needs to be protected from what they are capable of doing.

Theo: He never showed remorse. He only said he was sorry to the court because his lawyer told him to. He never apologized to me for what I was experiencing. There was fuck all I could have done! Every survivor needs to know, there was fuck all they could have done.

Kim: Yeah. (*softly*) That is the purpose of the freeze response; it's not to change the situation but to help you survive the situation.

Theo: Shit! That explanation helps.

Kim: Hate, rage, and the fight response that you probably felt toward Graham James during the abuse was managed by your psyche through "splitting." It is so difficult when you love and hate the person at the same time. Sorry for using your language, but this is what fucks people up the most. It can create tremendous shame, especially when the abuse is sexual in nature.

Theo: That helps me to forgive myself for having stayed connected to James for so long. That kind of confusion for a kid is beyond comprehension.

Kim: Inherent in the damage of sexual abuse is the psychological confusion that the survivor sometimes feels of love, enjoyment, sexual intensity, mixed with pain, hatred, and rage. The brain has to develop some unusual pathways to handle that mix of experiences, to associate them with one another. This would not be a typical neural network in the brain. In later life, previously unresolved confusing information can be expressed consciously or unconsciously as aggression, rage, and/or hatred.

Theo: So playing in the NHL was perfect therapy for me. A place to discharge my built-up aggression and rage in a somewhat controlled way. How ironic really, since it was my drive to get into the show that contributed to all this in the first place. But many people won't be as fortunate to have had this kind of outlet.

Kim: Some people will turn that anger and aggression outwards, which will hurt other people, and others will turn it inwards as self-hatred. If you can't access some form of outlet for your anger, you are likely to feel powerless; victimized over and over again.

Theo: This is an example right here of a safe, vulnerable, and healing conversation. I am able to stay present while we talk about this stuff and you are so good at holding the space for me.

Kim: I will never forget our conference in Winnipeg, when one of the participants began to share her story with the audience about her sexual addiction and promiscuous behaviour. She started to express her feelings of shame about not remembering their faces or names, and I began to watch you disappear from the room. You started to dissociate. But what was unforgettable and such a magnificent healing moment was that you caught yourself. You were able to express what you were experiencing to the woman and to the audience.

Theo: I remember saying, "Wait a minute, I am starting to leave the room as you are talking. I am so triggered by what you are saying. Although you are talking about yourself, you are also describing me and it is tapping into my shame. I am starting to check out."

Kim: It was a marvel to watch your body shift and relax as you vulnerably expressed what was happening for you. In therapy terms, we call what you experienced "dual awareness." It is profoundly healing when you can be both in your trauma experience and in the present moment at the same time. When this happens you are rewiring the brain! It breaks apart old neural networks and creates new ones. This is the power of mindfulness in a healing conversation.

Theo: I will never forget the feelings of gratitude, calm, and openness I felt after that shift. It was also exhausting.

Kim: Rewiring the brain through healing conversations is exhausting. You are taking old patterns and implicit memories and reorganizing them. This develops a sense of coherence to your thoughts and feelings at a time when your mind, body, and spirit are all in alignment. This is really the definition of healing, I think, when you take an old experience that is confusing, fragmented, stressful, or traumatic, and you make sense of it. Daniel Siegel says, "What is shareable is bearable."[xxv] That is the magic of the coherence that occurs when you have a lightbulb moment in conversation.

Theo: This is how we actually change those attachment patterns we spoke about earlier, right?

Kim: Healing conversations help rewire those implicit memories that are chaotic, disorganizing, and maladaptive, giving you a new state of being. A safe and trusting relationship would likely mimic all the qualities of a secure attachment relationship between a baby and his parents. If someone has a history of developmental trauma, they are not likely to know what this instinctively feels like. At first, they may not recognize this secure relationship as one that is safe. It might feel that unfamiliar.

As you're finding, Theo, you can change your brain and your

trauma response until you stop breathing. Of course, this takes patience and perseverance.

Theo: It is hard for me to imagine that I could deserve relationships like that.

Kim: The first step is to start believing it.

Theo: That is what this book is about, I guess. Changing people's minds.

Kim: We change our minds by putting feelings into words. Doing this develops important neural networks in the brain that help to integrate trauma. Understanding our feelings, tolerating our feelings, and being able to communicate them with significant people in our lives is often a culmination of all the steps of healing.

Theo: How does conversation actually change the brain?

Kim: The brain is able to change its structure in response to any experience a person has. Our experiences light up nerve cells in our brains, which even turn on individual pieces of our DNA. Repeated experiences change the very structure of our genes and that can strengthen the connections between activated nerve cells that are firing together. Dr. Donald Hebb said, "Neurons that fire together wire together."[xxvi] The more you practise anything, the stronger the neural network will be to support that thing you're practising.

Theo: I guess that supports Malcolm Gladwell's ten-thousand-hours theory where practice creates mastery.[xxvii]

Kim: Perfect example, and another reason to practise something positive instead of negative, and to pay attention to what our habits really are.

Theo: Are addictions a type of these neural networks that have hardwired together?

Kim: Yes, you betcha. Addictions are made up of obsessive thoughts. You taught me that. Every thought, including an addictive obsession, is represented by a neural network in the brain. Whatever you focus your attention on activates particular nerve cells. Changing your thoughts means changing your brain.

Theo: Knowing that is inspiring for me. It encourages me to pay more attention to what I am thinking about. There is something to the idea that our thoughts create our reality, since when we string thoughts together, they become a story. Then that story becomes part of our reality.

Kim: That's really cool. Making up a new way to tell a story is a perfect example of rewiring the brain.

Theo: So storytelling can be healing! The aboriginal peoples have been telling stories for centuries as part of their cultural heritage, and a way to preserve their history and communicate their lessons learned, too. One strength of my dad's, and his dad, was they both could tell amazing stories.

Kim: Cool. I remember back in Rankin Inlet that Inuit Elders would often be invited into the schools to tell stories and the little ones were always so engrossed. One man in particular was outstanding. His name was Mariano Aupilardjuk. He told the story of the time he visited New York City and came across a man sitting on the sidewalk—barefoot—in winter. He immediately gave the man his shoes, and openly questioned the value of a society that builds huge buildings but cannot find the compassion to take care of one of its own.

Theo: Great story!

Kim: That event touched him so much that he made it into his personal song, or "pisiq" that each Inuk can do when they have something they feel is worth passing along. Then these songs can be sung by people who respect them, far into the future, often with a big Inuit drum in the background. (*getting a bit emotional*) Sorry for the emotion, it's just that Aupilardjuk was a very close friend of our family and he passed away not too long ago.

Theo: Sorry to hear that. He sounds like a great man.

Kim: He was. Did a lot of work for suicide prevention, sharing traditional knowledge, healing, and trying to make the justice system better … but that song of his, it was aimed squarely at reminding everyone as human beings to have more compassion.

Theo: That's an example of a beautiful legacy.

Kim: It does matter what kind of stories we're telling. If, for example, we tell a negative abuse story over and over, in a re-traumatizing way, then the brain will become flooded with stress chemicals as if the event were happening again in the present moment.

Theo: Come to think of it, the stories I heard from my dad weren't necessarily always that coherent or full of purpose. But they were great stories though. My implicit memory must have loved hearing them, 'cause they looked so happy telling them and there was always a lot of laughter, even if my explicit memory can't recall all the details.

Kim: Do all you Fleurys have the gift of the gab?

Theo: Absolutely! And music too, I think. Must come from our Métis roots.

Kim: Speaking of your Métis roots, I loved it when you performed at the 2014 Indspire Awards for honouring outstanding Aboriginal achievement. I'm thinking of that scene where actress Tina Keeper, from the CBC series *North of 60*, walked in on you when you were in the bathroom peeing. How unexpected was that!?

Theo: It's funny that you mention it, but I think that's what keeps indigenous people so strong and resilient; it's their sense of humour. Not taking yourself too seriously is a bloody gift, I tell you.

Kim: Well, it's cool to see that First Nations people are reclaiming their rightful swagger. And the Canadian Indspire Awards sure get people talking about positive things. Inspiring.

Theo: Talking about telling stories and aboriginal folks, when the First Nations elders I know have been teaching, it is almost always in the form of stories. And with healing circles, it's all about sharing your story in a safe place.

Kim: Absolutely. This has been a principle of traditional healing circles since time immemorial. The structure of the healing circle demands respectful listening and invites reflection. Each person, spirit, is treated with equality. None of this is new; maybe the science helps explain why some of it works, but the practice of it is ancient. What is it about the healing circle concept that you think really hits home?

Theo: It's that everyone is respectful. No one would be defensive or antagonistic. So when they are relaxed and open, I feel relaxed and open.

Kim: That's amazing insight. Are you able to reflect how your mirroring is affecting your conversations when you're in them in the moment, or only afterwards?

Theo: I love it when I can figure it out in the moment, and adjust it if that makes it better. It is like an aha moment. That's one of the gifts I get from you when we're together having a conversation. You have a way of helping me to be consciously mindful of when and how my feelings are popping up or when I'm checking out. I know I don't always notice it though.

Kim: A theory I heard at an Attachment Conference in Italy suggested that only 25 percent of people are able to actively self-reflect on how their behaviour is affecting the person they are talking with, and make adjustments mid-conversation. Isn't that astonishing how small that percentage is?

Theo: No wonder the world is the way that it is.

Kim: It actually makes me feel better, because it suggests people are not actively trying to hurt each other; they're just focused on themselves. One thing that can give us all comfort is something that respected psychoanalyst Donald Winnicott said back in 1953. That to do a good enough job as a parent, we only have to connect with our kids 20 percent of the time. It's not like we have to be super attuned and actively compassionate twenty-four hours a day to be good parents.

Theo: Thank goodness. That would be exhausting.

Speaking of exhausting, this is what happens to me after a healing conversation like this. I need a summary to pull it together. Can you remind me of the basic ingredients of a healing conversation?

Kim: What would you say they are?

Theo: "Honesty," for sure.

Kim: "Boundaries" has to be in this list, probably at the beginning.

Theo: "Vulnerability" is what I often need to see in others before I can open up at all.

Kim: And "Compassion." Are those the four that make the most sense to you?

Theo: "Mindfulness" comes to mind too, but you know, mindfulness is underneath all of it. So, yeah, I think those four are one hell of a great start: boundaries, honesty, vulnerability, and compassion.

Kim: Boundaries have to be the start, because they are the guidelines that help us feel safe. They guard the physical and emotional space between ourselves and others. When they're crossed, we shut down.

Theo: When we're younger, we often don't know where they are.

Kim: Or maybe even what they are.

Theo: I didn't. Because my parents weren't paying attention, I didn't have any rules or limits imposed upon me.

Kim: Children figure out their boundaries as they develop and those boundaries need to change over time. An appropriate boundary for a two-year-old is different when you are five, ten, fifteen, or twenty-five.

Theo: I guess if you don't develop your boundaries you are kinda stunted in your emotional growth.

Kim: Boundaries define what we will accept or not accept from another person's behaviour. If our boundaries are too rigid, we prevent ourselves from experiencing life's fullness. However, if our boundaries are too loose, people can walk all over us without concern. Boundaries have to be flexible to be healthy.

Theo: In conversations, to know where our boundaries are means we have to be aware of when we're feeling uncomfortable.

Kim: It also means we have to tune in to when others are feeling uncomfortable. I have an example. One time, I was having lunch with a new colleague and she was asking me very personal questions. It felt intrusive and invasive. At one point, she asked me if anyone had ever diagnosed me with autism, since my eye contact was so poor with her. I said, "Well, people make very poor eye contact when they are anxious." I felt as if the listener was not at all attuned to my discomfort, so I had to protect myself. In hindsight, if my boundaries had been better, I would have commented on my discomfort much sooner.

Theo: That's a really good example. We are often so busy trying to please the other person that our boundaries become leaky. For me, one example that comes to mind is with the media. At some points, the media would antagonize me, trying to get shock-value stories and headlines about my abuse and anger. Well, I figured out that if I asked the reporter a question back, it would throw him off. They are not used to answering questions, and it was my way of protecting myself with a boundary. If someone wants to ask me a sensitive question, I think they know now that they have to treat me with respect, and I am always thankful when I get respect.

Kim: Anger is a good signal that your boundaries have been crossed.

Theo: Isn't that what you say, that all emotions are feedback?

Kim: They are. Now how about honesty?

Theo: The first principle of the twelve steps of AA is "get honest."

Kim: What did that mean to you when you first heard that you needed to be honest?

Theo: Taking responsibility for my feelings and my actions. And speaking the truth about them.

Kim: According to the television show *Lie To Me*, the average person tells three lies in a ten-minute conversation. Why do you think that is?

Theo: Maybe whoever made that up was lying. (*laughing*)

Kim: You're funny. They're including exaggeration, minimization, dismissiveness, and white lies in this statistic, so it doesn't mean we're all "liars." For example, when you ask me how I am in the morning, it is easier to say, "Fine," rather than tell you I just had a terrible bowel movement and am still feeling the effects of last night's curry.

Theo: Too much information is too much information. But it's true that the closer people are, the higher the odds that they'll answer with something other than, "Fine."

Kim: That's the point—it's the safety of the relationship that dictates the quality of the honesty.

Theo: Healthy relationships naturally have more safety, making it easier to be honest.

Kim: In talking about hard stuff, what happens when you sense the other person is not telling the truth?

Theo: I either call them on their bullshit, or I don't want to have anything to do with them.

Kim: I'm different. I notice the lie, hold that in my memory, and honour the lie as a signal that they are not feeling safe themselves. There are lots of times when you omit details from our conversations and an inside joke between us is "You know that I know that you know." I give you space to share when you're ready, and eventually you will come back to the topic. I trust that you will tell me the truth whenever you are ready, even though I almost always know when you haven't been totally honest with me in the moment.

Theo: I am so grateful for this quality in you. I interpret it to be unconditional acceptance.

Kim: Yes and no. The only "no" part is the anxiety I sometimes have of making you angry with me if I were to confront you with every piece of your bullshit.

Theo: There's a great example of honesty right there.

Kim: Thanks. It's something I've worked at. For the record, I think I am close to mastering the art of calling you on your bullshit nicely. I usually manage to set it up so you come to the awareness yourself.

Theo: I agree, and it's so much easier to hear it that way.

Kim: This honest conversation is also an example of being vulnerable.

Theo: What pains me the most about talking with some therapists is that they sit there and pretend they are perfect when sometimes I know they haven't done their own work. It's inauthentic. I've talked about it before, but that's a barrier to developing a relationship.

Kim: Author, Brené Brown is the queen of vulnerability, and she's awesome. In her book *Daring Greatly*, she says that vulnerability is at the core of all emotions and feelings. She defines vulnerability as being willing to step into uncertainty, risk, and emotional exposure.[xxviii]

Theo: What I'm coming to realize, especially through my relationship with you, is the critical role that vulnerability plays in healing. I think what makes our Forums so powerful is our collective vulnerability. It allows people to relate to each other on a personal level.

Kim: Those boundaries we spoke about are a balance. When a therapist is too distant, that will interfere with the potential for a securely attached therapeutic alliance. Early on in our relationship—yours and mine—I think my caution interfered with my ability to earn your complete trust. I am more vulnerable now and especially, when I am, I notice that our conversations have greater depth.

Theo: It also takes time. You had to feel safe that I was going to honour your boundaries too.

Kim: My ability to share some of my own relevant life stories seemed to help. As I became vulnerable through sharing, you became more and more willing to take emotional risks yourself.

Theo: I don't think this could have worked so well if you'd stayed rigid about those traditional therapist boundaries you told me about. It would have created too much inequality between us. I don't always respond well to authority. I also like it that you're not judgmental, just "discerning," as you say.

Kim: In order to keep our relationship safe, I also have to keep doing my personal work—being mindful and aware of my own projections and fears.

Theo: It's also easier to talk with you, just because you're a woman. Women have always been easier for me to share with. Just look at all the men who were role models in my life. My dad who was an alcoholic, Graham James who was a pedophile, many coaches and teammates who were really tough guys who seemed to respect toughness above anything else. My mom, although she was depressed and anxious, was at least always at home. She was a constant in that way.

Women are safer; they make me feel more comfortable. They're nurturing, compassionate, and they talk about their feelings. Men always seem to have ulterior motives to me. The problem with the nurturance from women was that sometimes I got it mixed up with my "little head" and interpreted this caring for sexual attraction. I needed to get laid so I had to make myself look like Prince Charming. In the end, what started out as a safe place to be myself, often turned out badly with promiscuity that I didn't intend.

The maternal feeling is really something I equate with safety. This might be why I am so over the moon with the sweat lodge. The sweat lodge for me is a comforting place and symbolically, it is supposed to represent the mother's womb. It is like a nest that I can come back to for safety, clarity, and affirmation.

Kim: When you're sick and physically vulnerable, if you weren't in a cave suffering by yourself, would you say you'd rather be comforted by a woman than a man?

Theo: Absolutely.

Kim: I only ask because in terms of strategy, would it be wiser at this point to make all your doctors and dentists and lawyers and accountants women? Or try to branch out vulnerably and try to cultivate safer relationships with men in those roles?

Theo: Never thought about it. I'm an equal opportunity employer. I honestly believe the best person for the job is the best person for the job. I'm more driven by success than gender comfort. Counting them now, though, most of the people closest to me are women. Guess I'm still being a little protective. And you know what, women get shit done. They're way more productive.

Kim: Fair enough.

Theo: My favourite example of vulnerability was during Dr. Gabor Maté's video lecture on attunement and addiction.[xxix] He gave a very personal example of how he turned into a little child when his wife declined to have sex with him. He's seventy-something-years old and he shared that it still turns him into a one-year-old child when this happens. He described how his early childhood experience during World War II resulted in a separation between him and his mother, which was tremendously painful. He links that experience of perceived rejection by his wife with his original separation from his mom. He described how this pattern instantly triggered him into abandonment. But being aware of this pattern today keeps his relationship safe and okay. His sharing of his own experiences with such vulnerability was bloody inspirational. It gave me such insight into myself.

Kim: I too love that story. Dr. Maté is a wonderful human being who has done much to shed compassionate light upon the world of addictions. Which brings us to compassion.

Theo: It is a hard concept to be selfless when you have been abused. Doesn't matter all the things you know, you still feel afraid that you are going to get hurt anyway. I am learning that I can't grow without being uncomfortable.

Kim: Compassion is a feeling of empathy for ourselves and for others. It is the emotional response to suffering, and it motivates a desire to alleviate that suffering.

Theo: I have often thought it is easier to be a prick, rather than put myself in the other person's shoes, especially when I am hurt.

Kim: When we are hurt is when it is hardest to be compassionate. This makes me think about the Victor Walk. When you decided to walk from the child sexual abuse statue in Toronto to the Parliament Buildings in Ottawa in May 2013, your initial intention was to increase awareness for justice.[xxx] You wanted people to read their victim impact statements on the steps of Parliament Hill. One day, I gently said to you, "You know, if you make this walk only about justice, you will exclude many of your survivors who are also offenders."

Theo: I remember thinking, "Shit, you're right." That was the reason my mission had to turn to healing. But in order to do that fully, I needed to find some of my own compassion for offenders. It has been an evolving aspect of our conversations ever since.

Kim: I was so proud of you during our November 2013 *Winnipeg Free Press* Online Cafe Interview, when the reporter asked about how you felt about Graham James today. You expressed that you were working on compassion and the thought of him now was no longer as disgusting as it once seemed.[xxxi] You even said you'd be willing to meet with him.

Theo: I have no reason to be afraid of him anymore.

Kim: From safety in relationship arises curiosity and self-discovery, and they allow us to see life in the present moment, rather than through the limited and often-clouded lens of past experiences.

Theo: I am shedding my past, like the snake sheds its skin. Hopefully, a bit more every day.

Kim: Interpersonal neurobiology says that healing conversations change lives.

Theo: And we've witnessed thousands of people who claim exactly that in our workshops, our presentations, the Victor Walk; everywhere we go where people are actively trying to feel better. So let's keep talking, and continue to encourage others to join in.

4

What We Say is More Than Words

"Happiness is when what you think, what you say,
and what you do arc in harmony."
Mahatma Gandhi

Kim: Deciding to tell your story in the first place is a huge part of the healing process. But it's also important to think about *how* you are telling the story and the effect the words and emotions are having on you.

Theo: Fucking right!

Kim: That's a great example. There can be a lot of power in the word "fuck." When it's said by itself, "Fuck!," it often resonates with anger circuits in the brain, suggesting irritation with the topic or the situation. That's not how you used it though; you used it to emphasize an opinion. According to what I could find on the Internet, there are seventy-six different uses for the word, "Fuck." It has permeated our language so much it could be used in just about every sentence and still be understood. For example, it can be used to express aggression: "Fuck you"; disgust: "Fuck me"; despair: "Fucked again"; incompetence: "You fucked it up"; and the list goes on. But often, the word "fuck" is used to exaggerate a statement, adding emotion or shock value. I think it's used to attract a bit more attention to what they're saying.

Theo: Jeezus. So most of the time when we say, "Fuck," it's more like saying, "Listen to me, here!" Hadn't thought of it like that. Sounds at least partly accurate, though. How else are we gonna get people to take us seriously sometimes? (*smiling*) You know, whatever reason I'm really saying it for, I still wanna be able to say it whenever I want to. The word just sounds right, don't it? (*laughing*)

Kim: Whatever you say. (*smiling*) There is no language police, and it doesn't offend me at all. When I worked with street kids in Winnipeg the word "fuck" was as common as the word "the." It's necessary to pay attention to what is behind the words we choose to say. It's connecting to what we're really thinking, feeling, and ultimately communicating, that is the key.

Theo: I don't think I used to think about what I was saying. My former wives would probably agree with this.

Kim: Many people don't; they just react. And it's a lot harder to think about what's coming out of our mouths when we're tired, upset, and—now I'm being overly obvious—when we're under the influence of something.

Theo: That's the danger of cell phone video cameras! Thank God they didn't have them back when I was out of control. Today, someone could wake up and hear themself on YouTube saying something completely idiotic that they have no recollection of.

Kim: The best way to prevent that is to try and connect with your words before you say them.

Theo: How we use "fuck" is one thing to think about; but what other words are worth thinking about?

Kim: It's not specific words so much, but the way we organize our thoughts that conveys the information about our feelings. One concept is how we use language to distance ourselves from the emotion of the topic. Instead of saying, "I am sad right now," you might say something like, "It makes people sad when ... happens." Notice the switch from "I" to "People" as a way of making it general rather than personal. And the language changed from the present tense to a hypothetical timeframe.

Theo: It's 'cause emotions are too hard. A bit of distance and generalities make it easier to talk about them.

Kim: But connecting how you feel to an experience in the moment helps you to *own* the feeling.

Theo: The very reason you become an addict is to help the feelings go away.

Kim: Good example of distancing language in that sentence right there. Notice how you didn't say, "I became an addict to help my feelings go away." The use of distancing words is a step up from alcohol and drug abuse, no question; but the goal is still to connect to your feelings.

Theo: I know. I *feel* okay with that.

Kim: I sense some sarcasm. "Sarcasm" according to *The Merriam-Webster Dictionary* is the use of words that mean the opposite of what you really want to say.

Theo: Ah, shit.

Kim: Sometimes when I'd ask you a question that happens to trigger a strong emotion, you'd start the sentence and then trail off with "Right?" or "You know?" and never clearly state your own experience. It was as if the emotional part was too hard to say and feel, but you still wanted to be validated and heard.

Theo: But I know that you know what I mean when I say "Right?"

Kim: I often do, because I know you. But it's a bit vague, and still leaves something to interpretation. I understand the use of distancing language as protection. I use it too. Please know I notice you've been saying "Right?" and "You know?" much less over the past two years.

Theo: I just had an aha! Many of the women I have been in relationship with are C strategy individuals who want connection. My distancing language must piss them off.

Kim: Excellent awareness. Connection-seeking Cs definitely want closeness and would feel dismissed when they perceive distance.

Theo: Fucking awesome.

Kim: Is that awesome awareness-wise, or do you like to piss them off?

Theo: Do I have to answer everything?

Kim: (*grinning*) Therapeutically, I call the way I often communicate with you the "sideways approach." To keep you safe from intense emotions that might re-traumatize you, I will come at charged topics "sideways," with information and ideas rather than head on in a way that might otherwise seem confrontational or too direct. This is why talking about how brains explain behaviour works so well for you; it is intellectual information that doesn't directly connect to the emotions. And then you can reflect on it after.

Theo: That works so well for me. It allows me to come to my own conclusions and awarenesses. It is empowering, rather than condescending.

Kim: Here's another distancing concept. I call it "sliding off." It happens when feedback is given and the receiver—because they are unable or unwilling to receive it—minimizes or dismisses what they are hearing. Even if the feedback is positive, many people are unable to take the information in. An example is when some people get a deliberate and well-deserved compliment, they just shrug and say, "Yeah, yeah."

Theo: Hmm.

Was that an example of the sideways approach there?

Kim: You're so smart.

Theo: Yeah, yeah. (*smiling*)

Kim: I know you are paying very close attention to the words I'm say-ing. Which is great. But for healing purposes, it's even more important that we focus on our *own* words. As a therapist, I'm trained to listen to others carefully, and that is why I'm looking for the real meaning behind what you say. In the beginning of our conversations, you frequently described yourself in self-deprecating and critical ways. You were definitely self-abusive with your own words.

Theo: (*with a sigh*) That's how I was feeling.

Kim: I just want to let you know that those negative words were poisonous and toxic to your brain, destroying brain cells and creating stress responses that hurt your body.

Theo: What the f...?

Kim: You didn't say a full "fuck." Trying to modify your language? (*smiling*)

Theo: Just thinking about it. But what you were saying there, how much can we really hurt ourselves with words? I mean, "sticks and stones will break my bones, but names will never hurt me." Is that all bullshit?

Kim: Harmful words hurt most when we think them about ourselves. When we constantly beat ourselves up with negative self-talk, our minds and bodies think they are bad and faulty. This type of inner dialogue creates chronic stress, and our chemistry reflects this. Over the past two years, I have seen you become much more aware and conscious of how you talk about yourself.

Theo: I notice this in myself. I think I'm getting calmer.

Kim: Had we gone to a brain imaging lab, we could have had a picture taken of your brain, and done before and after photos to see the progress. Functional brain imaging is becoming more popular as a way of prescribing specific activities and treatments to improve brain function. I think parts of your cortex would have gotten thicker as a result of your kinder self-talk. And I bet your amygdala (the place where we process painful emotions in our brain) would be smaller and less active. The less anxious you are—because you're not re-triggering yourself all the time—the smaller your amygdala gets.

Theo: Where could we have gotten this brain imaging done?

Kim: It's easier to access this type of imaging in the United States.

Theo: That would have been cool to look at, because so much of this stuff is hard to prove.

Kim: True. How we feel is not easily counted, even though it really counts!

Theo: Yep.

Kim: When you talk about yourself, it's not just the thoughts you have, but also how you string them together that is important.

Theo: Once I found out that I was damaging my brain when talking with such intensity about my abuse, over and over, I was able to mindfully regulate myself a bit when talking at speaking engagements. It allowed me to create a distance between the story and myself. The story isn't me anymore; it is just a story. I think I am finally comfortable in my role as the poster boy of childhood sexual abuse; it no longer defines me. I think of post-traumatic stress as post-traumatic growth.

Kim: I love that "post-traumatic growth" thought. You say your sexual abuse doesn't define you, but you say you're comfortable with being the poster boy for it. Those two thoughts don't seem aligned.

Theo: When I see myself as an advocate for abuse survivors, it's my post-traumatic growth that I'm looking at. That's why the abuse itself isn't what defines me.

Kim: That's really clear, and very healthy.

Theo: When I talk about my abuse now, it doesn't have the same venomous bite that it used to have. In the past when I was triggered, I didn't have the tools that I have now so I was relatively unpredictable. When I had one drink, I couldn't predict what was going to happen next, so there wasn't any predictability there. Now, I am aware that sexual abuse never was my core issue.

Kim: Wow! That is a significant shift in your understanding.

Theo: I know and experience my core stuff to be about abandonment rather than abuse. So maybe that's why the abuse part of my story has less of a hold on me.

Kim: When you are telling your story, how often do you loop back into the same thoughts? Or do you find yourself altering the story each time you tell it? As a professional speaker who tells your story so frequently, you have so many opportunities to reflect on this concept.

Theo: It does change a bit every time. It also depends on the audience.

Kim: When we tell the story of our trauma, we usually begin at the beginning. We start by talking about what happened. Too often when we tell the story this way, it is easy to get stuck at the beginning or in the middle. And rarely, if ever, do we get to the end of the story. The true conclusion to any trauma is the arrival at now, today. For that reason, for it to be a therapeutic experience, I suggested you try telling your story from the ending, revealing the fact that you've clearly made it. Has that strategy made a difference for you?

Theo: Yes. Last week I spoke to a room of five hundred people at breakfast. Every person in the room was glued for the entire forty-five minutes; not one person took their eyes off me. I started with where I am right now, feeling successful and finally in a position to inspire myself and others. Then I worked my way backwards to the trauma. I had to be very conscious when speaking and it was tough. It was pretty amazing though and I felt very different when telling the story. More empowered and relaxed.

Kim: The strength of this storytelling style is that you are updating your mind, and hardwiring into your brain a clear understanding that the trauma is over; that the event or events lie in the past. When you are rewiring the brain in this way, it helps to line up the dots between events and adds positive neurochemicals like dopamine (the pleasure chemical that we love) to the story. When the mind reorganizes the story of your trauma, it creates coherence and meaning to both the story and the way the nerve cells in the brain wire together.

Theo: We're rewiring my brain!

Kim: It is my impression, Theo, by watching and listening to you over time, that your story has become more coherent and clear. Dan

Siegel calls an integrated story a "coherent narrative," where the meaning is succinct and linked together in a logical sequence.[xxxii] Your body language softens, your eyes are more relaxed, your voice is more lilting in intonation, and your sentences stay all in the same tense of time. You used to switch back and forth between the past and present all over the place. These observations are indicators that your story is more integrated and comfortable for you.

Theo: Thanks.

Kim: Narrative is the linear telling of a logical sequence of events. Making sense of your story is a process of sorting through memory, linking the past and the present together with the potential future. Part of creating cohesive awareness is having a clear and succinct timeline of the events in your life.

Theo: We talked before how hard that was for me because of all my dissociation.

Kim: Now that you can better integrate timelines and more cohesively tell your stories, it suggests that you are less fragmented and plagued by dissociation.

Theo: Recently, I've been trying out something new when I speak with groups. I've been focusing on the process of healing, and moving away from the drama of the trauma.

Kim: To compare, just look back at a lot of the things you said in your book and the HBO documentary *Playing With Fire*. Short sentences, concise thoughts, often judgmental—all very under-standable and natural, and indicative of someone who'd been in your position. Also in parts of CBC's *The Fifth Estate's* "The Fall and Rise of Theo Fleury" on October 16, 2009, it was obvious that the emotions were so close to the surface you couldn't fully talk about them.[xxxiii]

Theo: That *Fifth Estate* interview was very emotional. It was just before I'd released the book and I didn't have the tools yet to understand what all was going on for me.

Kim: Completely understandable. But in the past couple years, as your comfort has increased, I've seen the connection between your words and your feelings emerge naturally. You're now expressing yourself coherently and in a more integrated manner. And what that means is you don't have to work so hard to contain your feelings. When you express yourself now, you're able to describe your emotions without becoming overwhelmed by them. I'm not exaggerating this; your speech has become slower and more fluid, and there is also a little less "fuck." (*smiling encouragingly*)

Theo: You are correct about my fucks. I don't want them all to go away though.

Kim: (*trying not to laugh*) Making a coherent story out of messy, complicated experiences makes your stories more manageable for your psyche.

Theo: And it must make it easier for the listener to relate.

Kim: Of course. But what we say is so much more than words. Our nonverbals are very telling.

Theo: Is this where you talk about me picking my nose?

Kim: There are many self-soothing behaviours and, yes, we'll talk about that too. There's always a reason for the behaviour, no matter how socially inappropriate those behaviours are. Therapists learn to watch as much as they listen, and combining these two and then relaying them back to the client is something we call "tracking." It's to help the client develop insight.[xxxiv] This tracking is almost the same as the attunement process between a parent and a child where the parent puts their mind in the mind of their child to help their child understand themselves.

Theo: What are you looking for when you are tracking me?

Kim: How you move, how you hold your breath, how you tilt your head, what your hands are doing, where your eyes are looking, whether you're leaning forward or backward, if you're slumping or sitting up tall, are you yawning or rubbing your face ... And on and on.

Theo: These things all mean something?

Kim: Paired together with the words you choose, these things mean a lot. Let's take yawning, as an example. Did you know, if you are talking about something difficult and you start to yawn, it's a way of reducing your anxiety?

Theo: What?

Kim: In their book *How God Changes Your Brain*, Andrew Newberg and Mark Waldman describe brain-imaging research that shows how yawning lights up a distinct neural circuit that also produces social awareness and feelings of empathy.[xxxv] Yawning connects us to other people.

Theo: I thought people yawned when they were bored or tired. And one of my ex-wives told me that she thought that I yawned every time I was lying.

Kim: Does that resonate with you? Was she right?

Theo: If she was, I wasn't conscious of it.

Kim: Well, hypothetically, if you weren't telling the truth, you might have been anxious, so yawning would have helped you with that. The structure in the brain that lights up when you yawn is called "the precuneus." This small brain part plays a central role in consciousness, self-reflection, and memory retrieval. When you actively yawn, you help yourself with all of these functions. Isn't that cool?

Theo: Even when it's not a natural yawn? If you force yourself to do it?

Kim: Absolutely. Newberg and Waldman suggest that we do it all the time. They suggest it's even more effective than meditation at calming us down.

Theo: That is the coolest thing. I will yawn on purpose now. (*yawning*)

Kim: Me, too. (*also yawning*) Four-dimensional ultrasound shows us that even a fetus will yawn as early as twenty weeks after conception. And they believe that yawning should be integrated into exercise and stress-reduction programs, cognitive and memory-enhancement training, psychotherapy, and contemplative spiritual practice.[xxxvi]

Theo: Imagine having yawning groups!

Kim: (*laughing*) The precuneus is also associated with those mirror neurons we talk about all the time. The cells in the brain that help us to connect with other peoples' feelings and actions. Yawning may even help us to enhance our awareness of others, our compassion, and the effectiveness of our communication.

Theo: That's a bit weird … But it does seem that whenever we see someone else yawn, it is contagious and we yawn ourselves.

Kim: That's an example of mirror neurons at work. You asked about yawning being a signal of being tired. Well, yawning does increase when you're tired. But what research has found is that exposure to light will also make you yawn, suggesting that it is part of the process of waking up. So, it's really a modulator. It calms you when you're stressed and makes you more alert when you're tired.

Theo: Yawning can be like adrenaline?

Kim: Mmhm. You're asking that question because you remember I told you adrenaline helps you focus your attention. But it's not just adrenaline that helps with this; dopamine does it too. Yawning is linked to the release of dopamine and oxytocin. Not as much as an orgasm of course, but in that direction.

Theo: I actually love a good sneeze. You? And a good fart! (*smiling*) Are you telling me the truth about yawning or just pulling my leg?

Kim: (*laughing*) It's bloody science!

Theo: Sometimes, I see the occasional person yawning in our workshops and think they must have travelled far to get there and they are just tired.

Kim: People sometimes yawn naturally because they are sleepy (especially after lunch), but they also do it when they are emotionally or intellectually overwhelmed. Yawning helps us to stay focused on the concepts and ideas we're finding important. Teachers everywhere can take some comfort that instead of interpreting yawns as boredom, they are in fact signals that someone is trying to stay connected to what they are hearing!

Theo: No shit. That's pretty neat.

Kim: Yawning will relax you and bring you into a state of alertness faster than any meditation technique. It also helps to regulate the temperature and metabolism of your brain.

Theo: (*yawning*) I am cooling off my brain! It's a better explanation than lying. What other things do you watch for when you're really paying attention to someone?

Kim: The feeling of helplessness/powerlessness is reflected in bodies that collapse and flop into a slumped position. Vulnerability and fear show themselves when the person pulls into a tight ball or sits on their legs.

Theo: Do I do those things?

Kim: Of the two I have just described, you are more likely to collapse. I am the one more likely to pull up into a ball.

Theo: At our Forums, Kim, you sometimes have audiences participate in the activity, "In your eyes, I see myself as…." Does this have anything to do with nonverbal communication?

Kim: Wow, that's an insightful question. When you look deeply into someone's eyes, you are instantly flooded with a whole bunch of nonverbal information. But what you see in another person is really a reflection of a part of you. Remember Anaïs Nin's "We don't see things as they are, we see them as we are." So looking deeply at another person is often like looking into a mirror. That activity you mentioned had people trying this out with a partner. Two people sit across from each other and look into each other's eyes for ten seconds, then they reflect on what they saw in themselves as they were doing this.

Theo: That exercise was mind-blowing for a lot of us.

Kim: It shows that whatever you see in the other is really just a piece of you. If you see someone as beautiful, then you are resonating with their beauty and it is also a part of you. If you see someone as anxious, then you are connecting to the anxiety that is also inside of you. Mirror neurons are at work.

Theo: I guess that ties into the concept of projections that we were talking about earlier. How you see an aspect of yourself and you unconsciously "project" it out onto someone else. I guess we have to be careful about this.

Kim: Exactly. When I am "tracking" as a therapist or as a friend, it is important to check in with the other person to be sure that what I am seeing is actually what they are experiencing. I don't want to project my own stuff onto someone by expressing something that I think I see, rather than what is really happening for them.

Theo: But what if, in all these observations, the other person has no idea that they are feeling the things you are seeing?

Kim: That's really common. Then you offer what you see as a possibility, with curiosity in your voice, rather than providing these observations as definitive and declarative states that are certain. That would be a bit disrespectful and invasive. This way, you are inviting the possibility for self-reflection rather than telling the person what they are feeling. Then this kind of connection won't come across as condescending and all-knowing. People definitely don't like that.

Theo: You often talk about what my eyes are doing. What are you looking at in my eyes when you are listening to me?

Kim: I mostly watch to see if your pupils are dilating (the black centres getting bigger). That would tell me if you are either stressed or really excited. It would be one of those two. I would have to know the context of our discussion, and check out your other facial expressions, to decide which it is. Pupils also change size when people are stoned, but I've certainly never seen you like that.

Theo: Do you remember that episode of *Lie to Me* about the psychopath? His pupils would dilate with excitement when he was looking at a photo of torture and dilate with fear when looking at a pretty girl. That is backwards, isn't it?

Kim: Yes, that is the opposite response that 99 percent of heterosexual men would have to such stimuli. But, as I mentioned, pupil dilation alone without the bigger context of facial expressions is not enough nonverbal information to make a judgement. In the case of that psychopath, it was his facial expressions in combination with his pupil dilations that gave him away.

Paul Ekman, the scientist behind the science of *Lie to Me*, describes seven universal fleeting facial micro-expressions that everyone on the planet expresses in relation to their emotions.[xxxvii]

Theo: That show is bloody incredible.

Kim: I was definitely addicted to it. Imagine if everyone knew this stuff! We'd know much better when people's insides and outsides weren't matching. What's clear in the show and the books on the topic is that we can trust the nonverbals more than the verbals. Former FBI agent Joe Navarro also wrote a great book on the topic, *Louder Than Words*. [xxxviii] It's worth reading.

Theo: What are those seven emotions that are universal signals?

Kim: Anger, fear, surprise, sadness, disgust, contempt, and happiness.

Theo: It's pretty clear that sometimes there's a lot riding on who's telling the truth and who isn't. Like when someone's saying they didn't kill their neighbour, but is expressing happiness with the corners of their eyes. Apparently, the science of this stuff is becoming more accepted than lie detector tests, and is used a lot in cases involving national security.

Kim: It's very interesting, isn't it? But for me it's not as much about finding out who's lying, as about where there is discrepancy between someone's inner feelings and their outer actions.

Theo: Why?

Kim: To help them reflect and understand themselves better.

Theo: You really are a therapist. Hey, I know one part of the body that never lies. There's a song about it by Shakira. (*laughing*)

Kim: Thanks for that. (*smug look*) I also look at where people move their eyes to when they are talking. Although this is not an exact science, in context with the words, it's becoming more understood that eye position can be helpful in appreciating the person's feelings about what they are talking about.

Theo: Sometimes when I am deep in thought, I know I look off into space.

Kim: That is very common. Dr. David Grand, the author of *Brainspotting*, calls this phenomenon "Gazespotting."[xxxix] Dr. Grand proposes that whenever we have an experience, we encode it into our brain with a particular gaze spot. When talking about that experience from memory, we are likely to look in the direction of that gaze spot as we retrieve the information. Many people will look down and to the right when they recall shameful experiences or up toward the ceiling when they honestly can't remember something. When I'm tracking this kind of eye movement, I am looking for repeated patterns of eye gaze that are associated with certain topics.

Theo: I can't feel where my eyes are when I am talking.

Kim: You're not really supposed to, because these are unconscious programs in the brain. I also look for the far-off gaze of dissociation, where you might be staring off into space or looking right through me. I rarely see that "gone" look in your eyes these days, though. I always say the mind is behind the eyes.

Theo: I thought I heard that people always look up and to the right when they are lying. Any truth to that?

Kim: There are conflicting thoughts about that observation. One theory that seems to hold water with me, however, is that when people are lying, they actually look right at you both to appear sincere and to observe whether or not you seem to be believing them.

Theo: Hmm. What about people who look away when you're talking with them? Or when they don't make eye contact at all?

Kim: We call this "gaze aversion." Looking away during an intense interaction helps to calm you down. In some cultures though, any direct eye contact can be perceived as inappropriate, so that's another reason we need to be mindful of who we're talking with.

Theo: I'd stare down some players just to increase the emotional intensity on the ice. Refs too.

Kim: Another thing to look for are incongruent smiles. Sometimes people smile when they don't feel happy at all.

Theo: (*knowingly*) Not hard to imagine.

Kim: It's the "false positive affect" I spoke about earlier. When the person is smiling, most of the expression is with their teeth and mouth. But for true happiness, look for the wrinkles at the corners of the eyes. If someone's smiling but their eyes are not engaged, this is likely a false positive cue, or they've had Botox. There are clearly lots of reasons people exhibit false positives. Probably the main reason is that it protects them from rejection.[xl] People want others to like them.

Theo: I can relate to that. I would have been smiling my ass off at my mom with sincerity until I figured out she didn't smile back.

Kim: Then you would have kept smiling more, but it wouldn't have shown in your eyes as much.

Theo: Right.

Kim: (*yawning to make herself more alert*) I want to say more about self-soothing behaviours.

Theo: I've got lots of them. What about when I rub my face all the time?

Kim: You do that.

Theo: What does it mean?

Kim: All the midline structures of our body are highly innervated—supplied with lots of nerves—so they're supersensitive—and are always available. So this is the quick and easy way to get instant soothing. Our nose, mouth, genitals, crossing our legs, clutching our hands … are all examples of places that we can touch or move to make ourselves feel calmer and more organized. People who pick their nose, suck their thumb, smoke, eat, drink, clutch themselves when no one is looking are all soothing themselves unconsciously.

Theo: Ha! Now, I am really self-conscious.

Kim: I know every time you need a puff of your cigarette, it's not just the nicotine you need. I think of it as a way for you to self soothe.

Theo: Why do we need to self-soothe?

Kim: To reduce stress. Stress is not just a feeling, but something that happens to the physical body. Your muscles get tense, your heart races, your blood pressure goes up, your stomach gets tied up in knots, and the thinking part of your brain becomes less available.

Theo: And so these self-soothing behaviours really change our body responses?

Kim: To some degree, for short periods. It's not just yawning that helps. All these things do, but to lesser degrees. Theo, you know we can't talk about self-soothing behaviours without at least mentioning masturbation.

Theo: Do we have to touch on that? (*awkwardly, but proud of having made a pun*)

Kim: It is another midline body structure filled with nerves, and a quite common behaviour in children. This is known to be normal. An article I just read on the topic says that children do it because it feels good and it helps them to learn about their bodies. If they do it excessively, however, it can be a sign of anxiety or emotional overwhelm."[xli]

Theo: Okay.

Kim: Of course, masturbation is much more complex than this; it has more to it than just self-soothing.

Theo: I get it. (*speaking briskly*)

Kim: Listening to your tone of voice just there reminds me to attend to more than just your body language. When we are under stress or uncomfortable, our tone of voice changes and can take on a quality of irritability and frustration. Just there you spoke more quickly than normal; but other times you often talk louder and more declaratively, especially when you are stressed. These are cues for me to change the topic or soften the intensity of the conversation.

Theo: When I talk louder, I must be wanting to get my point across. Maybe I'm not feeling heard.

Kim: What's interesting about that is when someone's voice reflects irritation, it immediately sets up a defensive reaction in the listener's right brain, which prevents the conversation from being fully productive. I'm remembering that it's the right side of the brain where all our early attachment stuff is stored. So tone of voice could easily trigger implicit memory.

Theo: So that's another reason why my former wives would have been triggering me! They'd each probably have more to say about it, but I know that when someone else's voice gets angry, it immediately stimulates me into a defensive response.

Kim: Good insight! No matter how subtle it is, expressed anger generates anxiety, defensiveness, and aggression in the other person. Anger directly interrupts the functioning of your thinking brain. (*taking a book out of her briefcase*) There's a quote in this book *How God Changes Your Brain* that explains the effect of anger on the brain clearly. Let me find it … here it is. When you're angry, and I quote, "Not only do you lose the ability to be rational, you lose the awareness that you're even acting in an irrational way. When your frontal lobes shut down, it is impossible to listen to the other person, let alone feel any empathy or compassion." [xlii.]

Theo: Hmm. (*thinking*) Now I understand what was happening in my brain during all the arguing and fighting I have experienced. My thinking brain wasn't thinking.

Kim: When I read *Playing With Fire* and when I first heard you speak, I noticed the intensity of the anger in your words and in your nonverbal communication. Recent brain imaging research has taught us that, when we express even the slightest bit of negativity or anger, it increases the negativity in both the speaker and the listener's brain. Contrary to popular belief, the expression and venting of anger doesn't help us to get rid of the angry feelings and negative thoughts. Although venting might feel good in the heat of the moment, it's been shown to actually cause more stress, and it increases aggression over time. Theo, do you notice if your feelings of anger are becoming less and less? Do you feel less angry?

Theo: Oh yeah! I've done a lot of work on my anger this year. The last time I came completely unglued was in a hockey game in Belfast, Ireland. I scared the shit out of myself. It was ugly. I was trying to break up a fight. People were getting injured and I called a guy out on it. All of a sudden, my own life felt like it was in danger. It moved me completely into reactivity and there was no thinking whatsoever. I never want to feel that out of control again. At this point, I am way better able to stop and think and self-reflect. Thinking more beyond my own perspective. How others feel.

Kim: Research shows that the best way to deal with negativity is to observe it with mindfulness. Try to notice your thoughts and feelings without reacting or judging them. I think of it like a cartoon bubble coming out of the side of my head saying, "There she is feeling angry again." This kind of self-observation places distance between me and the feeling. This takes the punch out of my anger.

Theo: You know what I came up with in my self-reflection about my anger?

Kim: Tell me.

Theo: It doesn't serve me. I don't need it anymore. It used to protect me. And what I've learned is that what sits underneath it are feelings of being abandoned, rejected, and unlovable. Sadness sits underneath my anger. Expressing my anger doesn't get rid of that. So what's it good for?

Kim: You must have thought a lot about that. Anger is necessary. Anger is a signal that a boundary has been crossed and it can be expressed in a healthy way if you are mindful. When you recognize that you're feeling angry, what is important is the ability to recognize if you're really under threat, or not.

Theo: I think being mindful forces us to wake up, 'cause it means we have to pay attention to all this stuff. If you are on anti-depressants, alcohol, and drugs, addictive behaviours mask the triggers even more than they would in the average person. Mindfulness is necessary to help you sit with the pain.

Kim: Mindfulness is a type of focused attention that allows you to see the inner workings of your thoughts and feelings, and then consider how you are affecting others.

Theo: You have to step away from being reactive in order to do that.

Kim: Our bodies carry the impact of both the positive and painful events of our lives. Our muscles, our nervous system, our breathing rate, and other physical processes develop fixed patterns that continue to speak to our brains about old traumatic and developmental wounds. The body has its own memories.

Theo: When we talk about trauma, it's the body stuff that I am the least consciously aware of.

Kim: That is so common. The dissociation you experienced separates you from your body, which makes it very difficult to be aware of how the trauma affected you physically. You've also been through a ton of physical injuries in your hockey career, which is very traumatic to the body. I know you say you have rhinoceros skin and don't feel physical pain, but your body still remembers all those injuries at some level. Pain and injury are stored in the tissues of your body, not just in your brain.

Theo: I'd rather feel physical pain than emotional pain any day.

Kim: I know what you're saying. But the brain doesn't fully know the difference between the two. They are both processed in the same brain structure—the insula. We are not able to clearly remember the sensation of physical pain (few of us women would ever have a second baby if we did!), but we are able to remember emotional pain way more than we want to.

Theo: When the skate cut my bicep, I was thirteen. I went into shock. But the emotional part of it was way worse, because I was so afraid it would mean I couldn't play hockey.

Kim: The shock you went into is an example of the body creating dissociation naturally.

Theo: Like all hockey players, when I'd get injured I'd want to get back on the ice as soon as possible. That's different from when I'm emotionally injured and want to stay the hell away from anything that could cause that kind of pain …

Kim: Whether you suck up physical pain or emotional pain, the body stores the experience in memory. However, what makes physical pain worse is if it's connected to a negative emotional event. For example, when you get hurt and lose the game seconds later, the level of pain will be processed differently than if you get hurt and then win the game seconds later. The memory of emotion sticks around much longer than the sensory memory of broken bones.

Theo: No question.

Kim: I was the guest speaker at a pain conference in Regina, Saskatchewan, and the theme of the conference was the link between emotional trauma and the treatment of chronic physical pain. The physiotherapists treating chronic-pain clients collectively made a best guess that 80 percent of their untreatable clients (the ones for whom traditional therapy had no effect because the pain was so high) were the ones with histories of emotional trauma.

Theo: So chronic emotional pain seems to make chronic physical pain worse?

Kim: There is emerging research on this, but it's just the tip of the iceberg.

Theo: Hmm, it's a reminder that we can't just treat the body; it's gotta be the mind, body, and soul for true healing to happen.

Kim: Whatever way we feel pain, physically or emotionally, it is feedback to let us know that something is wrong and needs attention.

Theo: I always knew I needed to let go of a lot of stuff, but I could never internalize what I needed to do. I think I learned some things in therapy, but I couldn't take in what I was learning and translate that learning into how to change my actions. Dissociation—the concept that we keep talking about—completely disrupted my ability to stay present. For me, the amount of dissociation I experienced every day varied in degree from subtle to significant.

Kim: This is true for many of us.

Theo: I still have difficulty at times staying mindfully present in a conversation and will revert to fiddling with my cell phone, just to anchor my anxiety. I will play games on my iPad when I could be interacting with my kids. These are subtle forms of mindlessness that I still engage in when I don't know what to do with myself.

Kim: When you begin to connect to sensations in your body, then you are experiencing what we call somatic mindfulness. It helps you to learn to trust your body.

Theo: Having Crohn's disease makes it hard to trust your body. I never know when my gut is going to act up. I can definitely feel that pain.

Kim: I totally understand. Guts have a very distinct pain pathway. Pain feedback from the gut is very difficult for your brain to suppress. Your body's survival depends on the strength of this pathway.

Gabor Maté wrote a book, *When The Body Says No,*[xliii] that explores the intimate connection between emotion, stress, and disease. The mind and body are intimately connected with each other. He says that in people who suppress their emotions and experience excessive stress that they don't acknowledge, their body can become confused, even to the point of turning on itself.

Theo: So when we deal with emotions, there's hope that the body will get well?

Kim: I truly believe so. What science tells us is that when you consciously label your moment-by-moment feelings, you reduce the activity in your brain's amygdala. Just by noticing your feelings, you turn off the stress response in your brain and in your body. Mindfulness changes your body!

Theo: So that's why I'm feeling calmer. Sounds a bit like Zen Buddhism, even though I really don't know anything about that. So, I'm trying to understand this. How does my amygdala help me process fear?

Kim: I have a great amygdala story. When we first moved to Victoria from the Arctic, we went camping. I was sleeping in the tent and probably breathing with my mouth wide open. I woke in terror to the feeling of something tickly crawling across my face. I opened my eyes and there were eight furry legs sitting on my nose. You can only imagine the drama in the tent. The amygdala processes the sensations that signal potential threat. Despite being asleep, my amygdala was screaming DANGER! And that spider flew across the tent in the midst of a level of pandemonium that my sleeping space hasn't known since.

Theo: Ha, I can picture the drama in my mind! (*laughing*)

Kim: The amygdala, which is at the bottom of my brain, rapidly sent alerting chemicals to the top of my brain to help me figure out what was sitting on my face. The top of my brain (cortex) said, "Oh, it is only a wolf spider and not a tarantula," and promptly told my amygdala to chill out. This is how the bottom of the brain works together with the top of the brain. Information flows back and forth all the time.

Theo: I'm not always sure that the top of my brain tells my amygdala to shut up.

Kim: Can you imagine if I had spent a minute or so allowing my frontal cortex to decide if the spider on my face was poisonous or not? If I took too long to make that decision, I could've been dead. That is why we react to threat so fast. Our survival depends on it. We react first and think later.

Theo: My whole life has been like that.

Kim: Mindfulness exercises the top of our brain and helps us to move beyond the autopilot of outdated and sometimes unnecessary survival reactions. In time, those reactive emotional loops that trap us in our previously destructive patterns just don't run the show as much.

Theo: So reflecting stops me from reactively hurting people when I'm hurt.

Kim: Yes. Nice connecting of ideas. Mindfulness will help you with your relationships, absolutely.

Theo: Self-reflection has helped me to wake up from my traumatic experiences and realize that everything isn't all about me. It's really helped me to become more present. It's hard work, but

I can catch myself when I am starting to check out. It is very tiring though.

Kim: It gets easier with practice.

Theo: I remember asking JJ, my first AA sponsor from Santa Fe, "Is there ever going to be a time when I will be able to think about only one thing at a time?" He said, "Yes," and I thought he was fucking lying to me. How would I ever learn to shut down my mind and think about one thought at a time?

Kim: So does this mean you can focus on one thing at a time now?

Theo: Once in a while. JJ wasn't lying. What I have learned is that when I am more mindful, I am a better helper because I can be present. Imagine if your therapist wasn't present during your session, there but not there, thinking about their own stuff; well, no healing is going to happen. That secure attachment figure has to be present to hear and be attuned to what you have to say. The intention of connection is necessary. Being present requires mind, body, and soul. Being attuned is a whole body experience.

Kim: Wow, you're sounding like me. What I hear you saying here is that you want to be a better helper.

Theo: It's my purpose. I honestly believe it's more important than my hockey career. I was put on this earth to help.

Kim: You just used the word "honestly." How does your own honesty help you to be mindful?

Theo: Being honest allows you to be present. The key to recovery from mental illness is honesty. When I was hiding everything and not sharing with other people, I had a lot of panic and anxiety. After writing *Playing With Fire*, the anger, anxiety, and resentment started to dissipate. Sharing your truth is the key to the healing process; it changes the distress.

Kim: I think meaning takes coherent shape when the truth is present. Without it, information is distorted. For example, some peoples' thinking is so distorted that they believe their own lies. You mentioned that Graham James believed everything he told you, as if he was so good at manipulating he convinced himself. When distortions like this happen, they can obviously be damaging and dangerous.

Theo: Even though Graham told me a lot of manipulative bullshit that he genuinely believed, it was still bullshit. I think people construct these distorted thoughts because of their own trauma, and the reason they do it is to be liked and feel like they belong. As a master manipulator, Graham was the whole package. He must have been planning stuff way more than anyone knows. As it was, it was like he was ten steps ahead of everyone.

Kim: What do you mean by that?

Theo: You know how the average child molesting pedophile abuses something like 260 kids in their lifetime?[xliv]

Kim: I've heard that number could be anywhere between 70 and 400, but it's extremely hard to get accurate statistics on childhood sexual abuse because the vast majority of offences never get reported.

Theo: Right, and I heard somewhere that on average molesters abuse 125 people before they even get caught.

Kim: Where did you get that figure?

Theo: I don't know, but the person who told it to me seemed really sure about it.

Kim: I'm not saying it's wrong; I've heard similar suggestions before. But I can't imagine it would be easy to put together statistics like that.

Theo: We'll never know exact numbers because people don't all report, as you say, but these indicative numbers, even if they are only indicative, are fucking huge! (*looking disgusted*) I don't know if those are Graham's numbers, but it would suggest there's a lot of scheming going on.

Kim: Do you know if Graham was ever abused?

Theo: I have no clue about his history.

Kim: It would be interesting to know the percentage of offenders who have a history of sexual abuse trauma themselves. I heard it was around 40 percent, but my suspicion is that it's higher.[xlv] And that study on pedophiles didn't report whether the molesters had experienced other forms of childhood trauma.

Theo: My guess is that Graham must have lost power somehow as an adolescent. It's like part of his emotional development got stuck there. He often behaved like a teenager himself, but could switch into the adult sometimes. It wasn't a black and white thing.

Kim: Confusing, eh? Sexual abuse is rarely only about sex. There is all the psychological stuff that goes with it. Power, control, manipulation, pleasure, selfishness; it's a mixed-up nightmare. Each person's story is unique to these factors. If they were all the same, it would be a lot easier to help people who've had these experiences.

Theo: Aside from his master manipulation skills, he had some great qualities.

Kim: This is exactly why people get confused. It's hard to split a person into good and bad when they are both. This is the first time I've heard you talk about Graham as a person, instead of as an abuser. You know what Dan Siegel would say about that?

Theo: He's the guru of mindfulness, right?

Kim: He's written twelve books on the topic. All of them helped to shape my understanding of this information we are talking about. I think he'd say that your practising of mindfulness on this topic is changing the chemicals in your brain.

Theo: For all those brain science geeks out there, what exactly is happening in our brains when we pay close attention to our thoughts and feelings?

Kim: I love brain science geeks. (*smiling*) When you start to rewire your brain with new thoughts through mindfulness, repetitive activation of the new brain pathways secretes growth chemicals (Brain-derived neurotrophic factor *uku* BDNF) that enhance brain cell growth and hardwires these new connections together. All this explains the concept of neuroplasticity, which is the ability of the brain to change itself in response to our experiences. In this exact case, your brain's experience is that you're beginning to think more mindfully, holistically, and compassionately about your complex relationship with Graham James.

Theo. Sounds complicated, but I know something's going on in there. (*pointing at his head*)

Kim: Dr. Norman Doidge, in his book *The Brain That Changes Itself*, is renowned for his explanation of how the power of positive thinking physically changes the brain.[xlvi]

Theo: It would be fun to sit at the kitchen table with all these people! Imagine the conversations we could have. (*smiling*)

Kim: Sounds like heaven to me. I think I'd like to invite Susan Gillis Chapman to that table too. (*excitedly*) She talks about how mindfulness gives us greater control of our conversations. How it teaches us not to just react whenever we feel hurt, so we don't make matters worse.[xlvii]

Theo: Anytime.

Kim: Hey! I just had a thought. Our mindfulness about the words/
thoughts in our brains are really important for our own brains
to change and heal, but we also use our words and thoughts to
communicate with others too.

Theo: You're only understanding that now? (*smirking*)

Kim: Very funny. Here's what I think: speaking gently and responsibly
increases the chances that what we say will actually be heard.
This is the concept of mindful communication. How I use my
tone of voice, soften my eyes, and relax my body also help my
listener to take in my message.

Theo: You do have a good therapy voice. Not squeaky or distracting in
any way.

Kim: I work at it consciously, and sometimes I use my tone of voice
to manage my own emotions. I slow down my pace of speech
deliberately when I notice myself starting to feel triggered. And
although you might not know it from this conversation, I make
my sentences brief when I need the listener to really listen.

Theo: I also know that you pause deliberately when you know I need
time to think. Some other people might just go on blabbing.

Kim: What you're describing is an example of attunement, where the
speaker tunes in to see how interested the listener is, and how
well they are understanding what's being said.

Theo: Something else I notice about your speech. When you're really
thinking hard, you enunciate more. Like every syllable matters.

Kim: That's true. How often do you catch yourself when you're talking
really fast or your voice is going up?

Theo: I think I catch myself more when I'm talking with you 'cause I feel the conversations are really important; it's harder to be mindful when I'm out buying groceries or ordering a caramel macchiato at Starbucks.

Kim: For sure. It all gets easier with practice too. I have another example. The words we choose. If the speaker wants to be understood, the words should be those that the listener understands and relates to. So if we're mindful, we'll slightly adapt our language to the audience every time.

Theo: I know I say "fuck" less around kids.

Kim: That's good. It's also the complexity of the language that matters. Some of this science jargon wouldn't sink in at all with some people. And languages themselves, how many are there around the world? Tons. But within each one, there are oodles of dialects. The more we can use the words and phrases of the local people, the more they'll be able to hear us. For example, if you're talking with people in a Hutterite colony, you're not going to say "Jeezus!" when you're surprised.

Theo: And when I'm talking with therapists, I try my best to use the words they use when describing psychological concepts.

Kim: It's just adapting to meet the needs of your audience. We aren't just moving our jaws for exercise, we're communicating because there are messages to convey. So there is some responsibility that the speaker carries, to increase the odds that they'll be understood.

Theo: Another thing to consider is that the message gets received. Just 'cause you leave a voice message doesn't mean they got it. Best for the communicator to check in and confirm, eh? Hey, how about texting and emails? What a different way of communicating that is!

Kim: Yeah, it makes all this interpersonal one-on-one stuff we've been talking about seem old-fashioned. How can you assess nonverbals when you're a thousand miles apart clicking away on a tiny screen?

Theo: But we all do it. And it's got huge advantages for speed and the quantity of information we can share.

Kim: Sure. And it has significantly changed the way we interact. One-sentence tweets versus eye contact … It's amazing to think of what this means to our interpersonal relationships.

Theo: It just means we have to be more mindful of how we text and tweet.

Kim: The problem often with email is that, because we don't see the entire context, any nonverbals, or hear the tone of voice, there is way more room for misinterpretation.

Theo: It's funny how we're more self-conscious on Skype than when we're in person. Why is that? I know. It's because we can see ourselves.

Kim: I actually find it distracting to see myself on the screen. I notice I play with my hair a lot. For people with negative body image issues, Skype is not easy. But what this modern form of communication is allowing us to do is to stay connected, all the time. As therapists say, connection through relationship is the source of healing.

Theo: So Mark Zuckerberg is a healer as well as a billionaire?

Kim: Facebook, with all the photos and streams of updates, has definitely helped connect the world. But like anything, it's not what you do but how you do it that matters.

Theo: It's all about mindfulness, full stop.

Kim: In our own healing, it's important to pay attention to our inner conversations.

Theo: And, to enhance our relationships with others, to also be mindful of our communication.

Kim: I just noticed you picked your nose there … (*asking with feigned curiosity*)

Theo: Kim, sometimes a nose pick is just a nose pick. (*laughing*) Now I'm going out for a smoke.

5

Relentless Positivity

"We'll love you until you learn to love yourself."
Alcoholics Anonymous

Kim: Thinking like a therapist—at the beginning of our friendship—I held the belief that it was necessary to see you through the eyes of "unconditional positive regard."

Theo: Hmm.

Kim: I first heard this term when I read the book *On Becoming a Person*, by Carl Rogers, who was a famous psychologist. He talked about how seeing someone through a positive lens offers them acceptance and support, regardless of what they say or do.

Theo: Shouldn't we all do that for everybody?

Kim: Yeah ultimately, with discernment, you're right. But when we first had the idea of working together, I committed myself to the process of seeing you positively, no matter what. At times, I wondered if I was sickly sweet, especially at the beginning, but in my heart I believed that you needed to fill up your tank of oxytocin from a nurturing, positive, safe, and absolutely non-sexual relationship. Changing your behaviour was not my goal. Developing trust and helping you reflect on why you do what you do, with a positive slant, was my relentless intent.

Theo: (*looking directly at Kim*) Hmm.

Kim: This positivity—when it really is relentless—is an attitude of grace that values you even though you have faults and short-comings. When you think of yourself negatively, your brain develops a hard drive that makes you see the world through that negative mindset. When someone comes along and sees you through these relentlessly positive eyes, it begins to show you a different way to think. As you change your thinking, so will your brain change.

Theo: I get really excited when I think of our conversations as rewiring my brain.

Kim: As we continue to say a million times, when you change your thoughts, the old brain cells that were wired together reorganize and new connections develop.

Theo: It is easier for me to consider the idea of receiving compliments when I think of them as rewiring my brain.

Kim: "Relentless positivity" is not the expression of compliments in the way you might be thinking about them. Many times, people give compliments wanting something back. Authentic positivity doesn't expect anything in return. There is no ulterior motivation.

Theo: (*teary and gazing away*) I feel shame even when you describe it that way. It connects to my unlovable and I'm-not-good-enough thoughts, making it hard to take it in.

Kim: Remember our recent conversation about negative body image?

Just because my loving husband tells me I'm beautiful to him doesn't mean I think I'm beautiful to myself. He's trying and trying to convince me, but until the day I believe it, the wires in my brain are still telling me otherwise. So I get it that your old wiring is resistant.

Theo: The closer the words are to your own beliefs about yourself, the easier they are to accept.

Kim: Very well said. I believe people when they say I have beautiful eyes, I guess … hmm. I'm working on accepting the other positive feedback.

Theo: So you're saying that unless I believe you (at least at some level) when you're positive about me, I'll be unable to hear it.

Kim: It would go in one ear and out the other, so to speak. I think receiving the positive energy of relentless positivity has more to do with how I say what I say rather than with the words I use.

Theo: It's not what you do, but how you do it.

Kim: As I've been describing, when I am talking with you, I constantly track your body language and facial expressions. I change my delivery depending upon the cues that you give me. You've come to learn and trust that when you get uncomfortable, I ease up. Attunement is the art of relentless positivity.

Theo: It seems to me that the same core issues resurface over and over, and you're relentless with your patience as I revisit them each time.

Kim: I am not expecting you to get rid of your core issues completely. I am hoping to help you accept them for what they are and notice them as they come up. And over time, they will soften their influence as you replace them with positives. It is unlikely that we will eliminate our core stuff from our personalities. I don't think anyone does. But we can definitely get faster at recognizing them.

Theo: I don't have to be perfect? (*making a funny face at Kim*)

Kim: I never expect that of anyone … except myself, as you know.

Theo: It's our self-image that really matters, eh. (*looking right at Kim*) Kim, you are awesome. Can't you see that?

Kim: (*looking down and to the right with shame*) When my hair is looking good, and I have my funky shoes on, I might agree … (*laughing*)

Theo: What I've learned from you is that comments like that are a deflection or a sliding off that dismisses what I've just said. It means what I said was hard for you to hear.

Kim: Can I say, "Yeah, yeah?" If I gave you a straight-out compliment like, "Your willingness to engage in topics that are so profoundly difficult for others to even touch on is really admirable," would you be able to take it in? Positive feedback is hard to accept.

Theo: True. But what am I supposed to say back to something like that?

Kim: People often confuse humility with downplaying themselves. This can easily become self-deprecating. True humility in the way I like to think about it is owning our greatness, while still being conscious about other people's greatness at the same time. It's not about comparing ourselves to others; the outcome of humility is that it creates more equality and respect in a relationship.

Theo: When we don't feel good enough, sometimes we exaggerate ourselves to measure up, in our own minds. It might come across as boastful to others … (*long pause*) When people talk like that, it could mean they are looking for basic acknowledgement.

Kim: For sure. In the past, arrogance was a significant trigger for me. It turned me off and made me feel angry.

Theo: Why?

Kim: Because I felt "less-than." Or worse, dismissed. I think it's that I didn't feel received or seen by the other person when they were boasting.

Theo: Say something else about that.

Kim: It resonates with my own insecurity

Theo: That's pretty vulnerable of you to say.

Kim: I'm learning from you in many different ways. Thinking about it from the perspective of the one speaking arrogantly, the only time we pump ourselves up and say how great we are is when we are actually not feeling good enough. What do you think?

Theo: Yeah, yeah.

Kim: That's a different "yeah, yeah."

Theo: Well, it was nice that you used the generic distancing word "we" instead of "you," even though the concept could have been linked directly to me.

Kim: There is a difference between humility and authenticity. When someone's really authentic, their brilliance shines through and there's no need to even talk about it. Speaking humbly just helps others to hear us, without the distraction of them getting triggered by an arrogant tone.

Theo: That's mindful humility! Great concept. I'll try it. I'm so great, I'll probably learn it really quickly! (*laughing*)

Kim: (*smiling*) You make me laugh.

Theo: So either pumping ourselves up or putting ourselves down is not an authentic representation of who we are, and both show insecurity to whoever's paying attention.

Kim: Well summarized.

Theo: So when you were being relentlessly positive to me, I know you weren't just blowing sunshine up my ass with some ulterior motive. I could feel the authenticity in how you communicated, and now that I think about it, your nonverbals were consistent. That helped me start to believe you. But it's not so easy with other people who we don't know as well, right? How do we know when someone is giving us a compliment that is real, versus a compliment that is because the other person is really wanting something in return?

Kim: We feel it. And it's in their nonverbals. Frequently, our positive feedback *does* have a hidden agenda, probably most of the time. At the root of it, we want to be liked, and we're all trying to avoid rejection.

Theo: You know I'm not a therapist, but it seems to me like all our feelings of rejection and abandonment seem to lead us back to our family-of-origin stuff.

Kim: Um hum. (*nodding*) When our ego needs to be fed, it is easy to get trapped by the seduction of compliments without noticing the allure and falsity behind it. When anyone's looking for compliments to feed their ego, they're more likely to miss the possible insincerity of the intent. Needing outside validation can become an addiction.

Theo: That is an intense one. Especially for those of us who like to be on the stage, huh?

Kim: Totally. I have been working on this one since I was three. I remember my very first ballet recital. It was at the Pantages Playhouse Theatre in Winnipeg. Right after my performance, I walked out onto the very edge of the stage in my red tutu and inquiringly asked the crowd, "How did you like me?" My mother was mortified!

Theo: Ha! That would have been hilarious! But you know what? I think I've been doing the same thing my whole life. I totally loved it when I knew the crowd was with me. That's a lot of dopamine!

Kim: When we don't feel good enough inside, the outside feels like it needs to be filled up with what's missing. I think to some degree I am still standing on the edge of that stage, sometimes wondering, "How did you like me?" But today I do it with more mindfulness. I'm also aware that whenever I get evaluation forms and 99 percent of them are perfect, I always still focus on that one that wasn't.

Theo: I can just see you in that red tutu!

Kim: It's a double-edge sword, though. That addiction to being acknowledged keeps us striving, eh.

Theo: My workaholic-ness relates to that.

Kim: If you don't get that relentless positivity as a child, you can still get it later on. What it helps a child to develop is a sense of who they are, through nurturing, soothing, and validation. This shows the child they are lovable and capable. A child feels loving kindness and positivity through the way the parent talks, uses their eyes, face, and actions. This nonverbal communication says to the child, "I love you and you are worthy of love!" The child's brain and body feel happy, calm, and relaxed. A good therapist or friend, like a secure parent, helps to rewire the receiver's brain away from shame to feeling worthy of love and acceptance.

Theo: So it's increasingly important for people like me to surround themselves with authentic friends.

Kim: Yes! That's very true for all of us. "Conscious friend choosing" is actually pretty rare. Stop for a second and think of all the people in your life to whom you are repeatedly exposed. Is the bulk of the nonverbals you get every day loving and accepting? No answer needed. Just something we can all reflect on.

Theo: There have been times in my life when the people I related to the most were other addicts, strippers, and other hurt people. Then, I seemed to attract relationships that were filled with blame and put-downs. I am consciously changing this habit. I am choosing to spend time with the friends and family who give me the nurturance we've been talking about. The more positive the energy the better. And then the more I have to give back to them!

Kim: I see you choosing new friends for sure, and they are reflective of your evolving inner state.

Theo: I'm definitely starting to notice a change in who I am naturally attracted to.

Kim: The people anyone surrounds themselves with are a reflection of where they're at in their personal development. Like attracts like. There was an interesting study on this principle years ago, but for the life of me I can't remember when or by whom. The concept is profound though. Two hundred people were brought in, none of whom had ever met each other. They were all told to mingle for a very short time and then pair up. What none of them knew going in was that one hundred of them were alcoholics, and the other hundred weren't. According to my memory of the study, fifty alcoholics paired up with fifty alcoholics, and fifty non-alcoholics paired up with fifty non-alcoholics. Remarkable, eh?

Theo: I can spot someone who's been abused a mile away. This is not surprising at all. Something about the commonality of the struggle in the other must be comforting to us.

Kim: Comforting in the familiar sense, for sure.

Theo: It must be from our implicit memory stuff …

Kim: I agree. Do you think this changes as we get past our demons? Can you ever see yourself naturally pulled to someone who has absolutely no history of abuse or addiction?

Theo: I have no idea. What do you think?

Kim: I think probably yes, but the jury is still out on that. What is most important is that whoever you are surrounding yourself with is also interested in doing their own work, so that the theme of self-awareness and personal growth isn't something you're stuck with thinking about and doing on your own.

Theo: I know what you're talking about.

Kim: The one with more skills is the one who has to take the lead. That's why it's so unfortunate when parents don't have the tools to take care of their kids. The child ends up trying to take care of the parent.

Theo: So true. In adult relationships, that can sometimes be frustrating.

Kim: Only if you feel you are not having any of your needs met by the other person. There's another aspect to this. Remember that movie on sex addiction, *Thanks for Sharing*?

Theo: Yeah, lots of triggers for me in that one.

Kim: There's a scene where Gwyneth Paltrow (a woman dating an addict) is in conversation with a woman who's been married to an addict for about twenty-five years. And she asks, "How do you deal with being married to someone who you know can fall off the wagon at any time?" She said that it was all about keeping her own side of the street clean. Insightful, eh? She'd married an addict after all. To be attracted to someone with that kind of history reflects back that you have to do your own inner work. For her to be focusing on her husband the addict all day long would create a no-win relationship. It would be anxiety-producing for her and shaming to him, and would totally distract her from doing her own personal work.

Theo: Whenever someone points a finger at me, there are three fingers pointing back at themself. I know this principle applies to me too, when I'm pointing fingers.

Kim: When anyone focuses only on the other's behaviour, they are missing a chance to better understand themselves.

Theo: (*rubbing his face*) That gets me right in my chest.

Kim: I know.

Theo: I know that you know that I know!

Kim: Remember, everyone's doing the best they can with what they have.

Theo: We can only hope they are. One of the things that is so hard for me is when someone blames me and I know it's all about their shit; it's just a projection, but they can't see it!

Kim: Until you no longer believe what they say, it'll continue to trigger you. My brother-in-law gave advice to his sensitive little brother when he was ten. He said, if someone's criticizing you, stop and consider the source. If he's someone you'd want as a best friend, listen to him. If he's a shit-head, don't pay any attention.

Theo: I feel disappointed when the other person can't see the real me.

Kim: It is disappointing. It's hard to feel misunderstood. When you are the recipient of a barrage of verbal abuse, sometimes the best thing you can do is drop the rope. Allow the other person to think they are right, or partly right, while knowing in your heart they are off-base. In response to their blaming, you might say something like: "Maybe there's truth to what you say. I'll think about that ..."

Theo: But then the other person will never get my point.

Kim: Who knows? Maybe they'll go off and think about it, too. But that's what "letting go" is. You can't always win, and people will not always see your side. As a strategy, I'd suggest you share your disappointment with those who care, and pick your battles with those who don't.

Theo: Will they ever get it?

Kim: Do you mean will they ever care? "Letting go" means learning to be detached from the outcome. To get to that point sometimes you have to sit with your shit, and look at it a bit more, and other times you have to give it up to the God of Your Understanding ...

Theo: You nailed it. It is the caring.

Kim: (*warmly*) Mmhm. To be aware that the other person doesn't care, or can't care, is very painful.

Theo: I think I like the relentless positivity better.

Kim: Me, too. Relentless positivity doesn't mean we always have to agree with each other though. But when we exchange feedback, it's about how we give that feedback so the other can receive it. And of course, it is the underlying care that matters. Respectful feedback from a place of positive intention, although it might be uncomfortable, is an awesome catalyst for reflection and growth.

Theo: I would rather someone be honest with me than just enable my destructive behaviour. I've lived through that enough already. And I know I willingly participated, for sure.

Kim: Enabling, or acting as a codependent, takes away the possibility for natural consequences to act as catalysts for change. Like giving money to a gambler, lying to an addict's boss to cover up absenteeism or pretending there's no abuse in the house where there obviously is.

Theo: Whoa, most of that hit home. (*rubbing the top of his chest*) I think my dad chose my mom as a partner—at a subconscious level—because some part of him knew he could get away with his shit.

Kim: Do you think a lot of people do that? People who study the dynamics of enabling say that the short-term pain, long-term gain approach is way better to curb people of addictive behaviours. So if someone pukes on the floor, let the puke stay there and don't clean it up for them. Having to clean it up themselves in the morning is a natural consequence. Although enabling behaviour comes from the intent to protect and keep the peace, it ends up keeping the dynamic unhealthy for everyone involved.

Theo: In truth, I appreciated the people who covered up for me. There were many of them, and I covered up for some too. But I know it wasn't right.

Kim: Often, codependents tend to combine their enabling with nagging. Even though they think they're helping, they often feel resentful. And their blame tends to shame the addict, which just reinforces the addict's self-loathing. Many enablers fear rejection and pushback from the addict, which keeps them compliant within the destructive pattern.

Theo: That explains pretty much every relationship I've ever been in.

Kim: It truly takes faith and courage not to enable someone you love. You don't have to be in relationship with an addict to experience this dilemma. I have to be mindful about not enabling my teenage daughter. Picking up her clothes for her when she can do it for herself, nagging and then helping with her homework, letting her borrow the car when she's late for work and only needs to go a few blocks. I think it's tough for parents to allow natural consequences be their force for learning …

Theo: I think enabling is most destructive when two addicts are in relationship with each other.

Kim: Ooh. (*exhaling*) I can see that. Cool when both of them can recognize their contribution to the dysfunction, though. Both parties need to see their personal contribution to any dysfunction.

Theo: I'm still pissed about the time Veronica and I went to a marriage counsellor in New York City and the therapist turned to Veronica and said, "You're fine, and he's fucked."

Kim: Took a long time to get you willingly back into a therapy office after that, eh?

Theo: What I know now is that the marriage counsellor didn't keep me safe. Even if that therapist was right about my behaviour at the time, I just felt more ashamed and isolated by her comment.

Kim: In relationships, both people contribute to any dynamic. Just talking in generalities now, but some people stay in relationships much longer than is healthy for them. Some people don't have the tools to make the relationship better, and some don't have the tools to leave when they should.

Theo: I don't believe in divorce. I think people should always try to work things through.

Kim: It's disappointing when it doesn't work out, eh.

Theo: Makes me both angry and sad.

Kim: (*big exhale*) We can work on our relationship stuff until we stop breathing. Do you want me to just listen now, or to give some suggestions for how people in relationships can communicate more positively?

Theo: Bring it on. For so many years my addictions were all-consuming. And I wasn't present to my relationships the way I needed to be. But, when I did try to communicate, it still didn't go very well. Remember, I didn't learn how to do relationships very well. I still think about what could I have said or done. Like after a game, should I have shot instead of passed or passed instead of shot? Whatever didn't go right used to get played over and over in my head. I know that looking back like that is self-deprecating. But I still wonder, in relationships, how I could have done it differently with the skills that I had.

Kim: Looking forward, all of us would do well to find ways to give each other feedback respectfully, with more kindness and compassion.

Theo: You know, especially at the beginning of relationships, there's a fine line between relentless positivity and enabling.

Kim: Ooh, that's good. I get what you mean. It was something I was very conscious of when we began this work together. It's easy to confuse relentless positivity with approval of a behaviour. If you're still doing something that I believe is hurtful to you or others, and at the same time I want to remind you that you're still wonderful as a person, I have to find a way to communicate those differences clearly. In a securely attached relationship, the child gets the difference between the parent loving "them" and disapproving of "their behaviour."

Theo: I don't have a lot of people in my life who have the confidence or clarity to really call me on my shit. But I like it when they do.

Kim: Why do you think they don't?

Theo: I think some people are intimidated by my anger. Others might be afraid of losing the relationship.

Kim: Very insightful. Another common challenging pattern in relationships can happen when one person puts the other person down repeatedly just to hold that person captive to the belief that they are worthless and can't do any better. Commonly, the intent of this pattern is to protect the verbally abusive person from being abandoned. It's unconsciously using aggression to demand connection.

Theo: A million memories just jumped into my head.

Kim: (*big exhale*) But we *can* speak our truth, offer support, reframe old beliefs, and reveal information without creating hurt for someone else. It is all in how we say it. It doesn't have to be harsh. But the reality is that there are all kinds of patterns in relationships that prolong our emotional pain rather than support our growth and well-being.

Theo: Ach, I just wish I didn't get so defensive all the time.

Kim: You mean if you are ever verbally put down, defensiveness is your go-to reaction?

Theo: Sure. My automatic response is to protect myself with anger and defensiveness. I don't like feeling hurt.

Kim: Remember, whenever we experience defensiveness there is a grain of truth in the accusation that is resonating within us. So it's giving us an opportunity to reflect.

Theo: Thanks for trying to reframe it, but maybe that just explains why I never liked playing defense. (*smiling*) It would have meant that I would have been wrong all the time! (*laughing at his own joke*)

Kim: It's hard when you feel like you have to defend yourself so much. Something I know about getting feedback of any kind is that it's easier to take in when you know the person saying it actually cares about you.

Theo: 'Cause you know that person is less likely to reject or abandon you. I know I receive feedback better from people who care.

Kim: For sure!

Theo: When I suspect they don't is when I get really defensive. I think it's getting feedback from people I trust that helps me to move forward. It is hard work. The hardest work you will ever do in your life is to take this journey of self-reflection and consciously change.

Kim: One of my psychiatry profs at the University of Manitoba repeatedly emphasized how important it is to "put someone together before we take them apart." Positivity helps to create that secure foundation. Like a frightened child, the shadow side of us will remain in hiding or in self-defense until it feels safe and comfortable enough to even look at what might be the crux of the issue.

Theo: A lot of this blasting of positivity has to be about timing. You were so nice to me at the beginning. Were you genuinely as nonjudgmental about my behaviour as you seemed back then?

Kim: I hope you don't think I'm "not nice" to you now?

Theo: Of course you're still nice, but it's definitely different now, more relaxed and balanced. And we laugh more. But that wouldn't have been possible for me without the amount of time we've spent together.

Kim: (*reflecting*) Some of your behaviours definitely triggered me in our early conversations. But I know those were my own judgments and projections, and it was easy for me to separate them. I knew, from my therapy experience, what was mine and what was yours. My initial focus was not on the issues, but on supporting your whole spirit.

Theo: Just curious (*looking like a troublemaker*) ... specifically, what things about me triggered you back then?

Kim: To quote your lawyer, "You're such a little shit, but I still love you." I quote him because I feel the same way sometimes!

Theo: Ha.

Kim: I can only say this after two years of such vulnerable, connected conversation that I feel safe enough to admit it. At this point, I know that my honesty will be received without harm to our relationship. Thinking back, initially I was really mindful about not becoming starstruck because of your number of Twitter followers. I think that may have made me try really, really hard to listen to you, so that I would be good enough.

Theo: That's honest. And I think I, and some people around me at the time, put you through the ringer. Kudos to you for staying present ...

Kim: I know something that made me do some of my own work. I had a hard time with promiscuous behaviour. When I heard your stories of sleeping with faceless women, it reminded me of my high school friends who fell in love with hockey players and were so hurt by them. Since it was one of my triggers, I had to be actively compassionate about it and go further out of my way to put myself in your shoes. This is a great example of relentless positivity. Despite my own blinders, I needed to step into your experience and understand the factors involved in the choices you made. Ironically, the process of mindfulness around this issue has given me tremendous insights into some of my own past dysfunctional relationships. Every piece of conversation that we all have has the potential to invite each of us into reflection.

Theo: Okay, now that I'm feeling brave and on a roll, what else about me is hard for you?

Kim: Why are you feeling brave?

Theo: Cause you're owning your own stuff and working hard at not judging me. I love that.

Kim: Okay, then. Here's the next one. It's kind of an ongoing trigger, but it's happening less frequently than it used to. Sometimes when you communicate, you come across as definitive and forceful. It's when your voice gets louder, you speak with a bit of anger, but lots of resolve; and you say things that can dismiss other people. However, I am reminded that this is just a defense that protects you when you're feeling vulnerable. The reason I can see it in you is because I have the same discomfort with being vulnerable. Although I may use a different form of defense to protect myself, I am equally as uncomfortable with being vulnerable as you are. What I am saying is that the parts of others we don't necessarily like are mirrors of ourselves. "In your eyes I see myself as ..."

Theo: Wow, you even make my arrogance sound not so bad.

Kim: When I truly have this mirroring concept in mind, I not only look at others with compassion, but I better understand myself.

Theo: Self-compassion is harder, isn't it?

Kim: It is always easier to be compassionate for others than it is for yourself. Kristen Neff is the self-compassion expert, and many of her studies have confirmed that finding.[xlviii]

Theo: I am actively working on self-compassion …

Kim: Now you get a turn. Do you want to tell me anything that you don't like about me, knowing that what you don't like in me is also in you?

Theo: Neat way to be vulnerable but still protect yourself there. Um, I don't like it when you are insecure about yourself. I don't like it when I feel that way either. I also don't like it when you worry about money. I don't like it when I worry about money.

Kim: See, even being honest with each other can be not so hard. People don't always have to tear each other apart with criticism and judgment to give feedback.

Theo: I feel sad when you are hard on yourself, because you are such a powerful agent of change for everyone you meet. I don't think you stop and appreciate all the people you are helping.

Kim: Touché. And that's another example of a reflection in the mirror. It's not only shared negatives that we see in each other, but we can see positives too.

Theo: Yep. We're both hard on ourselves, and we're both agents of change.

Kim: I just got something! In order to have the power necessary to carry the responsibility for monumental change, an ego *is* required. You are teaching me that big ego can actually be a real asset. Yours is like a necessary powerful force that is willing to move mountains to create change for others. If I match you in that strength of will, I am deeply honoured.

Theo: I always saw it in you. Remember what Nin said, "We don't see people as they are, we see people as we are." Remembering that helps us see good stuff about ourselves, as well as own our own shit.

Kim: You're right. It does remind us to acknowledge our own strengths when we see them reflected back from others. Another thing I know about you is that you read nonverbal communication very well. You have a great bullshit detector. If I am not being authentic, you will sniff it out. You require that I do my own work or you wouldn't believe or trust me.

Theo: You always allow me to come to my own ahas, and you are very patient with me when I flounder around, even though I think you know when I am deluding myself.

Kim: I stay away from pushing you for explanations that you are not ready to own. It is way more valuable when you come to the awarenesses and conclusions yourself.

Theo: You ask me questions, plant seeds in my head, and then wait.

Kim: I don't come at you head-on. Direct confrontation with too much need for you to change would feel like pressure to you.

Theo: I hate it when other people do that.

Kim: So as to not let you slip into a negative thought, I point out when I notice you're getting upset, like with the tracking we were talking about. Then I offer reassurance and inquire about the possibility if your response was connected to the past, rather than to something that was happening in the moment.

Theo: When you ask me a reflection question, you often start by saying that you're curious. I really like that. It is so non-threatening.

Kim: When I use that word "curious," it is to maintain an open lens of inquiry that invites all possibilities. I don't presume to know what's always going on for you.

Theo: Even though you often do. But that's an empowering habit you have.

Kim: I've got another strategy, this one's for fixing screw-ups. It helps me to repair a difficult moment if I've just put my foot in my mouth. Say I've just asked my colleague, "How's your wonderful husband doing?" and she tells me, "We're going through a really tough time and it's shit for both of us." I could salvage the moment between us, at least, by saying, "Oh I'm sorry that's happening for you. How must that feel, when people ask stupid questions like I just did?" Usually, just by showing interest and being fully present to my blunder will be enough to reinstate trust and respect.

Theo: I'd find it hard to think in the moment like that. When I put my foot in my mouth, the taste is so bad it even affects my sense of direction! (*laughing*)

Kim: It's helpful to have these kinds of strategies at the ready. There are other ways to keep things positive as well. When tension is mounting, I might say something like, "Your voice is getting louder when you talk about that," or "Your jaw is getting tight when you share this experience with me," or "You just turned your body away from me when I asked you that question." This kind of tracking helps you to develop your somatic mindfulness. And I know you're learning this awareness of feedback from your body very quickly.

Theo: When I manage to catch myself doing these things, it helps me to use my mind to slow down my reactivity.

Kim: You know, when you can consciously catch yourself slowing down your reactions, that's when you know your brain is changing!

Theo: Right on.

Kim: When I was at the Compassion Conference in Telluride, Colorado, they talked a lot about the effects of the word "love" on the brain and the body. When you hear, "I love you," and when you say, "I love you," certain parts of your brain light up and all the stress chemicals in your body calm down. Even when you just think loving thoughts, the same outcome happens.

Theo: I don't mind hearing it or saying it.

Kim: They've done all this cool research on monks who've spent their whole lives meditating and practising loving-kindness. What they've found from this research is that when we humans focus our minds on loving thoughts, our DNA changes at its core, making our bodies more resilient to stress and disease.[xlix]

Theo: The healing power of love.

Kim: The healing power of positive thoughts. When we think positive thoughts, we are constantly giving our own brain dopamine hits.[l]

Theo: You always tell me that dopamine is the chemistry of addiction, 'cause it's a feel-good thing. Why then are we not addicted to positive thoughts?

Kim: Well, apparently, our brains are like Velcro to all negative thoughts and Teflon toward our positive ones.[li] So it's the negatives thoughts that stick.

Theo: Doesn't that suck?

Kim: It seems that for every negative thought, it takes about three to five positive thoughts to override it. Magnetic resonance imaging is a funky brain X-ray type machine that uses a magnet to scan your brain. It can videotape what your brain cells are doing when you think and do stuff. If I were to say the word, "No" to you, the fMRI imager would light up your amygdala (your emotional brain) in less than a second. Your body would release all its stress-producing hormones and neurotransmitters in response to a word that we associate with something negative.[lii]

Theo: No wonder I hate to be told no.

Kim: When someone says, "Yes," our brains have very little response to the positivity. Positive words do not signal a threat to our survival, so our brain isn't as interested in that word. Significant repetition is needed for the brain to process "Yes" as a positive.[liii] Hence the need for relentless positivity.

Theo: This is what you are always trying to do, isn't it? Have me reframe my stories into something positive so I can override the negative.

Kim: That's the idea. Furthermore, when negative thoughts come into our brain, the stress chemicals that are produced have been shown to interrupt our normal thinking, especially logic and reasoning. It's like there's no one home upstairs when we're stressed.[liv]

Theo: Aside from making me stupid in the moment, do you think negative thoughts can actually damage my brain?

Kim: The more you stay focused on negative words and thoughts, the more you can actually damage key structures in your brain. Particularly the brain parts that are in charge of your memory, your ability to regulate your emotions, and your ability to feel your feelings.

Theo: When I know something is actually bad for me, it helps to motivate me to stop; so this information is good.

Kim: Sure, but it isn't enough to just get the concept. To change your brain for the better, you have to actually believe your new positive thoughts.

Theo: I can. I will.

Kim: Exactly. Did you know that for the first three years of your life, the right side of your brain is the dominant side and it is mostly oriented toward negative thoughts?

Theo: Of course I didn't. (*smiling*) Why is that?

Kim: I guess we need to pay attention to the bad stuff for our survival. The left side of the brain, which is typically seen as the positive side of the brain, only really starts to develop at around eighteen months.

Theo: I'm remembering that the right side of the brain is the home of the implicit memory of family-of-origin stuff.

Kim: You are so smart. That is why so many of our "issues" are related to that first eighteen months when the brain was overly watching for the bad stuff. It isn't until later that we really process positivity, when so much of our implicit memory is already in place.

Theo: Crap.

Kim: There is another time when the right brain takes over in development and that is during adolescence. I always say that they lose their brain! The surge of hormones flips a switch for a big growth spurt that reorganizes many of the previously established neural networks.

Theo: No wonder my teenagers are so frustrating. They lose their brain with all those hormones.

Kim: (*laughing*) It's unfortunate we all have to go through that stage, really. But this explains why adolescence is such a time that triggers their parents' own stuff. Implicitly, we all remember the feeling of being really stupid (when we were teenagers ourselves), and it kind of drives us a little crazy to see it happening in our kids, kids we're responsible for.

Theo: Maybe there should be self-help groups for parents of adolescents.

Kim: Some parents I know say that's what makes them drink. Another thing about adolescents that can help parents help their kids is to let them sleep. When the teenage brain is so busy figuring things out, they really do need their sleep. I've heard His Holiness the Dalai Lama say, "Sleep is actually the best form of meditation." And that's backed up by science. Sleep definitely helps consolidate memory.

Theo: And you know sleep deprivation in my teenage years was a huge problem for me.

Kim: A lack of sleep would have added to your anxiety for sure. Glad to hear you're sleeping way better now.

Theo: The difference is night and day. Notice the pun? (*smiling*)

Kim: Brilliant. (*rolling her eyes*) Back to the two sides of the brain. The right side has direct connections to the amygdala, the part of the brain that processes our emotions, and the left side of our brain does not have those connections. This means that talking, thinking, or anything to do with language—which is the function of the left brain—does *not* directly soothe the reactive brain. So when you're having a stressful argument, "Stop talking."

Theo: That's usually when I talk the most and the fastest, and maybe the loudest … I get your point.

Kim: It also means that when you're yelling, and people are stressed because of it, it's practically impossible for them to hear the point you want them to understand.

Theo: Shit! I wasted a lot of breath. And no wonder they didn't change their behaviour when I told them to.

Kim: (*smiling*) Sucks, eh. And that's not all. And this is unfortunate. Remember the right brain is biased toward negative emotions and pessimism? Because this side of your brain develops first, it's dominant and has the power of "veto" over the optimistic left brain, throughout our whole lives. This hardware issue means our basic design leaves us vulnerable to things like shame, guilt, and depression. It's like a default program on a computer.

Theo: I must have a very active negative right brain.

Kim: If I had to guess, I would say your right brain is quite operative. However, you also have many positive beliefs and those are a function of the left brain. Thankfully, there is a structure that works like a bridge (the corpus callosum) between the two hemispheres of our brains that flows information back and forth, balancing our negative and positive thinking. Like you, the brain is very interested in teamwork, making sure different parts of the brain are working in harmony as much as possible.

Theo: Are you telling me that I have a fairly well-integrated brain? How can that be possible?

Kim: I think your amount of resilience is amazing, but I also think of it as a bit of a mystery.

Theo: You are being too diplomatic. All the trauma, booze, cocaine, concussions, and stress that have fried my brain; it's a miracle I have any brain cells left at all.

Kim: You have a very high emotional intelligence and a powerful spirit.

Theo: Well, I know I'm not alone with all this, so that helps.

Kim: Loving thoughts, like these, also improve your physical health. You know how when you're upset, you can feel sick to your stomach?

Theo: I am very aware of the sensitivity of my gut to my emotions and I know my Crohn's disease is influenced by my stress levels.

Kim: Which are influenced by your thoughts. You know how I keep yakking about oxytocin as the chemistry of love and gleaming and beaming?

Theo: I really love that chemical.

Kim: Well, not only does your brain love it, but now we know that a whole bunch of other parts of your body do too. Scientists have found that our gut, immune system, liver, and heart also receive oxytocin. I think that it so awesome. What this suggests to me is that love affects your body, directly![lv] The more scientists study the brain, the more we realize how connected it is to the body. I think they are actively proving that love can heal our physical bodies.

Theo: So when they say "love your body," it is good advice.

Kim: Gives new depth to that phrase, doesn't it? Love is not just conceptual—it's neurochemical. Did you know that oxytocin is a natural antidote to stress? Yet another reason why being relentlessly positive with other people feels so good.

Theo: Healthy relationships sure feel better than unhealthy ones!

Kim: There's something called associative memory that we all have; enough positive exposure to someone who gives us an oxytocin hit will condition your brain to get that hit just by thinking about them. I read this study about girls between the ages of eight and twelve getting oxytocin hits when they heard their mom's voice on the phone.[lvi] (*smiling*) I love that idea.

Theo: Wild. But I'm guessing the opposite can happen. If you associated someone with fear, all you would have to do to get those fear chemicals going is to think about that person.

Kim: Yes.

Theo: Our thoughts really are that powerful.

Kim: Because they are that powerful, that's why it's important to think positive ones.

Theo: No wonder I'm feeling so much calmer these days. It must be the oxytocin that comes with the increased positivity.

Kim: What is it you tell me all the time about the way to really master something?

Theo: You know it—practise, practise, practise. Skate pass shoot, skate pass shoot, skate pass shoot, for ten thousand hours, at least. What are you saying here?

Kim: We also have to practise positive thinking. Especially those of us who aren't in the habit of it. When you are engaged in personal growth, the process is endless.

Theo: I guess it's like practising your golf swing. Tiger Woods is always tweaking something in his swing even though he is already so damn good at his craft. We can always get better and better.

Kim: Remember, it's not about eliminating your core issues. It's about accepting yourself, for all that you are. The same issues will come up over and over, maybe forever in this lifetime. But they come up differently as you develop yourself. Abandonment, unlovable, not good enough, whatever they are ... When you're first on this self-discovery journey, it can be like taking dynamite and blasting through things. But as you become more familiar with the process, your triggers become a lot more subtle. It does get easier. Instead of being triggered by all kinds of things and feeling like you're an open gaping wound, you get triggered by smaller things that don't cause front-page news. And you move forward feeling better and better about yourself.

Theo: I'm learning that sometimes I've gotta hear something over and over again before it sinks in though.

Kim: Like what?

Theo: Like that I'm a good person.

Kim: You're a good person, you're a good person, you're a good person ... Now you say it to yourself.

Theo: (*grinning*) I bet I could get addicted to feeling better and better.

6

This Healing Stuff Is Addictive

"The breeze at dawn has secrets to tell you.
Don't go back to sleep."
Rumi

Kim: When you were a young teenager, you probably would have traded your soul to make the NHL. Your motivation was that high. Like it was in your DNA.

Theo: Hockey was my everything; it was the only thing I could ever imagine myself doing.

Kim: And everyone who knew you back then knew that. Even when you made it, you were one of the most passionate players in its history.

Theo: Mmhm.

Kim: And during the time when you were being sexually abused by Graham James, the idea of disclosing the abuse and the potential risk that could have had on your future career challenged you to the depths of your core. To protect your dreams, as you've told me, you held the secret, and for that to happen, your addictions had to be in place. They created the safety for you to tolerate the shame.

Theo: I didn't feel like I had any options.

Kim: What's tragic to me is that in the end when you left Chicago without even telling them goodbye, it was your addictions that had even more power than your love of hockey. Ironically, it was the very thing you were trying to protect, your hockey, that was the thing that you lost.

Theo: Ah. Fuck! I know.

Kim: This is the power of the interconnection between shame and addiction. Addiction is really tough to crack when shame holds it in place, and being an addict inevitably brings more shame.

Theo: I couldn't keep playing and use, and I couldn't give up the mask for my pain. It was a no-win situation. It's like I couldn't hold on any longer. I left Chicago because I knew I was a detriment to the team; I was way too messed up and I really didn't deserve any paycheque for embarrassing anyone.

Kim: In *Playing With Fire*, you say that if you would've gone to treatment when you were still with the Blackhawks, even without playing, your contract with them would have still paid you $4.5 million.

Theo: Doesn't that show you how powerful addiction is? I chose my addiction over both hockey and money. Thinking like I think today, I realize that was crazy!

Kim: (*nodding*)

Theo: Do you know how much further that kind of money would go now that I am sober? Man, am I glad I'm past the booze and drugs today. Those were really shitty days.

Kim: That's the power of addiction.

Theo: I have to stay mindful to that power of addiction, every single day.

Kim: That requires tremendous vigilance on your part. In the end, all those various treatment centres you attended didn't really do enough for you?

Theo: Nope. Those retreat centres really just taught me a lot about other ways to get high! What do you think happens when hundreds of junkies get together and have a smoke after an enforced sharing circle no one wants to share in? They have their own sharing circles and talk about the crazy shit they did and how they did it. And I wasn't the craziest in there by any stretch. We all had our stories.

Kim: Anything stand out for you, that you learned from?

Theo: Aside from strategies to hide our addictions? Yeah, one guy really taught me just how fucked up people can get. He had a mission, like me, to try to chemically induce the perfect level of buzz. We were talking about hallucinations and I remember asking him, "So, how did you know when you were exactly there?" And he said, deadpan, stone sober, and expecting us all to be able to relate, "It's when I'd be looking at the TV screen, and all of a sudden it would split in two. Ya know what I mean?" Man his brain must have been messed up ... he eventually committed suicide.

Kim: (nodding) Very sad. When you did quit drinking and drugs, you went cold turkey. When you did that, did your personal life immediately get better?

Theo: For a bit. There was a huge blast of empowerment that came from the decision to want to get better. But old patterns of dysfunction don't go away by themselves just because drugs and alcohol are out of the picture. For years, and still today, I consider myself "a dry drunk."

Kim: Hmm. What's that like?

Theo: All the same qualities of being a drunk—without any fun. I don't mean I don't have any fun being sober. I do. What I mean is that there are no more moments when all the crappy stuff is being numbed out.

Kim: Doesn't sound ideal from a pain-in-the-moment perspective.

Theo: It isn't. But it's way better than the alternative. There's no comparison at all. And when I'm working through my stuff, the pile of issues I'd previously spent so much money and energy on masking *is* getting smaller. I must be getting dopamine hits every time I have an aha moment along the way, right?

Kim: Of course. You can get dopamine hits—pleasure through a brain chemical—from positive thoughts all the time. Probably the cheapest option of them all, 'cause thoughts are free. Dopamine hits are addictive!

Theo: The amount of money I spent on all my addictions over the years is fucking outrageous.

Kim: I can't even imagine. I remember when Bob and I went to an AA meeting with you last year. It was my first time as a guest. The experience was powerful and humbling for me. I was struck by the constant effort from everyone in the group that was required for them to stay sober. It really is constant work, isn't it?

Theo: It's the most important battle alcoholics will ever be in. AA teaches us, "Once an alcoholic, always an alcoholic."

Kim: (*nodding*) I'm sure it takes constant mindfulness.

Theo: The thing about alcoholics is that we're all egomaniacs with inferiority complexes. So for us to admit that we're alcoholic is important to say out loud, because it's about humility and surrender. And saying it to each other at every meeting that we're alcoholics is about our commitment, and our bonding. I have to re-make this commitment every single day.

Kim: By labeling yourself as an alcoholic, the intent is to keep you connected to the process and to each other. So in this instance, the use of the alcoholic label isn't about shaming yourself.

Theo: Not at all. Nothing to do with shame. It's just an acknowledgement of what I'm always working on. For me though, it took many years between when I stopped drinking and when I actively started looking for help. Initially, I was hoping I'd feel better just from being sober. But that didn't work. I didn't even realize it until later, but I'd only replaced those addictions with other ones. It's sad that it took so long, but it really just took me saying to myself, "I'm fed up with living in emotional pain, and I'm gonna seek out people who are able to help me get rid of that pain." I had to come to that decision all by myself. And that part only started a couple years ago.

Kim: You were really going it alone, weren't you?

Theo: Not alone now, by any stretch! But back then, you know why I wasn't trusting therapists; I'd had some bad experiences. And I was fairly pig-headed. I thought I was functioning okay, because I was comparing it to when everything was a gong show. Most people have no concept how insane people are and what they will do when they are in their trauma. Compared to that, with my non-drug-and-alcohol addictions, at least I was coping.

Kim: I'll never forget when someone close to you told me they thought that when you stopped drinking, that would be enough and you'd be okay. That was astonishing to me. It's the issues that need attention, not just the taking away of the hundreds of things that can cover them up. I think many people believe that the sobriety alone is the healing.

Theo: That is just the beginning. I know it. When you and I got into it, it became clear as day that my gambling, sex, workaholism, shopping, and food habits were just other ways of numbing out, and that I was still going to great lengths to cover up my pain.

Kim: There's a lot to understanding addictions. I think it really helps people to understand how addictions work in the brain, in order for them to appreciate the effort involved in truly changing the behaviour.

Theo: Thanks. It would bring a lot of compassion to the healing addicts out there if you could clarify all this.

Kim: Well, what are addictions? Everything that we do, if we can't stop it, we are addicted to it. Even our emotions. Believe it or not, some people are addicted to feeling hurt. Sounds nuts, but why do some people keep going back to abusive partners? People can be attracted to all kinds of self-harmful things; we can also have compulsions toward all shapes and sizes of tabloid-worthy habits; but it's only when these behaviours are uncontrollable that they cause damage in our lives and get to be called "addictions."

Theo: Right. Just because someone looks at porn once in a while doesn't mean he's addicted to it. It's only an addiction when he's missing work because of it, or his family leaves him because of it.

Kim: Good example.

Theo: The science of addiction is fascinating. You say our brains are a natural pharmacy. I like that analogy. My substance abuse days taught me a lot about being a chemist.

Kim: Our internal pharmacy is stocked with chemicals, and the brain is designed to keep itself in a balanced state. Inside these skulls of ours is a soup of chemicals floating around, constantly changing in response to the world around us. It is those chemicals that are part of the communication highways in our brain. In fact, many of the drugs in a real pharmacy are made to mimic what we already have in our brains.

Theo: There's a lot going on in there. (*pointing at his own head*)

Kim: Every millisecond, your brain takes in information and an electrochemical reaction happens in response. It is kind of like old-fashioned telephone wires sending signals from one receiver to another. Makes me feel old even describing it that way!

Theo: I'm not that much younger than you; I remember those. (*with a compassionate smirk*)

Kim: Your brain is about the size of two of your fists put together and weighs about three pounds, full grown. It's at least 75 percent water and is the consistency of a soft-boiled egg. Sounds basic, but it's the most complex thing in the entire universe. It's made up of some one hundred billion brain cells, called neurons. Each of these nerve cells looks a bit like a tree with many branches that fire electrochemical impulses. When any branch comes close enough to a branch from another neuron tree, signals are passed from one to the other. These interconnecting nerve cells create a freeway of communication, moving from branch to branch.

Theo: I can picture that in my mind. And I remember the images of them from the movie *What the Bleep Do We Know!?* The little green arms connecting to each other, going "zap" with an electrochemical charge.

Kim: That movie shows an incredible animation of the brain that helps people grasp its complexity. To put it into perspective, we each have about 1,000,000,000,000,000—a quadrillion—such signals of information lighting up in our heads all the time. One quadrillion. That's a lot of messages, and they impact every single thing we do, think, and feel.

Theo: Makes me wonder how many trees got chopped down in my brain from all the various types of damage I put it through.

Kim: You know that new trees can grow, right? That's what "neuroplasticity" means. The brain's designed to be able to adapt.

Theo: Thank God.

Kim: The chemicals that are responsible for this communication between neurons are called "neurotransmitters." Serotonin, dopamine, adrenaline, opiates, GABA (gamma-aminobutyric acid)—these are a few of the important neurotransmitters when it comes to understanding addiction. Like members of a team, these chemicals work together to regulate us. But of all of these, dopamine is what is at the heart of all addictions. It's the chemical of reward, and it makes us want to do things again and again. That's why I call all forms of addiction "dopamine-seeking."

Theo: How are drugs and alcohol like these chemicals you are talking about?

Kim: Well, the drugs we become addicted to have everything to do with these chemicals. Let's start with alcohol. How do you remember it first affecting you?

Theo: I was addicted from the first sip I ever took. It made me feel relaxed. But once I started, I couldn't stop.

Kim: Alcohol certainly changes the way we feel. But did you know that the first thing alcohol does is stimulate you?

Theo: I would get a little dopamine hit of excitement even if someone said, "Let's go for a drink." I was like Pavlov's salivating dog. I get the concept of alcohol exciting me.

Kim: You got it. At first, alcohol releases dopamine in the brain and this is what gives you pleasure, excitement, and addiction. It feels rewarding. Later, after the alcohol has been in your system for a while, its effects become sedating and relaxing.

Theo: That's what I felt.

Kim: The neurotransmitter that gets released by alcohol that makes you feel calmer is called GABA. GABA is our "chill out" chemical and it quietens the brain, temporarily reducing worry and tension, which means we feel more uninhibited.

Theo: That is why I drank, to "shut up my brain."

Kim: You know how you're highly distractible and a seeker of stimulation?

Theo: Yeah, that part of me makes me think of the movie *Up*! You know where the dog is distracted by the squirrels? I recognized myself in that. I like to refer to people who are distractible like me as having "squirrel brain." Our attention will go toward anything that comes along!

Kim: Well, GABA slows down your squirrel brain so you are less distractible. It allows you to think of only one thing at a time, even if the thing you may choose to be thinking about under the circumstances is relatively senseless.

Theo: I've seen a lot of people act stupid in bars. They say things over and over they certainly wouldn't say when they're sober. Looking back, some of those places I went to were cesspools of debauchery.

Kim: Do you miss that lifestyle?

Theo: Not in the slightest. And you know what I'm realizing? Women who are wasted don't hold any attraction for me anymore. In the past, I would have been all over them like a fat kid on a Smartie.

Kim: Where does that expression come from?

Theo: (*proudly*) Russell, Manitoba!

Kim: I just don't relate to that. I have no personal experience with drunken people passing out in bars, having fights, spending hours in strip clubs. All that slurred speech and the stuff you see in the movies is foreign to me.

Theo: All those people in bars are just people; there's no mystery to it. They all have their stories. I don't know how many strippers I've sat with and just talked about their stories, and it's all trauma. One woman that comes to mind was abused by her brother for years and then got roofied—someone spiked her drink—and woke up with five guys doing their thing to her. I can still feel her pain. But I know every single person in the world has a story, and I'm not sure the bar is the right place for me to be hearing about them anymore.

Kim: That's an intense story. And good awareness on your part.

Theo: Kim, I'm not proud of it, but I am most certainly an expert on the topic. In the interests of science, what do you want to know about what it's like to be an alcoholic?

Kim: The part I can understand is what's going on with the chemical reactions in the brain. When I think about it for myself, I just imagine that drinking too much would make me feel sick and dizzy, and I would hate that.

Theo: You are obviously not going to be an alcoholic.

Kim: Like all of us, I have other addictions, but that's one we don't share.

Theo: So everyone is addicted to something?

Kim: I think we are. But not all addictions have such destructive effects. When people are addicted to a TV show or gaming or exercise or our cell phones, even if those things still negatively impact parts of our lives, there isn't the same level of negative connotation associated. For someone to truly have no addictions, considering all the reasons people have for developing them, that person would have to be pretty extraordinary.

Theo: Even pretty extraordinary people have addictions! (*smiling*)

What would you say your choice of addictions are?

Kim: You really want me to make a list?

Theo: I'll share mine if you share yours … (*smiling like a troublemaker*) No, you don't have to.

Kim: It's okay. I've said before that I'm not proud to be a workaholic. When I've got headaches, I take too much Tylenol. Sometimes I need to get dopamine hits from shopping online. I do love funky shoes. Bob says I'm addicted to buying books about the brain; they're always coming in the mail. I've been addicted to the TV show *Lie to Me* because it's so damn interesting, and I've also been accused of having an addiction to the character of Harvey on the TV show *Suits*. (*laughing at herself*)

And one more I can think of, I think I'm addicted to emotional intensity. I'm writing this book with you after all.

Theo: This is fascinating.

Kim: Why? Do you see a pattern in what I'm describing?

Theo: Don't know about that. But you also seem to have some addiction to healing. (*smiling*)

Kim: Sure. It's another way to get a dopamine hit.

Theo: When you have any downtime, you fill it up with new stimulation. I bet you don't sit in the hammock much. I guess you're a dopamine seeker, too.

Kim: You'd be right. What addictions do you have that we haven't already talked about?

Theo: Whew. I don't have a list ready. I think we only skimmed the surface of some of them. Alcohol is the easiest to talk about though.

Kim: Okay, so why do you think you chose that one?

Theo: I didn't take my first sip because I wanted to be addicted to it. But I liked it, a lot, because it made me more confident and I worried so much less about what others thought, especially girls. And alcohol was so readily available.

Kim: (*nodding in agreement*) Not counting caffeine, alcohol is the most widely used drug in the world; well ahead of tobacco.[lvii] For better or worse, just about every culture in the world has found a way to feel the effects from the fermentation of plants. According to the 2014 Global Drug Survey, alcohol is also the most common drug to send people to the emergency room, as well as the thing that friends and relatives of users worry the most about them consuming.

Theo: I believe that. I read recently that one-half of all the traffic fatalities are related to the abuse of alcohol. It's obviously terrible for our livers, our hearts, our immune systems, our mental health!

Kim: What was the worst part of it for you, personally?

Theo: By far, it's that it stopped me from getting the help I needed. I used it to cover up issues that were eating away at me.

Kim: Hmm. You've said your drinking didn't help your most personal relationships.

Theo: Not at all. That is an example of an understatement. But think about it. Just about every social function, business function, and most family gatherings have alcohol. Even the Church has found a way to work it into ceremonies. It's everywhere. If we stopped and were mindful about how much we are actually consuming and what it is doing to us, how much less would we drink?

Kim: No question, it totally permeates our culture. Just look at advertising during sporting events, wine lists at restaurants, toasts at special occasions. It's all expected. But as a researcher on this topic, part of the reason I have been turned off alcohol is from knowing what it does to the brain. And there's another reason. For me, there is also a history of alcoholism in *my* family, and that didn't do anything to endear me to it. What's wild is the level of enabling, or maybe you could call it denial, across our society. Denial was so huge in my family of origin, that we've only just begun to talk about it. My dad was seventy years old before he first verbalized that his dad had been an alcoholic.

Theo: Hmm.

Kim: And I know alcoholism isn't rare. A study from the US says that about 43 percent of all adults have at least one alcoholic in the family.[lviii] And another study recently found Canadians are drinking more than 50 percent above the global average.[lix]

Theo: And of course, some communities we work in have much higher percentages than that.

Kim: Just looking at statistics, the highest percentage I've seen is a remote community in British Columbia that has 85 percent of its kids being born with FASD—Fetal Alcohol Spectrum Disorder. And when that level of alcohol dependence happens in a community, a whole slew of social problems comes with it, which often take generations to resolve.

Theo: Yeah. That cycle is very hard to stop if everyone around you is doing it.

Kim: So true. But closer to home for me, we have a teenage daughter, and we all well know how alcohol affects the behaviour of teenagers whose brains are already going through a lot just from growing so fast. And, thinking of teenage boys who often take the most risks, who would want anyone near their kids when they're feeling more relaxed and confident *just* from being under the influence? Teenage boys can get the feeling of being relaxed and confident in other ways that are much more appealing to a mother: like doing well in school, being physically active, volunteering in their community …

Theo: You really are a mother. But you know, hearing this, which I know is all true, makes me feel guilty. Because as a young man, I was not very responsible.

Kim: I didn't mean to trigger you into guilt; I let one of my own personal judgments slip in there.

Theo: I can relate. I also have a fifteen-year-old daughter.

Kim: Are you an overprotective father?

Theo: Not at all. I only have three shotguns, two machetes, and one castration utensil hanging by the front door. Thankfully, I haven't used them, yet. In truth, Taytm's so responsible I'd trust anyone she loved.

Kim: I know that you know that I know that you're a softie underneath.

Theo: WTF? Not even close. I'm a crazy lunatic nut job who would use a castration utensil on an out-of-line dickhead without any hesitation. And I'm not afraid to go back to jail. (*slight chuckle*)

Kim: Even sober?

Theo: Especially sober. If some boy was acting as out of control as I was when I was younger and I could see they were hurting Tay, I might even do it premeditated.

Kim: I can see you're joking a bit, but there's also some seriousness to what you're saying.

Theo: This is one of the hard parts of coming back from a serious addiction. You know you've been an ass, and now you can't seem to tolerate those same behaviours in others. I feel like a hypocrite, but my protection instinct to people like my own kids is really strong. Most addicts are ashamed of themselves.

Kim: Of course. And I think it'll all be okay. Tay is an awesome kid and I think she could defend herself very well without you, if she ever needed to.

Theo: In many ways she's tougher than me. I really love her.

Kim: This reminds me that our kids learn from our negative patterns positively as well as negatively. I sure did. I watched my dad smoke and I decided, "I'm never going to smoke." Many times our kids overcompensate far in the opposite direction from the behaviours they see in us that they don't like.

Theo: Being a parent is a huge motivator for wanting to get clean. I know that families are just as affected by alcoholism as the addict is themselves.

Kim: It is important for families to have information about addiction as it can increase the possibility for repairing relationships. I'm remembering Al-Anon is available as a support group, but I think understanding the neurochemistry of addiction can also help. It decreases the shame all around it.

Theo: It certainly was the case for me. Especially when you talked to me about the connection between my alcoholism and my mom's addiction to Valium. Because my dad was such an alcoholic, I never even thought of my mom as an addict.

Kim: Yeah, we've talked about that a lot, because it seems to be an important link to understanding yourself as you were growing up. In our society, we don't always think of prescription drugs as addictive in the same way as when we talk about booze or street drugs. But there are many prescription drugs out there that are highly addictive and have serious consequences.

Theo: My mom still relies on Valium to this day.

Kim: When I think about your addiction history, I have a belief that it started for you when you were just a little speck in your mom's tummy. There are conflicting research studies about the effects of the use of Valium during pregnancy, but some suggest that it causes a syndrome similar to FASD, as well as ADD.[lx]

Theo: I hate labels. But I think I get your point.

Kim: To understand what might be going on for you, I looked up what Valium does, and what we know about how it affects the developing fetal brain. Without giving a chemistry lesson, this is what I found out that we know for sure: Valium is a prescription drug that increases the amount of the natural neurotransmitter GABA. GABA chills you out. Valium is prescribed to help reduce anxiety.

Theo: You talked about GABA when you were describing the brain chemistry of alcohol. You said that alcohol also increases GABA. My mom was prescribed Valium when she was a teenager for her anxiety. I guess Valium and alcohol are not that different in their outcomes.

Kim: They both have a sedating effect.

Theo: I never thought of my parents as having the same addictive needs; their behaviours were so different.

Kim: It is interesting, isn't it? When you start to understand what these drugs do, it gives you greater insight into a person's suffering.

Theo: Shit. You know, I just remembered a story. When I was playing in New York and they sent me to a treatment centre, one day that place had a family day. So I called up Veronica—who was still my wife at that point—and told her when you come here for this event, I want you to also bring my mom and dad. So she did. And they both came. My dad was right on, totally engaged in the process, and my mom practically had a nervous break-down. She was a mess. Complete denial. That was when I first connected with the idea that my mom might be an addict too.

Kim: That must have been hard for you to see.

Theo: I'd known something was wrong; but I'd never thought of my mom as the one with addictions, because my dad's were so obvious.

Kim: Back in the Sixties when your mom was pregnant with you, they had no idea that these kinds of substances or drugs could hurt a developing baby. That kind of science didn't exist back then.

Theo: Are you saying that my mom's addiction to Valium could have affected me even before I was born?

Kim: (*in a soothing voice*) Well, what we know now is that everything a mom experiences affects a baby's development. A baby is attached to its mom through the umbilical cord and placenta. So all the chemicals moving around in the mom's body are transferred directly to the baby.

Theo: So when mom is doing Valium, baby is doing Valium?

Kim: In a sense, yes. Everything a mom consumes transports across the placenta to the baby. Specifically when a mom takes a psychotropic drug (one that crosses the blood/brain barrier), the baby's brain says, "Wow, there's a lot more (or less) of a certain chemical in here than I normally need." Of course, an imbalance of too much or too little of any particular natural chemical will cause the brain to have to adapt. The problem is that fetal brains and bodies are not formed enough to handle these chemicals the way an adult can.

Theo: So how does the developing brain handle this stuff?

Kim: Well, when there is too much of a chemical in the spaces between brain cells (synaptic spaces), the brain does what it can to get rid of the excess. In the example of Valium, there would have been too much GABA—the chill-out chemical—floating around. In order to deal with what it doesn't need, the brain either produces less of its own GABA, or the brain cells grow new receptor sites in order to mop up what can't be used. These receptor sites are kinda like suction cups.

Theo: I remember seeing those receptor sites in the movie *What the Bleep Do We Know!?* They were described like keyholes, and the neurotransmitter chemicals fit into them like keys.

Kim: Exactly. This is how the brain cells absorb the surplus of any chemical like GABA when you take a drug. There are different types of receptor sites on neurons, and each one is very picky about what it will absorb. Only certain chemicals will fit into a specific lock. So when a mom takes a drug like Valium, there will be too much GABA inside the baby's brain; the developing neurons will likely accommodate to its presence by growing new receptor sites.

Theo: So what does this mean? When my mom was taking Valium, how would I have been feeling in her tummy?

Kim: You would have been one chilled-out, blissful fetus. When she had lots of GABA in her system, you would have felt practically sedated.

Theo: (*laughing*) Well, I don't ever remember feeling chilled out since then, except when I was drinking.

Kim: That makes perfect sense, because when a baby is born, its direct link to its mom through the umbilical cord and placenta are cut. The drug that mom was consuming no longer gets to baby's brain and so those recently grown receptor sites have to die off back to their genetically designed original state. That is what we call "withdrawal."

Theo: I know the feeling of withdrawal. You feel terrible. The worst I ever felt was in the Tucson rehab clinic, coming off a drug I'd been prescribed, Clonazepam.

Kim: Which is like Valium, only more intense.

Theo: I know! I know what it is! It sucked. Because it was a downer, the rebound effect was unbelievable. When it was gone, I felt shaky and more anxious than ever.

Kim: (*sympathetically*) Withdrawal happens to babies, too. Just like an adult, the baby's brain misses the presence of what it was experiencing. Not because it was good for the baby, but because it had become used to it being there.

Theo: I would have missed that GABA chilled-out feeling as a baby?

Kim: Likely, when you were born, and physically separated from your mom, your brain would have noticed the absence of the GABA immediately. This could have left you feeling agitated, hyper-alert, and irritable for a while until you accommodated back to your more natural state.

Theo: I don't think I know what you mean by "natural state." Most people would never describe me as calm or relaxed. Most would say I was like the energizer bunny, always doing crazy shit, except when I was playing hockey.

Kim: That makes sense to me. I was reading an article about Valium that described how GABA decreases the brain's natural dopamine levels.[lxi] So if you didn't have enough dopamine in your brain, you might want more. I've always thought of you as a dopamine-seeking junky. You love intensity, need cognitive stimulation, have all kinds of addictions, and love physical activity. These states and activities are all sources of dopamine. And you were addicted to cocaine, which is almost chemically identical to natural dopamine.

Theo: How does being an excitement-seeking dopamine junky relate to GABA, which mellows you out? That doesn't make sense.

Kim: (*smiling*) GABA and dopamine have a close relationship. What I've learned about GABA is that when it goes up, dopamine goes down.[lxii] GABA's job is to calm the brain down. (*gesturing with her hand from up high to down low*) And dopamine's job is to add more stimulation (*gesturing with her hand from down low to up high*), so that we have motivation and focus to do anything.

When there is consistently too much GABA in the developing brain from a drug like Valium, the developing dopamine system would have trouble working.

Theo: Let me get this straight, are you saying that my dopamine-seeking behaviours could be related to the Valium I was exposed to before I was born?

Kim: That is what I'm thinking. Although there isn't enough research to prove it yet, I believe that, even years later, brains remember the presence of all that prenatal chemistry that was in there (*pointing to Theo's head*) when you were tiny. I suggest that even now, your brain is likely highly sensitive to the tiniest changes in your GABA and dopamine levels. Even now that you're sober, your brain is probably still trying to balance out these chemicals.

Theo: Hmm. I'm sure it is. (*thinking*) Are you suggesting that I was predisposed to becoming an addict?

Kim: Based on these ideas, that is exactly what I am suggesting. But, please remember that your mom had no idea that Valium would be so addictive to her and potentially harmful to you. She likely had her own reasons for needing to calm herself down at the time.

Theo: Now I know I didn't have a chance. My road to all these addictions was set in motion when I was a fetus. Even if your theory is only a possibility, it makes me feel way better about myself, because it helps me believe that my addictive patterns weren't all my fault.

Kim: It makes sense to me because whenever our brains have trouble managing dopamine levels, we are instinctively driven to try and find a way to balance it. You might end up seeking dopamine in all kinds of different ways to try to raise it if it's too low.

Theo: I guess dopamine is my favourite chemical!

Kim: Well, we all love it really. Remember, dopamine is naturally produced by your brain whenever you are doing something that feels good.

Theo: Is that why dopamine is the chemical of addiction, because it is connected to pleasure?

Kim: You've got it. It is the chemical that makes you want to do something over and over. That is just the way an addiction feels. You get a rush of dopamine in response to pleasurable activities like food or sex.

Theo: Or hockey. (*smiling*)

Kim: For sure. I think when you were playing, you were getting massive doses of dopamine.

Theo: Well, it sure felt good. There's no drug better than the feeling of winning an Olympic gold medal for your country with your teammates, and then seeing your dad in the stands cheering for you. Over the moon happy. That's the best feeling on the planet, as far as I know.

Kim: When I think of you being happy playing hockey, I think of you sliding on your knees with your arms in the air after scoring some big goal for the Flames. Kind of epitomizes pure joy in sport.

Theo: That was a hell of a lot of fun. I think you're talking about the overtime goal in Game 6 against the Oilers in the 1991 playoffs. That Flames team was so awesome! (*smiling*) But if that top of the world experience was all about my dopamine levels being off the charts high, what would I feel like when my dopamine levels are really low?

Kim: Without enough dopamine, you could feel sluggish, depressed, distractible, unfocused, or even uninterested in life.

Theo: I didn't like to stay in those places for long, or at all. I still don't like those feelings. But I remember one time when I was super chemically messed up. Don't know if it was up or down, but it was way out of whack. It was the first year I was with the Rangers and I was really just hanging on. I'd been to LA and then Tucson to start the process of therapy the NHL made us do; I had started peeling off the layers of the onion. I was doing all this therapy. But because I wasn't coping well when I got out of therapy, I went back to my old habits of being a chemist between the ups and downs. And my personal life at that time was just a shit-show. One night, I went to line up in the face-off circle, and I just fucking fell over onto the ice from the anxiety.

Kim: That's unbelievable.

Theo: Maybe it was exhaustion, too. I have no idea. It was from the anxiety, exhaustion, all of it. It was just a fucking mess. I also didn't know if I might have had a concussion. Who would be able to know? I just didn't know. 'Cause there were so many things going on in my life; but it was more anxiety than exhaustion. I couldn't sleep. That was the worst. New York was probably the worst when I couldn't sleep. So after the face-off circle debacle, that's when they put me on the Clonazepam.

Kim: Ah. So they were focused on trying to decrease your anxiety.

Theo: It was only half a milligram. But they gave me the whole bottle! So the way an addict reads a pill bottle is when they say take one every four hours, we take four every one hour. That's the way an addict reads a pill label. So, I was taking a lot of it. And I'd mix it with cocaine, right?

Kim: Are you kidding me?

Theo: To level off. 'Cause upper, downer, upper, downer … 'Cause the alcohol certainly wasn't working enough on its own.

Kim: (*exhaling*) I'm watching your body get tense and hearing your speech get faster.

Theo: No shit, that was a horrible time. (*sinking in his chair*) I definitely felt depressed and separate from my body. I had to go off the ice. I couldn't play that night. I was so wound up from my attempts to keep regulated from my staples—booze and cocaine—I don't think my system knew which way was up, and I definitely wasn't keeping track. The Clonazepam drug the doctors gave me didn't help at all, though. Made everything worse, even more up and down. (*beginning to re-traumatize himself*) Couldn't even stand on my feet in the face-off circle. (*slumping and holding his knees*)

Kim: I can see this is hard for you to talk about. I'm seeing you go into a ball.

Theo: That's what I'm most ashamed about: the moments when I wasn't helping my team.

Kim: You had a pretty huge addiction. You obviously needed a lot of help. The timeline is confusing, which tells me there's a lot of trauma attached to these memories. This is a very difficult topic and we don't have to unpeel every layer in one go.

Theo: Yeah. (*exhaling*) You know, I was thinking it'd be a good idea to get my medical records from back then to understand what exactly I'd been prescribed. I couldn't get them the last time I tried, but I think some laws have changed since then about access to medical information. It might be helpful for my own self-awareness if I could see more about what might have been going on from a chemical perspective.

Kim: It would be great to have a look at those, and with a physician you trust who could help you interpret it all.

Theo: Hmm. I know a lot of dangerous chemicals got added to my brain as an adult. But I'm guessing my brain was already chemically messed up from the start … I'm wondering how those two are connected.

Kim: Please remember when we talk this way about brain chemicals and babies, I don't want you to think you were doomed by your early experiences. Our brains can change as long as we are still breathing. We can always remodel our brains by changing how we think, feel, and act. We are incredibly adaptable.

Theo: Well, thank God! So this is what you mean when you keep saying we can rewire our brain.

Kim: The same neuroplasticity that happened in the fetus's brain, the way we can change how our neurons work, can keep on happening in our brains throughout our lifetimes. We are able to transform ourselves throughout our lives.

Theo: You don't just mean transform our personalities; you mean we can transform our actual brain matter?

Kim: That is exactly what I mean.

Theo: I remember when we met with Dr. Nicole Letourneau in Calgary and she talked about a mom's stress affecting a baby's developing brain. Although enlightening, that was a downer conversation. I need to be reminded that my brain can change.

Kim: I remember what she talked about. "Whatever moms experience, babies experience." If your mom was stressed out when she was pregnant, her body would have produced a lot of that stress chemical, cortisol. For you as a fetus, if there was a lot of cortisol hanging around you, it would have been like having a bath in toxic waste.

Theo: I know that I don't want too much cortisol in my brain because it's a stress chemical.

Kim: It's actually a killer of brain cells. Additionally, both of the stress hormones—cortisol and adrenaline—have significant effects on our heart and on our immune system. When those stress hormones are chronically high, you deplete the immune system of its ability to protect you from illness. This is why chronic stress can make you sick.

Theo: That was hard to hear. There is no doubt that my mom was stressed all the time.

Kim: This is relatively new science and, without scaring you, it is important this information gets shared. Stress is not good for anybody. When a mom is chronically stressed throughout her pregnancy, the chemicals in her body will ignite or "turn on" some of the developing baby's brain stress response genes. The mom's stress environment says to the baby "prepare for stress!"

Theo: You mean, I was a stressed out-fetus, too?

Kim: I think you alternated between being stressed out and sedated, just like you described your mom to be.

Theo: That was a pattern that stayed consistent throughout my addictions.

Kim: You wouldn't have been the only stressed-out fetus in the world. Carrying a baby for nine months is often not the most relaxing time for anyone.

Theo: I remember when my own kids were in the oven ... there's always a lot of change going on in relationships when that happens, right?

Kim: Sure, and when you were made, you were the oldest of your brothers, so your mom wouldn't have ever been through pregnancy before.

Theo: I can only imagine what her life was like back then.

Kim: Sometimes, taking certain medications are necessary and without them, a mom's well-being is compromised. She was following her doctor's orders. But if you were exposed to that, and then chronically exposed to stress as a fetus and later as a child, with developmental trauma issues, there's no doubt you would have been primed for anxiety and less resilient to future stressors as an adult. We now know that early exposure to stress influences how well or how poorly someone responds to stress for the rest of their life, unless they become actively engaged in managing their stress over time.

Theo: I can say with certainty that I haven't always managed stress well. (*making a funny face*)

Kim: This is what you are really engaged in working on now, though. And the way you manage your stress today is already light years ahead of how you might have responded to stressors even a couple of years ago. A testimony to the fact that early exposure to stress does not mean you are doomed.

Theo: Good to know. Stress has definitely contributed to my addictions.

Kim: Remember, addictions are about covering up emotional pain and stress. And people who start out their lives with early exposure to stress will have less tolerance to it later in life. So they get stressed more easily than others.

Theo: Like a rattlesnake? They're really sensitive in some ways too.

Did you know their tongues are so sensitive they have their own sense of smell and that's one of the ways that they navigate?[lxiii] (*smiling*)

Kim: I didn't know that rattlesnakes were such sensitive creatures.

Theo: But I'm still trying to understand what I would have started out with. Would my dad have contributed to my brain development when I was a developing fetus?

Kim: You've said in some detail how your dad was an alcoholic and abusive back then—he likely had his own patterns of history and trauma that contributed to his behaviour. He also probably didn't know, because no one knew it back then, that it's not just women who contribute to their kids' brains. Dads do play a part, with the DNA they provide with their sperm. Alcoholism is partly genetic, and we know it takes two people to make a baby.

Theo: I can just see his sperm swimming backwards, upside down, going round and round in circles … Jeezus, a wobbly egg and a drunken sperm, can you picture it? (*smiling*)

You know, what you just said, most people don't know that men also have to be responsible about this stuff.

Kim: The challenge is that the time in a fetus's life when the brain is growing the fastest, and so is most vulnerable to things like alcohol (which is worse for a baby's brain than even cocaine), is the first three weeks of pregnancy.

Theo: This is the time when most people don't even know they're pregnant yet!

Kim: This is the point! New studies are all over it, but they suggest that if a couple are thinking of making a baby, it is *highly* recommended that neither the mom *nor the dad* have a drop of alcohol even before they start actively trying, and then absolutely zero for the mom during pregnancy.

Theo: Hmm, that would require quite a bit of mindfulness and maturity, even if we would have known about it. (*thinking about it*) But dads aren't connected directly to their babies when they are developing in the mom's tummy, so how does an alcoholic dad's sperm affect a baby? This of course would be something I would think about.

Kim: There is cutting edge research that talks about how alcoholic dads affect their babies. At least, in alcoholic mice. The sperm from the alcoholic male mice were altered in their DNA, and were shown to affect the development of the pup mice.[lxiv] More research is emerging on this topic all the time.

Theo: Holy shit. I think my kids are okay. They're smart, athletic, and all.

Kim: It's kinda like rolling the dice at the casino. Some kids will be okay and some maybe not as much. Genes alone don't determine anyone's fate. And there is so much science today that no one could have known; we simply can't judge ourselves for all the choices we've made. And remember, we talk again and again about how judging isn't helpful to ourselves anyways.

Theo: Right. Good reminder. Getting back to my dad, I can imagine his sperm DNA had "alcoholic" written all over it; but I also know he contributed to my mom's stress, even when I was *in utero*.

Kim: Do you remember when Dr. Nicole talked with us about the long-term effects of maternal depression on attachment? She shared her new findings about dads and their impact on the well-being of moms too.

Theo: I was trying so hard to process everything she was saying, but I kept checking out. Talking about maternal depression must be a sensitive topic for me. Can you remind me how her story went?

Kim: She reinforced everything we've been talking about regarding how depressed moms contribute to their kids' insecure attachment. What was exciting for me is that she shared a finding describing how when dads support their stressed-out pregnant partners, these moms had consistently lower levels of cortisol stress chemicals inside their bodies. The less cortisol floating around in the mom, the less cortisol damaging the fetus's developing brain.

Theo: I remember Bob sharing with me his philosophy, that the best way for a dad to support his kid is to love the mom. That, I remember. But what you're saying is that Nicole's science is backing that up, even before the kids are born. (*thinking it through*) So when dads emotionally support pregnant moms, they are supporting their baby's future mental health.

Kim: That is the message. I agree that the best way to support a child, by far, is for both of the parents to love one another. I think that the gift of modelling what a full healthy relationship is like, after the child is born, is what Bob was thinking about.

Theo: Sometimes in dysfunction, a parent will focus entirely on the child and not at all on the other spouse. That dynamic alone causes stress in the home.

Kim: And it could increase unhealthy attachment patterns in the kid, not to mention what it could do to the relationship between the parents.

Theo: All this is a lot to think about ... and what my own role's been as a father and a husband. Heavy shit.

Kim: Well, it's true that each one of us has our own path and everyone's got their own stuff to work on, including our kids and spouses.

Good news is that no one expects perfection. And better news is there's always the possibility for repair.

Theo: Yeah. (*changing topic*) Getting back to alcohol, I still don't understand everything about that. What about drinking during pregnancy? My mom didn't drink when she was pregnant with me, but I'm curious, what does this behaviour do to the fetus's developing brain? People ask me this all the time and I'm not sure I really understand it.

Kim: It's another form of prenatal exposure, probably the most common kind. When a pregnant mom drinks, alcohol sits in the fat and water of the developing baby's brain and it just takes up space. The brain develops around the alcohol and leaves the brain with holes in it. There is a term commonly used to describe an FASD brain, called "Swiss cheese brain."

Theo: The brain grows with holes around the drops of alcohol?

Kim: Not that literally, but that's the concept. The brain doesn't have a way of getting rid of the alcohol the same way it can absorb drugs that are mimicking the brain's natural neurochemicals. That's why prenatal exposure to alcohol is so much worse than exposure to anything else. Alcohol is completely foreign to the brain, so it just sits there, essentially.

Theo: Are people who are exposed to alcohol as a fetus really handicapped?

Kim: How bad the alcohol affects the developing brain depends on a lot of things. The amount of alcohol a mom drinks, how often mom drinks, how early in the pregnancy she drinks, and for how many years she has been drinking; all of that matters.

Theo: How common is it?

Kim: I think it's under-identified. My FASD expert friend Penn Thrasher in Port Alberni, British Columbia told me that approximately 10 percent of the children in Canada have been formally diagnosed with FASD. This is the label that we give to kids who are known to have been prenatally exposed to alcohol. For this official diagnosis to be given, the mom has to disclose that she was drinking during pregnancy. FASD is a spectrum, so some people are affected just a little bit and some people are affected quite a lot. There are also many prenatal-alcohol-affected people out there who are not diagnosed.

Theo: What does it look like when you have the diagnosis of FASD?

Kim: It can affect your memory, your ability to learn, your motor coordination, physical health, behaviour, and mental health. Many adults with FASD also have mental illness. Some kids have different physical features because of it, like an undeveloped groove between the nose and upper lip, a thin upper lip, wide-set eyes, and a smaller head circumference. The most significant finding, though, is that prenatal exposure to alcohol has been shown to increase the prevalence of alcohol abuse later in the baby's own life.

Theo: Holy shit.

Kim: Well, there's more. When world-leading FASD speaker Diane Malbin presented back in 2007 at the International Conference on FASD in Victoria, British Columbia, she shared a few of her experience-based opinions. She said she believed that 100 percent of birth moms to kids with diagnosed FASD have at least some personal history of trauma, and were self-medicating with alcohol while they were pregnant. And, of those, about 50 percent of them were first affected with FASD themselves. It seems it is a cycle that is passed on from one generation to another.[lxv]

Theo: I remember when we had our first speaking engagement together in Nanaimo, in November 2013. The day before that, I got to play with the senior FASD hockey team. I was stunned at how capable they were. You always told me that FASD kids can have difficulty with motor coordination, but many of these guys were so capable. It was like playing hockey in a regular game; they understood all the plays, had all the hockey jargon, and were so motivated to play. It was a real eye opener for me.

Kim: We are just beginning to understand how changeable the brain is. Those guys are proving that even individuals with developmental disabilities like FASD are doing it, and they can keep changing it as long as they live.

Theo: That possibility for improvement gives us hope. I often wondered about women who drink during pregnancy and the guilt they must feel. This information about the brains being able to change for the better would give them some comfort.

Kim: I hope so.

Theo: (*thinking deeply*) What I really get out of this conversation is that, once again, "It's not my fault." There was so much going on in my life even before I was born that influenced my behaviour and contributed to my addiction history. I am not thinking of this as an excuse, but as a way to feel less ashamed of myself for all my destructive behaviour.

Kim: Remember the difference between guilt and shame. Guilt can be helpful as a motivator for change, but shame for the way you are as a person can prevent you from feeling like you will ever be anything better. You don't have to go there. It's key to take responsibility, but offer yourself some compassion too.

Theo: I am trying to understand how my kids' brains might be affected by my drinking.

Kim: Some kids will be more affected than others by exposure to alcohol. Science is only beginning to understand which kids are more likely to be affected by prenatal exposure than others. A lot has to do with how each child's specific blueprint of genes interacts with the alcohol. This understanding of how genes interact with the environment is a science called "epigenetics."

Theo: I always thought you were stuck with the genes you have. I'm a Métis Canadian, and our family history links directly back to Gabriel Dumont, Louis Riel's right-hand man.

Kim: He was a brilliant rebel of a political figure, wasn't he?

Theo: I think I inherited his shit-disturber genes.

Kim: In truth, genes are only the templates of information that are passed down from one generation to the next. What diseases we might get, what talents we could have, how smart we are likely to be; these are all examples of qualities that we often assume we are just born with. But, from the moment of conception, from the exact instant that your dad's sperm and your mom's egg got together, this minuscule "you" was being affected by every single thing in the environment around it.

Theo: When you say "babies are affected by everything in their environment," I think about air, trees, water, soil, global warming. That isn't what you're talking about though, right? (*smiling*)

Kim: The "environment" we are talking about here is anything at all that influences the reaction of a piece of DNA. Consumption of alcohol would be an example of a person's biological "environment." Air, food, water, and toxins are parts of the environment for sure, but there are genes in your DNA that say how you'll respond to the presence of alcohol in your body.

Theo: Really? Why would our body need genes to respond to alcohol?

Kim: Everything your body might experience needs a gene in order to know how to respond to it. So both men and women who drink will potentially alter the genes that respond to alcohol and pass those genes on to their kids. This research is just emerging and it still generates debate in the field.

Theo: Abstinence from drinking seems to be the only way. The elders who are survivors of the residential schools talk about lasting effects of trauma over seven generations. Why is alcoholism connected with trauma psychologically?

Kim: As you know, people who've experienced trauma often self-medicate with alcohol because it chemically reduces the feelings of stress and anxiety, temporarily covering up their pain. The transgenerational trauma you are describing in our Canadian First Nations peoples happens when emotional and behavioural patterns of trauma are passed down from one generation to another, even if the initial traumatic stressors are no longer directly happening.

Theo: Right.

Kim: Trauma is carried across generations in many groups of individuals such as Post-Holocaust survivors and many of the world's cultures that have experienced genocide or persecution. Adverse childhood experiences are passed on from one generation to the next through their stories, attitudes, and attachment patterns. Remember, the gleaming and beaming of one generation will always affect the gleaming and beaming of the next.

Theo: So my drinking was not only connected to my abuse, but the quality of my upbringing, my prenatal exposure, and my genetics. I guess that was in backwards order. Did I get them all?

Kim: I think all of those say something about how you learned to cope with and soothe your own stress.

Theo: I always think about how I was instantly addicted when I took that first sip. It was around the time I was being abused by Graham James. So much stress at that time.

Kim: At some level, it's likely you remembered what it felt like to have GABA in your system. Your brain had probably been missing its presence since birth. That first hit of alcohol likely turned on the memory of the feeling of GABA and you were "home." Calm, safe, and comfortable. An experience you were not having much of in your life at the time.

Theo: I guess that is likely true for many alcoholics. You know, I loved the Alcoholics Anonymous process; it was tremendously important for me. But the AA process didn't get at the root of my trauma. Until you get at the source of your pain, you are still gonna have to find various coping mechanisms to make the anxiety go away.

Kim: That's right, you would have still felt that you needed soothing somehow. Taking the alcohol away is only part of the story for any alcoholic.

Theo: It comes back to the idea that we can all rewire our brains through healing conversations. A caring, secure relationship can help any anxious brain from needing to seek substitute mechanisms that end up making our lives crazy.

Kim: I think making your relationships as healthy as they can be is important for healing ...

Theo: I loved how I felt when I started drinking. It was like a magical veil came over my brain and stopped the pain. But the wonder of alcohol didn't last 'cause it would make me tired. So after a while I started to need to add cocaine to help keep me awake, so I could go on drinking.

Kim: That makes sense to me. Alcohol produces GABA in your brain, which sedates you and cocaine produces dopamine in your brain, which stimulates you. When you started combining cocaine with the alcohol, the stimulating effect of the cocaine would have helped keep you awake.

Theo: I love understanding what I was doing. And I told you I was like a chemist! It was a delicate balance between the two. Doing lines of cocaine definitely allowed me to drink more and for longer. I'm an alcoholic first, and in hindsight I know I used cocaine to support my alcoholism.

Kim: Over time, chronic alcoholism damages the brain's dopamine system.[lxvi] This means you would have had less effect from your own internal pharmacy of dopamine, so you would have needed more of the artificial chemistry in order to feel the same outcome. Using cocaine would have supplemented your craving for that dopamine.

Theo: I was already a dopamine seeker, needing more of it. Are you telling me that drinking all of the time would eventually make me need even more?

Kim: (*nodding*) Although the way you describe it sounds like an over-simplified explanation, it is fairly accurate. Chronic drinking can potentially lead to more dopamine-seeking behaviours, which would only increase your addictive patterns.

Theo: This is now making sense! No wonder I had such a combination of addictions. I was trying somehow to regulate my dopamine.

Kim: Neurobiologically, that is an explanation.

Theo: You know I'm not using this as an excuse, right? Just self-understanding.

Kim: I get that. And remember that cocaine is probably the most addictive drug out there, given that it is almost like pure dopamine. Because it ties directly into that reward centre in the brain, it results in an intense compulsion to keep using it. Cocaine gives you a short-lived "hit" of being high, but many people crash afterwards.

Theo: Not me, I wouldn't feel a crash. The cocaine would level me off the alcohol, so I wouldn't be as drunk.

Kim: That also makes sense. I think because your brain was already deficient in dopamine, it would take quite a lot of cocaine for you to have an excess of that in your brain. It seems like the cocaine evened you out. Not that I am suggesting, by any means, that you keep seeking cocaine to make that happen.

Theo: Fascinating how this all fits together. And don't worry, I have no desire to get back into that rodeo.

Kim: I wasn't really worried. But it's worth knowing that addictions, especially addictions to cocaine, have been linked to early infant developmental trauma and specifically attachment issues. Studies on rats who were deprived of snuggles from their moms have very low levels of dopamine in their brains. These rats became extremely easily addicted to cocaine when it was fed to them.[lxvii]

Theo: A lack of gleaming and beaming also lowers dopamine? Shit! It's a wonder I have any dopamine in me at all.

Kim: Many addicts report a history of challenging childhoods as a part of their experience. Please remember that this is not about blaming and shaming, but a possible explanation for how things might have unfolded. None of these things are cause and effect; there are too many variables for it to be that black and white.

Theo: This is helping me, though.

Kim: You are an ongoing success story for sure. Every time you dopamine hit yourself with an aha or a positive thought or a healthy relationship, you are counteracting your addiction chemistry. When you find healthy ways to feed your dopamine seeking, you are healing yourself from the inside out.

Theo: Drinking made me forget; cocaine made me feel like superman; but crystal meth is something that made me more scared than anything else in my whole life.

Kim: Say more about that one!

Theo: First off, none of my addictions really helped me. And we didn't mention hash. I took lots of that, which just made me comatose. I don't recommend any substance. But, crystal meth was the worst thing I ever put into my body. I only took it once, by accident, thinking it was cocaine, but I thought I was gonna die. It was the only time I dialled 911 on myself. My heart was racing and my head was pounding like I was going to explode. And it messed up my brain in a way that lasted for a long, long time. Maybe part of it is still there.

Kim: What do you mean? What kind of residual effects are there for you?

Theo: I don't know for sure, but ever since that time, something changed for the worse. It upped the anxiety factor for years. And now, sometimes when it's a bright day, I can't stand the brightness and have to close the curtains before I can join a conversation. I was never like that before. And some of the guys I met in the rehab centres who'd spent years on it … it was just fucking scary what it does to you. Stay away from crystal meth; it's bad shit.

Kim: You're right. From a brain perspective, it's absolute poison. To boost its potency, people put in battery acid, drain cleaner, lantern fuel, and antifreeze.

Theo: Who in their right mind would choose to put that in their bodies?

Kim: The very thought of having Drano in my body terrifies me.

Theo: Heroin is another drug that I have seen really mess people up.

Kim: Heroin and Morphine, painkillers, are very much like our natural brain chemical painkillers that we call endorphins. All of these are known as opiates.

Theo: I've never tried heroin.

Kim: Good, 'cause it's a tough addiction to kick and has wrecked the lives of many. Opiates help make pain bearable. They don't treat pain, they just change our perception of it. We produce natural opiates (endorphins) in order to tolerate both physical and emotional pain.

Theo: I haven't had much experience with painkillers. I could tolerate a great deal of physical pain, so I wasn't exposed to them.

Kim: Physical pain and emotional pain are processed exactly the same way in the brain. The brain does not know the difference between physical and emotional pain.

Theo: I have a very high pain threshold. I would rather have physical pain than emotional pain, any day. But many hockey players got hooked on painkillers.

Kim: The other thing to know about our natural painkillers is they are also part of the gleaming and beaming chemistry. You get a big endorphin hit when you get a hug. Hugs actually make the pain feel better!

Theo: I guess I never need to try heroin. I can just go around hugging people. (*smiling*)

Kim: Works for Bob's mom actually. She volunteered through her church to give free hugs at a Gay Pride Parade and said it was one of the happiest days in her life! Her highlight was witnessing her British church friend—who wasn't used to hugging at all—do the same. She said her friend was glowing for a couple weeks afterwards from the natural high of all the hugs, and it had nothing at all to do with the parade itself!

Theo: There's no way on earth that hugs would have helped me when I'd just lost my teeth and the roots were exposed.

Kim: How do you know? Did no one hug you? (*laughing*)

Theo: I was in too much fucking pain, I wouldn't have let them near me.

Kim: Next time, give it a try. (*still laughing*)

Theo: Fuck off.

Kim: Are you getting sick of my theories yet? 'Cause I have one more.

Theo: I am going to need a yawn to stay awake. Or maybe I'll just rub my face. (*thinking*) No, I think I'll yawn. (*big yawn*) Fuck, that felt amazing. Now, what were you saying?

Kim: (*ignoring him*) Nurturing relationships, like opiates, soothe pain. Oxytocin, the chemistry of love, interacts with the opiates the most. Oxytocin increases the brain's sensitivity to endorphins. So the more love you have, the better you are able to deal with emotional pain. It is a good thing to be addicted to "healthy relationships."

Theo: I certainly think this is working for my dad. You know what he's up to today?

Kim: No. Your parents still live in Russell, Manitoba, right?

Theo: They sure do! My dad's leading the AA chapter there, and he goes to the local bullshit table three times a day. People in small towns like to say they're going for the coffee, but you and I know they are going for the relationships. It's the same in all the small towns across our great country. There's always a table in every town where the local wise people go to solve the world's problems. And they are really skilled in shooting the shit! Practise, practise, practise! (*laughing*) I'm so proud of my dad. I think of him as the king of that bullshit table in Russell.

Kim: Bob tells me about those tables. He's worked across the prairies developing wind farms and, as you know, he has a huge respect for the interconnected support networks those little towns naturally provide. He says those bullshit tables are the heart and soul of the community, and are to be treated with absolute reverence. So kudos to your dad!

Theo: But any insider, and my mom, will know it's also the best place for gossip. (*smiling*) And in the evenings (or mornings or afternoons) depending on the town, it can also become where people imbibe a bit in the drink.

Kim: And therein lies the conundrum about drinking with close friends. As human beings, we really want and need to connect with other people, and it's socially accepted that alcohol is part of that picture, but that element just isn't comfortable for everyone.

Theo: Most people can just pay attention to moderation, but that doesn't work for alcoholics. I'm getting really good at ordering virgin Caesars and virgin Mojitos. At least, I like the taste.

Kim: It's good you have those two to go to, 'cause it'd be tough to never have anything to drink when you're at all those functions with people around you who are drinking.

Theo: Yeah. But my memories of what one drink will do to me keeps me firmly away. It's not far from my mind.

Kim: When I heard Dr. Gabor Maté say that people who have difficulty forming intimate relationships are at risk for addiction, it strengthened my conviction that healthy relationships are a powerful healing force for change. Even the bullshit table can be a healing place!

Theo: Of course it is. 'Cause laughter is healing!

Kim: It's funny you say that, 'cause Bob always said he never needed an alarm clock when he slept at the Auberge St. Leon Motor Inn, in St. Leon, the Wind Capital of Manitoba. At 8:00 a.m. sharp he'd hear full-on belly laughs from their bullshit table every single morning except Sunday; and we'd go join them, of course! (*smiling*)

Hey, I've got a question for you: If oxytocin, the chemistry of love and relationships, is the antidote to stress, and addictions are linked to low levels of oxytocin, then—

Theo: (*cutting her off excitedly*) Then all we need is love. I know it's not that simple. But that's a big part of the message.

Kim: "Love" isn't just a word; it's something we have to believe and feel. (*suddenly curious*) Theo, how does an addict know when he's an addict?

Theo: I'll never forget this eighty-something-year-old lady I met at an AA meeting in Tucson. She got up and introduced herself as an alcoholic and shared that she'd had one glass of wine a day for forty years. After the meeting, I went up to her and asked her politely, "If you only drink one glass a day then, why are you here?" And she said, "Because for those other twenty-three hours of every day for forty years, that one drink was all I was thinking about."

Kim: Addiction is a compulsion of the mind. It's all about your thoughts. Do you think you'll always be an addict?

Theo: Yes. I am addicted to many more things than just booze. Gambling, sex, and food are also on my list. Do you remember when we were all on Bowen Island? What was I doing on my computer when no one was looking, because there were a few moments when I couldn't stand the lack of stimulation and the quiet?

Kim: You were gambling.

Theo: Yep. I like the mental stimulation of it. And it's not just the risk involved in gambling I enjoy; I also like going to the casino to see my buddies. But I get my biggest hit just thinking about the possibility of winning.

Kim: I know that a gambling addiction can be devastating; people have lost everything they have to this addiction. Do you have to love money for an addiction to gambling to happen?

Theo: No! You just have to like winning and I certainly love that.

Kim: How else do you get that winning feeling these days?

Theo: I love golf. I just got my second hole-in-one! I'm hitting the ball better than ever before. I think golf allows me to escape the intensity of people—like the ice rink. A place and activity where it all comes naturally and success flows.

Kim: Nice. So you play golf to relax, use gambling to ramp up. Is it all still a matter of balancing natural GABA with natural dopamine?

Theo: I guess it is. But golf can also be huge for dopamine. When I enter tournaments, I absolutely play to win!

Kim: Ever since Charlie Sheen announced to the world that he's addicted to winning, something about the word "winning" puts me off a bit. You?

Theo: Hmm. I bet you I could beat him at golf.

Kim: (*laughing*) Okay. Food. Tell me what your relationship's like with food.

Theo: It was always a love/hate relationship. I didn't take care of myself at all. The pain from my Crohn's disease has meant that when I ate whatever I wanted to, I'd pay for it after. This has been a literal pain in the ass since about 1994. I wonder whether, if I didn't have Crohn's, if I would've got to over 250 pounds. I love good food, always have.

Kim: But you're in good shape now. To look at you, I wouldn't think you have greasy French fries and ice cream for breakfast.

Theo: However good that sounds, no, I don't. Not often anyway. It all changed for me last spring when we did the Victor Walk. Ten days of straight walking. To have energy for that, I took some good advice and started juicing. Since then, I've been trying to learn everything I can about nutrition and mindful eating. As much as I can, I'm working with Sherry Strong, a food philosopher in British Columbia, on her *Return to Food* program.[lxviii]

Kim: I'm very grateful for you introducing me to her as well. Her premise—that it's best for us to eat foods that are the simplest to gain from nature around us—makes sense. And it does give us more energy, doesn't it?

Theo: For sure! It's harder to follow when I'm travelling, but starting the day with lemon water and having more natural smoothies is at least a great start.

Kim: What strikes me as the biggest aha about food is that the whole relationship thing with it is really a mind/body integration.

Theo: You have to care about yourself to eat really well …

Kim: So true. Okay, there's a big elephant in the room left when we talk about addictions. It's the one with perhaps the most shame attached to it.

Theo: Sex is not so easy to talk about.

Kim: It is a powerful source of dopamine, and other good chemicals. But it can be a source of escape, rather than a source of connection.

Theo: There's a flood of thoughts coming into my mind, and I'm starting to check out.

Kim: Let's leave that for another conversation. I think this is a lot of addiction already.

Theo: A person can only let go of so many addictions at one time. We didn't talk about smoking either …

Kim: Yes. There's a lot to be said about that, too, and I think it's important to celebrate each small step of success along the way. That's why AA has you count the number of days of sobriety. You've come amazingly far from the out-of-control Theo back in New York, Chicago, and Santa Fe.

Theo: Yep. And I'm having more fun now. Not the over-the-top-party-in-a-limo-with-ten-prostitutes fun, but genuine good feelings, at least once in a while. When I did that party stuff, I was good at it, but I was sad, sad, sad underneath. Now, when I get invited to Mario Lemieux's box at a Penguins' game before his Fantasy Camp to raise funds for his charity, and I look over and see Mark Recchi, Rick Tocchet, and Gary Roberts and we're shooting the shit about our playing days, I am stone sober, but fucking happier than a pig in shit. And playing music and golfing with my sons and establishing stronger relationships: all this is healing and it's addictive!

Kim: From all this talking about addiction, what do you take from it?

Theo: Thinking over my lifetime, (*pausing to think*) I think I was actually addicted to hockey.

Kim: I think you were too.

Theo: Until I was addicted to other things more.

Kim: And now you've become addicted to healing.

Theo: Right. Okay, I got it! (*smiling*) Maybe I'm thinking of food because I'm hungry, but if my addictions were like a hamburger, my two buns would be hockey and healing, and my patty would be all the drugs and booze and damaging stuff in between.

Kim: (*smiling*) How do you come up with this shit? But, you know what that says, right?

Theo: What? That I got great buns? (*laughing at his own joke*)

Kim: That we can have power over our addictions. We can choose to replace them with healthier ones.

Theo: (*thinking of hockey and healing*) And, that I got great buns. (*still laughing*)

Kim: Oy vey. (*rolling her eyes*)

7

God of My Understanding

"We are not human beings having a spiritual experience. We are
spiritual beings having a human experience."
Pierre Teilhard de Chardin

Theo: Addiction is a spiritual disease, one in which a person loses all
faith in humanity. To me, true spirituality is all about relationship. Most addicts are traumatized in their family of origin situations, so what they really lose faith in is relationship. That's a
setup for addiction. The trauma causes emotional pain for which
the best answer is spirituality.

Kim: Which, as you say, is the deepest form of relationship ...

Theo: This is what I'm beginning to really believe.

Kim: You've been saying this healing stuff is addictive, and I fully agree
it is. But like any addiction, it starts with a first time. Do you
remember when you first decidedly got hooked on the feeling
of healing?

Theo: September 18, 2005 was my awakening.

Kim: That's when you asked God to take away your desire to drink and use drugs?

Theo: That was the day.

Kim: Why specifically then?

Theo: It had to do with my relationship with my second wife, Jenn, before we got married. We were just going around in circles with dysfunction. I knew if I didn't do something radical, I would lose her, and if that happened, I believed I'd lose everything.

Kim: You describe your surrender to a higher power as the turning point.

Theo: Yeah, it was definitely my spiritual connection to the "God of My Understanding" that helped me have the strength to overcome my desire for drugs and alcohol.

Kim: (*looking up something on her iPhone*) Hold on a second. Here it is. "Spirituality" is defined in Wikipedia as an "attempt to seek meaning, purpose, and a direction of life in relation to a higher power, universal spirit, or God."

Theo: Spirituality is like a warm blanket. And it's the spirituality part that's returned me to sanity. Remember, the definition of insanity is doing the same thing over and over and expecting a different result.

Kim: Right. What I think spirituality reflects is a search for the sacred in all aspects of life. Spirituality plays an integral role in the healing process of the mind, the brain, and the body. The "God of our understanding," if and however we choose it to be defined, can be an instrumental force of support that softens our burden and strengthens our will. Our individual definition of spirituality can be as unique as our DNA.

Theo: Amen!

Kim: So when you think of the God of Your Understanding, how would you define that?

Theo: I think spirituality is the piece that is most often missing when we are trying to heal from addiction and trauma. Once we find our connection with a higher power, though, we seem to be able to "nail it" and find an inner peace. I don't think you can have true sobriety without spirituality. Spirituality helped me to stop my obsessive thoughts.

Kim: I think it is very difficult to define spirituality.

Theo: I think we get spirituality mixed up with religion. Religion contributed so much to my "fucked-up-ness." My dad was Roman Catholic and my mom was Jehovah's Witness. All the different rules that were in my head about what's good and what's bad really fucked me up. What I learned at church when I was a kid was that I was born a sinner and needed to seek forgiveness from a punishing white haired guy in the sky. On Sundays, I would go and pray to God to forgive me for all my sins and stop me from going to hell. On Wednesdays, I would go to my mom's Jehovah's Witness meetings and learn that the world was coming to an end any day. The apocalypse was near. I was so afraid. Completely traumatized by these negative thoughts. When you are eight years old, what are you supposed to believe? The first thing I remember about the Jehovah's Witness God and the Roman Catholic God is that they both made me feel afraid.

Kim: I think religion can be a path to God, but often it comes with many rules and conditions.

In their book *How God Changes Your Brain*, Newberg and

Waldman talk about how some religious activities focus on fear in a way that I hadn't heard before. They describe the effects of this type of fear on a very important brain structure that relates to spirituality, called the "anterior cingulate." This structure is like a bridge between your rational thoughts and your emotions. In neuroscience, the anterior cingulate is known as the seat of compassion.[lxix]

Theo: Let's see if I've got this right. So in our brains, there's a little thing called an anterior cingulate, and it's located right between the place where we have our ideas and the other place where we feel our feelings. And its job is to allow us to have a sense of compassion for others, right?

Kim: Yes, and this relates to our spirituality. The anterior cingulate gives us the ability to walk in another person's shoes. When we watch another person suffer, the anterior cingulate helps us to care. Brain imaging studies have looked at the cingulates of Tibetan monks with years of practiced meditation. What they found was that when the monks were engaged in peaceful, meditative thoughts of loving kindness, their cingulates lit up like Christmas tree lightbulbs. But when fear-based religious thoughts dominate …

Theo: That little thing gets damaged?

Kim: Yes, that is what Newberg and Waldman found. And when it does get damaged, it makes it harder for us to have acceptance of others.

Theo: Wow! That helps me to understand why there can be such intolerance, which I have experienced as negative judgment. That produces shame.

Kim: Newberg and Waldman have more to say about fear-based

religions. They report that subscribing to these ideas may create symptoms that mirror post-traumatic stress disorder in their followers. According to their research, fear-based religious followers exhibit higher degrees of anxiety and neurosis. In essence, when you are afraid, you don't have the brain space to care about others' needs. Fear gets in the way of having compassion.

Theo: Well, that further tells me I'm fucked. When I was little, the Jehovah's Witness thinking poisoned my mind with all kinds of terror. As a kid, I would wake up every morning thinking the world was going to end. That is my first conscious memory of being physically terrified.

Kim: Most kids are afraid of spiders, but that sounds like a whole different ball game for you. I know fear is fear and terror is in the eye of the beholder, but I don't think I've ever been exposed to that constant a stressor.

Theo: I guess I took it literally, but that thought sure made me anxious.

Kim: Kids do take these kinds of thoughts literally; your anxiety would have been understandable. Newberg and Wallace suggest that people who are very anxious to begin with often seek out the more fundamentalist religions, because those ideologies offer a highly structured belief system that serves to help reduce their feelings of uncertainty.

Theo: That's interesting. Joining a fundamentalist religion won't be my path though. I'm on a far different road from that. It's the spirituality I'm attracted to, not the religion part.

Kim: For me, understanding the relationship between fear and the need for increased structure allows me to have compassion for why some of us seek the religious paths we do. Ultimately, it would be great if we could all have compassion for each other.

Theo: I am not there yet, but I am a work in progress.

Kim: Why do you think spirituality is important to healing from trauma?

Theo: Because to me, spirituality in its purest sense is a relationship with a universal being. Whatever I am in relationship with is an aspect of my spirituality. Relationship with people, energy, plants, animals, and nature are examples of how I feel my spirituality.

Kim: I am reflecting on the conversation you had with my friend Marie from Atlanta, Georgia, when you were expressing your strong feelings about religion being a source of the world's shame. You were passionate and angry when she questioned you about the strength of your conviction.

Theo: Hmm. I was feeling that I needed to defend myself and my beliefs.

Kim: She suggested to you that your message would be better received if you could express your beliefs with a little more tolerance of others' beliefs.

Theo: Since she comes from the Deep South, I assumed she was defending the high and mighty Church, and I guess that got my hair up. The trigger for me was related to my thought that it was the Church that had made me feel so ashamed all these years. The Church left me empty in my heart. I personally still have anger at organized religion. I think it can be one of the biggest forms of abuse. If God is a loving God then why does the Church talk so much about punishment?

Kim: What happened next in your conversation with Marie was an example of a minor miracle. I suggested that the previous anger you carried toward the justice system had now been moved to

religion, as your next target. You were stunned with that awareness and immediately did a lot of work around it.

Theo: I realize now that I was pointing my finger at Marie and getting
big in my chair. I'd crossed my arms and leaned way forward
into her space. No question, I was on my angry soapbox.

Kim: I watched Marie do something really skilful at that point. She
held her own space, but also stayed in place with your anger. She
was able to acknowledge it without judging it, which is why you
were able to feel safe but still be angry.

Theo: That was incredible how she did that. She was uncomfortable
but she didn't fight back and didn't back down from her own
position either.

Kim: Then you regulated yourself and said, "I got it. I just connected the
shame from my sexual abuse to the shame from my upbringing
in church. So if I am going to fully forgive my abuser, a piece of
my work has also to be finding forgiveness for the Church and
all the shame of it."

Theo: That was big, I'd never thought of it like that before. Fear-based
thinking is really a trigger for me ...

Kim: What was it about your concept of Church that made you feel
ashamed?

Theo: Well, sex is completely evil, didn't you know? (*smirking*)

It's a lot more than that. How I was seeing it, the Church was
all about fear, and shame, sin, sin, sin (*looking down and to the
side*) But you know, thinking about it with my adult head now,
not just my triggered emotional reactions, I know the Church
does good things too. I appreciate that the people in the con-
gregations are there to get support and offer support and build

their communities. I have no reason to shit on any one of them. It's not like I actually hate any religion. And whenever people are supporting others, I'm all for it.

Kim: You are definitely one who believes in community. Everything about your mission is about bringing people together. And at their core, religions are all made up of people who are trying to lead more peaceful and connected lives, in their own ways.

Theo: That's just it! In their own ways. If I am going to stand up there and say, "I suggest you consider choosing a God of your own understanding," and then I am judgmental about what that looks like, I am talking out of the two sides of my mouth.

Kim: You don't like being told what to do, do you?

Theo: Are you kidding me? Of course not. Who does?

Kim: It's pretty clear that you've got some anger and confusion toward your religions of upbringing. And you were triggered by Marie when she hinted that you could have more tolerance for others' beliefs.

Theo: I was angry and I lashed out a bit, because of my own crap; nothing she had done.

Kim: Perfect example of a trigger. The next emotion I immediately observed following the anger was embarrassment for having gotten angry.

Theo: I felt bad that I had offended her. I actually felt ashamed at the possibility of having offended her.

Kim: Then you immediately repaired the situation. You ran through the entire process of telling your story, experiencing emotion, sitting with your shit, and repairing the relationship in ten minutes instead of ten years. That's why I call it a miracle.

Theo: It all reminds me that life's not fair. I know it to be true, but it still pisses me off. Our discussion was a perfect example of what the trauma survivor has to face when they come out of the closet, so to speak. I get angry when I talk about topics related to shame and I'm tired of having to justify and defend myself all the time.

Kim: There is *shame* and *anger* wrapped together right there in a single sentence. That's what happens for survivors of abuse; those two feelings often get linked.

Theo: I don't want to be judged badly about how I do spirituality, because it's something I've thought a lot about and it's working for me. It is what has kept me sane.

Kim: And if you lost your conviction about your spirituality, you might feel lost again?

Theo: Yup, and then I would have no rudder at all.

Kim: This is another beautiful example of why some people hold on tightly to their structured beliefs—for their own survival and support.

Theo: Another mirror of reflection … I guess that experience helps me understand why others defend their beliefs.

Kim: When we feel connected and own what we feel, it is quiet and grounded and there is no need for defensiveness. The conviction is inner and doesn't need to be spoken or imposed on others.

Theo: Yeah. Turns out the impact of my religious upbringing is stronger than I thought.

Kim: Even though you may still have some remnants of judgment about other religions, I see you as increasingly compassionate toward others all the time. Let's go back and try to define what spirituality means to you now.

Theo: Relationship with a universal being. I used to regulate myself with my addictions or by playing hockey, but now I think I need relationship with a universal being to help me with this.

Kim: Yup. As you continue to shed your fearful thoughts, you will be increasingly able to see others as less threatening. This will allow you to have more compassion for others, even when you perceive them as hurtful. Your anterior cingulate will grow as your compassion expands.

Theo: Then may my anterior cingulate—and all of our anterior cingulates—continue to get bigger and bigger!

Kim: Great intention! Our anterior cingulates are the true hearts of our neurological souls.

Theo: One more thing that has been a challenge for me is that in some religions we can only get to God through some form of authority: a priest, a guru, a rabbi, or whatever. In these cases, we are not taught to have a personal relationship with God. There's always a middleman.

Kim: I can see how you would think that a middleman could detract from your personal relationship with your God. You also show distaste for authority once in a while.

Theo: Yup, that's true.

Kim: Do you think that God could be like a secure attachment figure? Nurturing, soothing, and comforting?

Theo: What a beautiful concept.

Kim: Having a relationship with the God of our understanding doesn't have to be based on a religion. It can be about connection.

Theo: Well, yeah. Works for me.

Kim: When was the first time that you were directly angry with God that you can remember?

Theo: When I was little, I loved Father Paul at our church in Russell. He was a wonderful human being. I felt so pissed off at God when Father Paul died of a heart attack. I thought God was supposed to prevent stuff like that from happening to *good* people. Religion starts with the idea that something is wrong with us, right? So if you work hard to be good and still die for no reason, what was the point of working to be so good? When Father Paul died, who really was so good, I thought God had abandoned me. But it was me that made the choice to leave God behind. And I certainly didn't seek any God of My Understanding for a long, long time. I didn't even know that was an option. Even if I did, I was too hurt and angry to think I'd find one.

Kim: Father Paul was like your middleman.

Theo: Wow, hadn't thought of it like that. Maybe when he died unfairly, I decided the whole church had abandoned me. Never got any spiritual connection back until September 18, 2005 when I really needed it and asked God for help.

Kim: Kind of all or nothing, eh? Yet another example of how our childhood beliefs guide our adult lives. The God of my childhood was from the movie *The Ten Commandments*. Cecil B. DeMille's talking ray of light in the clouds, telling Moses what to do in a booming, deep, male authoritative voice. In my childhood mind, He was there to punish us when we are bad and maybe reward us when we are good. I thought prayers were like letters to God being mailed to the sky.

Theo: Ha! I can see you watching *The Ten Commandments*.

Kim: (*pulling out her book again*) I put a note in this book to remember to share something cool with you. It's from Newberg and Waldman again. (*reading*) "The moment we encounter God or the idea of God our brain begins to change.... The more you focus on God, the more God will be sensed as something 'real.'"[lxx] I think this is awesome. The more you think about something as real, the more it becomes real.

Theo: I get that. Since I was six years old, I believed, "I am going to play in the NHL, I am going to play in the NHL, I am going to play in the NHL."

Kim: (*putting the book away*) Then these guys go on to say that there is actually a brain part called the thalamus that helps us to differentiate between what is real and what is not. Their brain imaging studies showed that when people were connecting to the God of their understanding repeatedly, their thalamuses lit up, making God "real" to them.

Theo: When I started going to AA, they always talked about "higher power, higher power." My sponsor JJ would ask me "How is your higher power stuff going?" I would say, "Not so good," thinking, "What the fuck are you talking about?"

JJ would say, "You know you get to pick your own God."

I would think, "What? How can I do that?" So different from what I had learned. I thought he was nuts.

Kim: Does the term "God of My Understanding" fit the way you think about your God?

Theo: After I had my spiritual awakening, I had to attribute my success to that; I didn't have anything else to call it.

Kim: It's a really hard thing to describe, isn't it?

Theo: I feel like the God of My Understanding is my connection to everything. I like that description, because pretty much my whole life I was disconnected from myself. Having a God connects me to my own life.

Kim: Why do you attribute your success to something out there? Why don't you attribute it to something in there? (*pointing to his heart*)

Theo: All my authority stuff, I guess I still believe in it at some level. Ownership of my own success wouldn't be right because I don't believe that anyone is ever doing anything all by themselves. At the end of the day, I realize I know what I am doing. I get that it's part of me and I am plugged in. But I would rather give the credit to Him rather than to myself.

Kim: So do you feel spirituality is a co-creation thing?

Theo: That's what I'm buying into, because I know there's a higher power that's way bigger than me, but that I also have free will. I'm still trying to figure it out. Whatever it is, I am warming up to the idea that the less I react and the more mindful I am, the less hurtful I will be. And the less threatened I will feel.

Kim: There are religions that specifically practise mindfulness, like Buddhism.

Theo: Kim, you haven't said what you really believe.

Kim: I believe we are all connected. And we are all better off when we treat people with compassion.

Theo: Do you go to church?

Kim: No. But that doesn't mean I don't appreciate some of the helpful things churches do. I also had one of those tragic break-ups with the Church, when I was about fourteen. When I was younger, we were huge Anglican church-goers, active in the church community, and friends with the minister. Sunday school, and all that. Then one day, we got a letter from someone on some committee from our church saying that our minister, the one whom we'd had over for supper so many times, was being moved, as he had been accused of sexually molesting someone in our congregation. "That's it," my dad said. "We aren't going to Church anymore."

Theo: My church let me down too when Father Paul died and I lost a friend. Do you also kind of miss that connection?

Kim: Not really. I've found my own way to create a sense of spiritual community in the relationships around me, and I'd definitely say I am a spiritual person.

Theo: When you think of Jesus, what kind of a man do you think he was?

Kim: (*smiling*) I played Mary Magdalene in our high school's *Jesus Christ Superstar*. I've always been very attracted to Jesus' spirit. If I stop and connect with what I believe about who he was, I feel inspired and accepted and more whole. That said, I don't feel I need to go to church to access connection to what is divine.

Theo: Me neither.

Kim: So what about you. Do you go to church now?

Theo: No. I think it would fall down if I walked through the door. (*laughing*)

Kim: I don't think it would fall down. Given what you were taught when you were little, today do you see yourself as an evolutionist or a creationist?

Theo: Hmm. Neither.

Kim: Well, do you take the Bible literally when it says God created the earth in seven days with Adam and Eve starting up the world's first dysfunctional family?

Theo: Kim! (*accusingly*)

Kim: We know no one is perfect. No family is perfect.

Theo: I think I just stood up for Adam and Eve! I guess some of those Bible story messages are still with me.

Kim: All the tape recordings that played over and over in our heads are part of our implicit memory.

Theo: I just got something. Adam and Eve, original sin. That's what began the concept of shame. Maybe we should call it original shame. But I admit the Bible also has stories with messages of love and compassion in them too.

Kim: So do you believe in the seven-day story of creation?

Theo: We went to the Calgary zoo. I love the monkeys. There is no question I believe in some evolution. And I think we can evolve our own beliefs, too. (*mischievously*) Why the big bang started is still up in the air, and who's behind it? It's a mystery to me. So what I'm happy believing is that the God of My Understanding had some hand in kicking it off and we've all been trying to survive better ever since. You must have a similar belief, right?

Kim: The motto of my whole business is "Supporting the conscious evolution of the human spirit." So, absolutely. I think we each have the capacity to consciously change our genes and evolve with mindfulness. We're not in this wondrous adventure of life alone, though. I think there is magnificence and mystery around how we're all magically connected, much more than we know. And every time I walk in nature, that's when I feel most thankful for being part of it.

Theo: So that minister of yours, was he ever found guilty?

Kim: You know what, we still don't know. It wasn't talked about, other than, "We're not going to church again."

Theo: Interesting how one negative event, or even accusation, could be so powerful. The Church has to know that this is a significant issue that takes away from its purpose.

Kim: It's all about trust. Even if two hundred church members are loving and caring, all it takes to wreck the peace is one person, and as you say, we don't even know what the full truth is. Bottom line, when trust like that is broken, sometimes it never comes back.

Theo: True.

Kim: Whatever our feelings toward the church, and whatever our reasons for them, it's clear that it's a huge part of our society. It's perhaps ironic and fitting that it's because of the Oblate Sisters and the Aulneau Renewal Centre—their restitution mission in Manitoba—that we were first brought together at that conference in Winnipeg. The church, directly or indirectly, does bring people together, and that's a good thing.

Theo: That's the part I always liked about going to church, the people. The new Pope's cool though, eh? Pope Francis.

Kim: His deep humility and his belief in serving are very appealing. I wish him well. But if I were to have dinner with the leader of any world religion I'm familiar with, I think I would invite over His Holiness the Dalai Lama. To me he is a combination of wisdom, patience, compassion, silliness, and optimism. And also humility. I am sure Pope Francis and he would get along well.

Theo: I don't know much about the Dalai Lama other than what you tell me. I think the concept of accepting things as they are sounds peaceful, but I don't think you could ever get a team of Buddhist monk hockey players to compete with the same intensity. If they are okay with losing the puck, how could they win?

Kim: I don't think they would be sore losers, though. And to achieve such detachment from the "need" to win could be interpreted as having already won. Not that I'm advocating any religion over another—whatever people choose. What I wish is that their choices encourage them to be decent to everyone, including themselves. At their cores, I think all religions are saying the same thing pretty much, and it's a loving message at the root. It's how they've been interpreted and often used in the name of political will that frustrates me with the institutions.

Theo: Yep. The reason I don't go to church is that I don't think my kids need more fear and shame heaped on them; there's already enough of that. I personally believe Jesus would be sad to see that people think they are following his "way" more by staying away from church than by going to it.

Kim: I don't think he'd mind how and where you connect to love and compassion. So please don't feel guilty about it. Like you say, there's enough of that going around already.

Theo: (*nodding in agreement*)

Kim: (*shifting in her chair*) I'm thinking of AA and how often it talks about spirituality. But you didn't even recognize the God of Your Understanding until … (*searching her memory*) you said it was about nine years ago. How did these two concepts come together for you?

Theo: After I initially got sober in Santa Fe, at the clinic, I really tried to stay the course on my own. But it wasn't working for me.

Whenever I drove the bus, metaphorically, the bus crashed. As I mentioned, I'd started my relationship with Jenn and was actively back in addictive mode. Doing lines of coke, drinking, gambling. We'd just missed our run at the Allan Cup with the Horse Lake Thunder. That's like the Stanley Cup of the Canadian Mens Senior AAA Hockey and the wild team I was playing on in 2005. Our home rink was located six hours northwest of Edmonton, if you can believe it. After we didn't win the Cup I was feeling really low. Jenn and I were fighting all the time. I didn't want to fuck up again. I found myself on the bathroom floor in a ball and crying like a baby. Screaming at God, "Why the fuck don't you help me? I can't stand you!"

I called God every name in the book. I was really suffering. I went up one side of him and down the other. It was so painful to reach that critical point yet again where I felt like "Haven't I hit rock bottom enough?" I remembered that AA taught me to ask God for help. I'd never really tried it before. I was so desperate I thought, "Let's try it." So I got on my knees and said my prayers and begged God to help me. "I know God that you don't give us more than we can handle, but I am full. I can't handle any more. Please take away the obsession to drink and do drugs."

Then I went to bed.

When I woke up in the morning, I passed a mirror on the way to the bathroom. I hated mirrors. I never looked at myself. This time I stopped and gazed at myself. I looked different. Softer, wiser, clearer. It was so strange. I felt so different. I thought "God … There you are. You heard me."

I haven't had a drink or a drug since, in nine years. Really what I was doing was starting the process of forgiving myself. What had I been doing? Self-abuse. It was time to stop the self-abuse and come to the realization that it was time to forgive myself.

Kim: I call those moments "a shift." Change in consciousness, transformation.

Theo: Shift happens. (*laughing*)

Kim: (*ignoring his brilliant wit*) What came out of that shift?

Theo: Contentment, faith, belief in myself. It taught me that when I have a struggle, I can "give it to God."

Kim: Sounds like an experience of "grace." To me, grace is assistance that comes from a higher place.

Theo: AA calls it a "God shot" or a spiritual awakening.

Kim: Grace can come in different forms. A person, an idea, a message, or a special opportunity. Faith is an interesting concept. It doesn't have to be only about God; it can be a belief in science, love, faith in ourselves, or faith in each other. All of these thoughts and beliefs will result in the same brain activity. It seems that having faith in the human spirit is what drives us to survive.

Theo: Are you telling me that optimism and hope are survival skills?

Kim: According to our brains they are. Faith also helps your physical health. If you strongly believe something, it's been shown to stimulate your immune system. That is what the placebo effect is all about.

Theo: Cool.

Kim: What do you think about the concept of hitting "rock bottom" as being necessary for connecting to God or more particularly, for healing?

Theo: I think hitting rock bottom can come as a one-time crash or a series of visits from hell, each one tipping us more forcefully from our avoidance to becoming awake.

Kim: Pain is a great motivator. But we often tolerate it for a long time before taking action. You talk about people who are spiritually dead as "sleeping." What do you mean?

Theo: I think to be spiritually connected is to be awake. It means we have to become aware of ourselves, our thoughts, and our feelings. There is so much more to us than we can see or touch. People who walk around in denial or are disconnected are spiritually dead and missing all the wondrousness of living.

Kim: Finding spirituality is like waking up. Do you meditate?

Theo: Can you see that? (*grinning*) I just imagine myself wearing tight yoga pants and it doesn't feel right.

Kim: Don't even go there! That is a disturbing visual image. (*laughing*)

Theo: I couldn't meditate if I tried. I have squirrel brain. My thoughts are scattered in a million directions all at the same time. The idea of sitting without moving and keeping my mind still sounds like absolute hell.

Kim: So you never tried it?

Theo: Of course I tried it, once at a drug and alcohol treatment centre. Talk about a setup. Newly sober, a hundred addicts in one room without our addictions to calm us, not one of us could focus our minds in any way whatsoever. It was hilarious! Complete gong show. "Try to think of nothing at all," they said. As if! Zero chance for success. We were so stressed out from the instructions, we were all bouncing around in our seats to the point where it might as well have been our exercise class!

Kim: (*trying not to laugh*) That actually makes me mad that you'd be set up for failure in that way. It's against my relentless positivity belief to give anyone such a difficult task without them having the tools.

Theo: It was ridiculous. No one could sit still for even a few seconds.

Kim: When I try to meditate in the way I think it should look, I get anxious as well. I try to perform meditation as if there were some perfect way to do it. But I doubt myself and wonder if I am doing it wrong. The God of My Understanding would think we are so silly to be worrying about this kind of stuff.

Theo: He or She is probably thinking we're worrying about many things we don't need to be worrying about.

Kim: Remember I told you I had the opportunity, a few years ago, to travel to a Buddhist Temple in India to spend a week with His Holiness the Dalai Lama? The deep vibrational feeling of the Tibetan monks chanting "Aauuummmmummmooooaaahhh," and the utter joyfulness of the little child monks in their sunglasses and cellphones are two things I'll never forget. (*smiling*)

Every day we would listen to His Holiness speak, but we had to do it sitting on this hard marble floor. I was so stoked to be there and my expectations of what it was going to be like were off the charts. I guess I thought I would come back completely transformed; I don't know. Although I hugely admire His Holiness and the concepts he was talking about as I understood them, my truth was I hated just about every second of sitting on that floor because of my physical discomfort. My butt hurt so bad. I kept wanting to fall asleep. I so much wanted to lie down. Then my self-talk started beating me up for failing as a holy person. Every time my mind would wander, I would try to bring it back.

Then, I realized that some pretty cool ideas were bouncing around in my mind. Was this my mind running wild or the insights of meditation? How could I tell? Why couldn't I empty my mind of thoughts like I thought I was supposed to? Just as I was asking myself this, the next sentence out of His Holiness's mouth was "Meditation does not mean ignoring, letting go of, or not having thoughts."

"Amazing synchronicity." Here I thought I was doing it wrong, but it turns out random thoughts were okay! My expectations of needing to able to clear my mind completely was actually the barrier to the very connection I was looking for. Those cool thoughts I was having were actually providing me with the inspiration and connection I desired. Once I let go of my expectations, I realized that I was totally capable of benefitting from meditation in the way that I'd hoped.

His Holiness is a radiant being with such humility, very grounded and loving. I wasn't disappointed in my experience in India one bit. It just took me a little while to surrender to whatever was happening. And once I did, I was in the flow.

Theo: Expectation is the big word there in your story. When we expect to get something, or be able to do something, it's like we put a cork in that natural flow. (*warmly*) I know you have high expectations of yourself.

Kim: I'm torn between keeping them too high and just accepting what is. To figure this kind of stuff out, do you think it is important to have a daily practice?

Theo: I am talking in my head to God all the time. And no, I am not psycho. Conversations with God are a part of my "practice." It is how I exercise my connection and keep myself in relationship with God. Sometimes, I actively say the serenity prayer,

"God, please grant me the serenity to accept the things I cannot change, the courage to change the things I can, and the wisdom to know the difference," and sometimes I am just yakking away to God in my thoughts.

Kim: I love it. Did you know that when you intensely and consistently focus on your spiritual values and goals, you increase the blood flow (that is a good thing) to your frontal lobes and the anterior cingulate? When these two brain parts work together, they help the emotional brain to relax! It makes you feel calmer naturally. Isn't that cool?

Theo: That explains a lot. When I connect to the God of My Understanding, I definitely feel calmer and more "regulated" as you say. How do they know this shit?

Kim: Brain scientists put people in brain imaging chambers and look at how active their brains are under different conditions. In this instance, they had people think about spirituality (as they understand it) and looked at which parts of their brains were lighting up.

Theo: That validates what I run around this country yakking about: "Spirituality is the missing link." Now you are telling me that it really does affect your brain, your emotions, and your behaviour!

Kim: That's why I love this stuff!

Theo: What about prayer? What does that do? Some mornings, I consciously get down on my knees and actively pray. It feels good. When I begin to speak at a conference, I invite the Grandmothers and Grandfathers into the room for spiritual support. Some of the shit that comes out of my mouth could never come from my own head. I know I am spiritually guided, especially when I say things that I don't normally say.

Kim: In most of the scientific studies I can find, prayer and meditation are very similar physiologically; they both happen in the same part of the brain. Once again, it's the frontal cortex and the anterior cingulate that come on line. When these parts of the brain are exercised over and over, it helps you to focus your attention.

Theo: I could definitely use more of that.

Kim: Makes me wonder why we don't all meditate more often. Interestingly, meditation can be separated from its spiritual roots and can simply enhance your cognitive brain and improve how effectively you think. Daily meditation is believed to increase our ability to focus and improve our memory.[lxxi]

Theo: Does that mean spirituality makes your brain smarter?

Kim: In some ways, yes. Focused attention through meditation or prayer builds new neural circuits in the brain and enhances motivation. The more you practise, the stronger these neural circuits become.

Theo: I am not lacking motivation.

Kim: You certainly aren't. Optimism and motivation tap into the exactly the same neural network as faith in your brain! I think you're kind of primed for "faith."

Theo: Do you know of any really easy meditations? It would have to be simple and quick.

Kim: I do know one. I just learned it from this same book I've got in my briefcase. When you pray, meditate, or just relax for a few minutes, repeatedly touch each of your fingers to your thumb, in order from pinky to index finger, saying "sa ta na ma."[lxxii] When you do this repeatedly, it dramatically increases the amount of activity in the front of your brain, which helps you to focus your attention and become more mindful. Apparently, it's a highly effective form of meditation!

Theo: You mean all I have to do is touch each finger to my thumb over and over again? That will help my brain?

Kim: Yep. In the ancient language of Sanskrit, "sa ta na ma" actually means "birth, life, death, rebirth." What we are really meditating upon is the cycle of life.

Theo: Cool.

Kim: It's good to keep in mind that meditation only helps keep the brain healthy if you think about positive things. If you were to do this exercise while thinking about something negative, that would not be helpful.

Theo: (*touching his fingers*) Sa ta na ma. I can remember this one. Probably won't do this when I'm driving, but I could do it at a red light …

Kim: We could talk about the value of mindful driving … Driving on long highways for me is definitely a time for self-reflection. I think the key with new effective habits is to find ways to work them in that realistically fit with your lifestyle. Otherwise, it's very hard to succeed with it. Realistically, you could do this "sa ta na ma" while you're watching a commercial on TV.

Theo: Ha. That could work. One of the things that really connected me to my spirituality was when I returned to my Aboriginal roots. The sweat lodge. The sweat lodge is a tradition of cleansing. It's supposed to help you get rid of toxins in your body and in your soul. The sweat lodge is a holy place of connection with God, spirits, and those who have passed on before us. It is supposed to be like Mother Earth's womb. In the sweat lodge, there is teaching, storytelling, praying, confessing, sharing, and community.

Everything that happens in the sweat lodge is safe.

Kim: What is it about the sweats that spiritually works most for you?

Theo: I think it's that everyone there is committed to the idea that they want to feel better, and it's fully understood going in that not one of us is perfect. And there's some element of surrender and connection to all things.

Kim: I like those thoughts too. And I think that so much of spirituality is linked to storytelling. When we talked earlier about healing conversations, I think that the stories we tell about ourselves are a form of connection with our spirit. Our stories embody the content of our lifetime, our connection with ourself. I believe that we find God within our own being; when we connect with our own stories, I think we're connecting with God.

Theo: I wonder if this partly explains why I am so connected to the Aboriginal traditions. Sitting in the sweat lodge and telling stories is very powerful for me. I feel less alone. Listening to other people share with true raw emotion as they talk about pain can be the road to healing. Pain either paralyzes us or motivates us. I have experienced both.

Kim: I think that sweat lodges can be like healing conversations, enhancing relationships … (*pausing to think*) I see all the time that First Nations spirituality is a big part of your journey.

Theo: No question! The aboriginal world often has a way of bringing in new information, or saying things in a different way … so the message gets through.

Kim: What are you talking about when you say that?

Theo: Well, I got a story for you. I spoke at a conference in Bella Coola, British Columbia, which is a very remote community where there is only one way in and the same way out. And it's one of the most beautiful places I've ever been to.

Kim: I've been there too. Such a beautiful part of the world!

Theo: It really is. At the conference I spoke at, sitting together in the audience listening to my story were perpetrators and survivors, which I didn't know would be the case. It was all pretty intense stuff. But when I first got to Bella Coola, I got there a day early. And so I was just kind of sitting around and this young man came up to me, and he was about twenty-four years old and he said, "Would you like to go on a hike?"

And I said "Why yes, absolutely."

And he said, "Well, I'm kind of the local historian for the community," and I thought that was kind of strange, 'cause he was only twenty-four. But he explained to me that this honour was passed down to him from his father and his father before him. I said, "Okay, let's go!"

We hiked up into the mountains and as we were hiking, there was this roaring stream beside the pathway so I reached in with my hand and pulled out some water and I drank it. It was just so pure. And so we hiked a little bit further and we came to a clearing where there was a whole bunch of carvings that had been traced back thousands and thousands of years. They were of all sorts of animals that had been carved right into these big huge rocks. So I just happened to be standing over the carving of a frog … and the first thing he says to me is, "Have you ever seen a frog hop backwards?"

And I said, "No, I can't say that I ever have."

He says, "So while the frog can look to the left, and the frog can look to the right, it's always moving straight ahead."

And I kind of thought to myself, holy shit, that's me! And I really didn't think too much more of it, at that time. But then, I started to use the story in my speeches, talking about the frog, and the concept of moving forward, and takin' baby steps, slow and steady, that kind of thing. So I go to Winnipeg, fast forward nine months later, I'm speaking at the Thunderbird House, at a similar conference. So I get there a day early and they invite us to do a sweat. And they have a sweat lodge right on Main Street in Winnipeg.

Kim: I know that place, a lot of activity there.

Theo: Sure is. So I went to the sweat. And it was like every other sweat I've been involved in: lots of spirituality, lots of drumming, lots of traditional songs, you know, a sharing circle. It was awesome.

So the next day I spoke at the conference, and again I told the story of the frog. And when I was done speaking, the spiritual leader who ran the sweat the night before grabbed the microphone out of my hand and said, "You'll never guess what walked into the sweat lodge last night!"

I said, "I have no idea."

He said, "A frog ..."

And as soon as he said that, they shut the entire conference down and they did this ceremony. In this ceremony, they presented me with a pipe. You know to receive a pipe is one of the highest honours in the aboriginal culture, and it carries tremendous responsibility. Then they gave me my spirit name in Cree, "Tanti," which means the frog.

Kim: What an honour!

Theo: Huge. I guess they recognized that my spirit animal is the frog.

Now it's part of something I'm proud to identify with. So, everywhere I go now, I start telling the story of the frog. It's kind of getting interesting, 'cause now I'm in Halifax and I look over on my nightstand and there's this statue of a frog. Everywhere I go, this frog is always appearing.

Kim: Neat how that can happen.

Theo: So, I was in a Métis Community in Northern Alberta and I was doing another sweat. And I was talking to the spiritual guy who was doing the sweat and we were just having a casual chat and I started talking about this frog. And he's like, "That's interesting." He said, "Does your daughter have respiratory problems?"

I said, "Yep, she's got kind of a mild case of asthma."

"Well," he says, "The next time you see a frog," he says, "Take that frog and put it on her chest."

So I did that. And you know what, Skylah hasn't really ever had a problem since.

Kim: I completely resonate with this kind of synchronicity.

Theo: Then I was in Calgary, and I was speaking with the Meadow Lake Tribal Council and there were nine different bands from around that area. And again, I told the story of the frog. And when I was done speaking, this elder woman came up to me and she said, "Did you realize that the frog is the healer of children?" And so everywhere I go, this story gets better and better and better …

Kim: And on many different levels.

Theo: So then when it came time to organize the Victor Walk from Toronto to Ottawa, I didn't want it to be about me. I wanted it to be about what we were raising awareness for: healing from childhood trauma. So "Victor the Frog" is sort of, I guess, the mascot, or whatever you want to call him; he's the "spiritual leader" of the Victor Walk. So he has his own Twitter account, his own Facebook page …

Kim: Ha! Does he?

Theo: Yeah! Do a search on twitter for @victorthefrog. (*quite serious*)

Kim: That's awesome. (*smiling*) And it's all about going forward, never back, right?

Theo: Yeah. It's just moving forward. The frog never moves backward, 'cause he doesn't know how to. I think there's only one frog in the world that can actually hop backwards, not sure which kind that is. But he's always stuck in his old shit though.

Kim: (*laughing*) That's funny.

Theo: We can learn from animals too, right?

Kim: That's a good example of it. You know, Amanda Lindhout, who was living in Calgary and then became a free-lance journalist all over the world, would say the same thing. She told a powerful story in her book *A House in the Sky* about her time being held captive in Somalia for 460 days. She'd been through hell and was just about spiritually broken, when, on the verge of taking her own life, she got a sign. It was a bird that came to her window, the first of anything she'd seen from the outside world in three months, and it symbolized to her that she would be released, that she would be free. Again, it can be animals that encourage our feeling of connectedness to a greater picture that helps us get through …

Theo: And they can give us little bits of guidance when we need them.

Kim: Just had a question pop into my mind. How do you know, with certainty, when you are plugged in to your higher power?

Theo: It's a feeling more than a thinking, I think. It's when I trust that I am being cared for. When I surrender to the God of My Understanding, it's then that I feel that I am looked after. Whatever shows up is what is supposed to happen. It helps me to feel supported and directed. That is what it means to me to carry out God's will. It is the following of the signals that are in my life. When there is struggle, then perhaps I am going in the wrong direction. When there is ease, it is like a force pushing me along, reminding me I am on track.

Kim: Mmhm. I think that when I am connected to myself and deeply in harmony with what I am feeling—when my own insides and outsides are matching—that is when my actions are most in sync with God's will.

Theo: Once you grasp something greater than yourself, synchronistic events start to happen. That softens the blow for me when it comes around the topic of abuse. We are always looking for excuses for our bad behaviour. I don't want others to feel sorry for me. But when I realize everything that bothers me about someone else is really "me," I have to internalize it first before I can work with it. I see those who bother me as examples of synchronistic events that teach me more about myself. This is spirit in action.

Kim: Sometimes, it is a whisper with subtle direction. Events or signs in the world around you often show up to let you know that you are aligned with your intent. That is when you feel like you are in the flow.

I remember one time, I was working at a camp for kids with special needs in the Nineties. I was struggling with an important question: "Do I move away from teaching this work with kids with special needs and move in the direction of talking about spiritual healing?"

As I was walking along the beach there were two parallel wheelchair tracks in the sand. All of a sudden the two parallel tracks merged into a single path. That was my message that helped me to think about the two ideas as an integrated possibility. I realized I could do both, mindfully bridging the fields of therapy and spirituality, without having to give up either one of them. To me, this is what spiritual synchronicity is: the whispers of information from the divine that provide us with guidance.

Theo: Even if those thoughts came from inside your own mind and were not coming from anywhere else, it still helped you to find your purpose. That is what is at the core of our healing: finding our purpose.

Kim: Nicely said.

Theo: I believe our spirit has a plan for us. By connecting to that plan, that purpose, I am connecting to my spirit.

Kim: Being in alignment with your purpose is the call of your spirit. When I think of you on the ice, I think of spirit, because that's your happy place, where you're connected to yourself! It doesn't matter whether you are an Olympic hockey player or a healing motivator, when you are aligned with what you are doing, you are listening to your inner voice.

Theo: Sometimes, things we want, or think we want, don't happen right away. If we think of God as a mailman or a gift giver, we will be disappointed when things don't happen. That's when it is easy to blame God.

Kim: I don't believe there is a chalkboard in the sky with a divine plan for each one of us. I prefer to believe that we are not pawns on a chess board. There is a great deal of free will and a need for participation in our own lives. Our future is affected by each and every passing moment.

Theo: Over the past two years, by being connected to the "process" of these healing conversations, I've learned a great deal about having patience. Things will happen when they're supposed to.

Kim: A great example of being aligned with our purpose occurred when you and I were sitting in one of your favourite restaurants in Calgary (La Brezza Ristorante) working on this book, totally engrossed in a really sensitive and emotional conversation. At one point in the discussion, when we were being brought the bill, we noticed a woman in her late fifties sitting alone at another booth, just close enough to us that she might have heard tiny bits and pieces of a concept we were trying to make sense of.

Theo: For sure! Meeting her was like that song from The Police's album *Synchronicity*.

Kim: Which one?

Theo: "Synchronicity." (*smiling*)

Kim: Of course. (*shaking her head*) When we both got up to leave, you scanned the room as you always do, and I saw you two share brief eye contact and without speaking out loud, she slowly mouthed the words, "Thank you." We both thought that was pretty neat, and went on talking.

But about ten minutes later, we were still continuing our conversation in the parking lot, and that same lady approached us, looking right at you. She had tears welling in the corners of her eyes. Her voice was quivering, but her message was strong. She said, "Thank you for all that you do. For giving those of us without a voice a voice. You have changed the lives of so many. I am grateful."

We were a little dumbfounded, but the timing of it really reinforced that this kind of discussion is worth trying to document. How do you explain that? (*pausing*) Some kind of beautiful in-the-flow moment reminding us that we are on the right track, maybe?

Theo: And the depth of her situation, or how little or how much help we were really able to provide her, we'll never know!

Kim: We don't need to know, do we. Even if the tiniest amount of comfort is received, it's worth speaking up, one hundred times over. The grateful anonymous lady in the parking lot is only one example of countless times we have been together and experienced the force of spirituality at work. Being in the flow means wanting to get up tomorrow morning and keep it going.

Theo: Absolutely!

Kim: So to try to capture your personal beliefs, spirituality for you comes from feeling connected: in relationship, in conversation, in aboriginal culture, in some Christian principles and stories, in a mix of your own beliefs that serve you in moving forward. Is that it?

Theo: For me, I feel more empowered pulling different ideas and concepts together than accepting one concrete set of beliefs and behaviours. And I appreciate that my interpretation of my beliefs can always change. I prefer a world in which everyone can choose what works best for them.

Kim: My father-in-law Philip Spensley has a way of thinking about God that appeals very much to me. He says "God is the energy that connects all living things." So when he prays to God, he's really praying for the greater good.

Theo: Nice. But didn't you say he was a Montreal Canadiens fan?

Kim: Yep. But he, my husband, and the whole family believes that the Montreal Canadiens winning *is* in the interest of the greater good, like the stars coming back into alignment, and when all is well in the world.

Theo: Kim, spirituality can only extend so far.

Kim: (*laughing*) But you do realize hockey fans pray too, right?

Theo: Prayer helps. Some teams just need to keep the faith.

Kim: I've heard in Montreal that hockey is like a religion.

Theo: They have their St. Patrick; and now there's Jesus Price.[lxxiii] Hey, I thought you didn't pay attention to hockey?

Kim: My husband cares about it, and I care about him, so ... We have a friend from Pointe-Claire, Quebec (Scotty Taylor) who came up with a wise way to put it. He says "When you get married, it's the job of the husband and the wife to take care of each other's hearts." I acknowledge that hockey means a lot to Bob, so I can at least pay a tiny bit of attention. Can't really help him get his team to win though, can I?

Theo: We know we can't all get what we want. There's only one Stanley Cup winner a year. (*tongue in cheek*) But why do you think God sometimes seems to punish some people, thinking here of Toronto fans, more than others? Is it for some lesson?

Kim: Do you really think that we are here to learn specific lessons? I ask this question because I struggle with the idea that there is some kind of pre-set design out there for us.

Theo: If not, then why do we seem to be presented all the time with struggle? Eventually, if things are as tough as they can be, like when we're in heavy addiction, we have to make one of two choices. Continue doing what we're doing, or stop the behaviour.

If we continue as is, it may kill us, but there is little fear in keeping on with it; it may be absolute toxic crap, but it's familiar. But if we stop masking the pain, we have fear of the unknown. And self-doubt, 'cause it's new territory. But my experience has been that there is absolutely nothing that you cannot overcome.

Kim: Comes back to faith, doesn't it?

Theo: Sure, but I can see where that falls apart for a lot of people. When we're brought up not knowing how to have a relationship, having faith in it doesn't make sense to us. So we've gotta find some other way to learn it.

Kim: That makes sense.

Theo: If everything is by design, and maybe it is, then the reason I am across from you in this moment is because we share in the commonality of the struggle.

Kim: Even if there isn't a great design planned by the white haired man in the sky from my childhood, we are definitely sharing in the commonality of the struggle. We have the same purpose.

Theo: When you are little and there's someone in your corner, you feel safe. When you carry your burdens all alone, it makes any trauma all that more damaging. I've seen so much evidence of attachment issues in my travels around the country. And it makes sense to me why aboriginal communities struggle so much. But the spirit itself is free of struggle and conflict. If we can just get to that while we're alive and have enough strength to help others …

Kim: It is the ego and what happens to us along our path that is the other shit that gets in the way.

Theo: Do you realize your language is changing the more you hang out with me?

Kim: Ha. You caught me saying "shit." I have noticed that. Every one of us on the planet is affected by the habits of who we hang out with. But here's a question: to reach your highest level of healing through spirituality, do you think you heal better alone, one-on-one, or in groups?

Theo: As I've said hundreds of times, I've been in every group with the name Anonymous at the end of it. Essentially, they're all pretty much the same. They're humbling, and they serve to remind us that we're not alone with our problems. And there are other people who care. But by themselves, at least for me, they don't go all the way and were never as intensely personal as a good one-on-one. The Anonymous groups provide some tools, but they didn't help me understand the connection between trauma and coping through addiction. That piece really came from my time with you. I really like the sweat lodge, as we mentioned. Like the self-help groups, it's the concept of being a team that appeals to me. I know there are many people walking with me on this journey—not only the journey of sobriety, but also of peace and wellness. That sense of team is priceless. But ultimately, it's my own connection with the God of My Understanding that is all that I am. Without the spiritual side of my healing, and feeling connected to this greater good, I don't know where I'd be.

Kim: You have so much to do that can help others find the help they need; just reminding yourself of that fact keeps you spiritually connected.

Theo: You know, for the first time in my life, I have some pretty solid spirituality and I don't question anything going on. So all these things coming together don't surprise me. I would say that for me, even though I've been talking in many communities and with thousands of people, the one thing that I kept leaving out of my story was spirituality. Now that I have it, look what's happening! I'm able to connect with people all over the country more effectively. I gotta say, the reason I am here and in this position is because of my spirituality, not because I am sober. Being sober is just a by-product of spirituality. When you're connected to your passion and purpose, the rest falls in line … (*suddenly pensive and a tiny bit ashamed*) except of course for those moments when it doesn't.

Kim: (*compassionately*) And that's a whole other chapter.

Theo: (*touching his fingers to his thumb and smiling*) Sa ta na ma; sa ta na ma; sa ta na ma …

8

Shame Revisits

"Things do not change; we change."
Henry David Thoreau

Kim: No matter how hard you work on yourself, you're still going to revisit this place. Or another way of looking at it is that shame sticks around even when it's not invited.

Theo: Shame is like crazy glue that keeps us stuck. It's the number one barrier to healing; it gets in the way of getting better.

Kim: My experience in understanding shame is that it begins in infancy. It's in the context of those early infant-parent relationship patterns where those first feelings of shame arise.

Theo: Abandonment, rejection, and feeling not lovable. Those core issues seem to be the result of my original sources of shame.

Kim: The wonderful Brené Brown in her book *Daring Greatly* suggests that as children we store shame as trauma. These experiences change how we see ourselves and they profoundly affect our feelings of self-worth.[lxxiv]

Theo: I love Brené Brown, I watched her TED Talk.[lxxv]

Kim: Her ideas really fit with what we've been talking about; it's early developmental trauma that sets our coping strategies in motion.

Theo: I believe every time I get triggered and react with a strong emotion, I am revisiting some aspect of my old shame.

Kim: So awesome you're even aware of it. It isn't easy for people to make those connections. One astonishing fact about the brain is that it feels social rejection the same way that it feels physical pain. Rejections are painful. The same parts of the brain that give us empathy for others feel it when others don't have empathy for us. In case you're interested, it's the insula and the anterior cingulate where this happens. When you experience repeated rejection, abandonment, and shame, your capacity for empathy toward others wears down over time.

Theo: That really explains how hurt people hurt people.

Kim: I know that we say that a lot. But it reminds us to have conscious compassion.

Theo: (*nodding*) That definitely makes sense. One of my earliest memories is that my dad always made me feel ashamed when he came to the rink when he was loaded. I wanted him to be the same as all the other parents.

Kim: What did you do when he showed up that way?

Theo: I just avoided him. We had such a sense of team back in Russell that I didn't want to stand out. But he was always bragging about what I was doing. It didn't fit in with the philosophy of what everybody was trying to teach us about teamwork. Although I know today that it was pride that he had for me, he didn't know how to express his feelings in a way I could receive them. The way he expressed them made me feel ashamed.

Kim: I'm pulling together what you've been saying. Your mom wouldn't have given you much gleam and beam; at home your dad was highly unpredictable; and when he tried to praise you in public, it backfired. I'm sorry you and your dad had that experience.

Theo: That's just the way it was between us.

Kim: I think it's key to understand how little kids perceive shaming. As infants and children, we read the earliest cues of shaming in the nonverbals of our parents and the people around us. A scorning look, a dismissive turn, a harsh voice are all cues that affect a baby's and child's mood and nervous system.

Theo: I am still sensitive to that stuff. I react so automatically to that information. At the end of the day, shaming totally sucks.

Kim: As early as the first couple of days, young infants begin to dissociate when they are receiving cues of disapproval. The only strategy they have is to retreat inside themselves. Imagine if all you had to look at were facial cues of disgust or absence, you wouldn't have a very positive mirror in which to see yourself.

Theo: When I listen to that explanation, I can feel that sensation of disappearing even as you talk about it.

Kim: You just tapped into the feeling of shame. That is hard to do actually; shame is a slippery experience to connect with. It is so uncomfortable that we want out of it as fast as possible to avoid the depth of pain that it touches. Most of us bypass that feeling immediately. Brave of you to connect with it even a little. Because only when you connect with it can you deal with it.

Theo: (*rubbing his face*) When I connect with the feeling of shame, I feel frustrated at wanting to connect deeply with others and not being able to. It is so empty. I feel ripped off.

Kim: I think that is where so much of your anger comes from; feeling ripped off. What was missing?

Theo: No one was there for me. (*looks away and rubs his nose*) My chest feels heavy and I feel a bit nauseous.

Kim: In this moment, you are connecting to the feelings of what you were missing as a child—right here, right now. But right now you are not that child.

Theo: (*becoming a bit teary*) It feels like I am defective or put together badly. And yet of course I know that's not who I am.

Kim: You are describing exactly what shame does to you. It keeps you locked into self-loathing and disgust until eventually it defines you. You have both to know in your mind and feel in your heart that you're okay, in order for that feeling to be authentic.

Theo: Hmm. I was looking for a specific memory that caused me to have these feelings. It makes me feel better knowing that shame's encoded in implicit memory, so it's about what I was feeling when I was really young and I don't have to beat myself up for not remembering details.

Kim: That's what happens to all of us. When rejection or shame happens to you in infancy, it won't have any words, just feelings. We can't always find a specific moment or an example of an experience that caused the original feelings to creep in. We can't erase implicit memories, but we can definitely learn to become observers of them rather than reactors to them.

Theo: I was looking for some old tape to play back in my head of specific shameful experiences, but I think that there were so many, piled on top of each other, that it became like a big pile of shit.

Kim: Shame starts out by being something we receive from another, but eventually we do it to ourselves.

Theo: I always say that when the abuse stopped, I abused myself. I guess that would be similar.

Kim: That dynamic is not at all uncommon. I know that I can be my own biggest critic.

Theo: I am with you. I think that so much of my drive comes from that place of inner judgment. And then look at how I was coached when I was older. It was all about shaming.

Kim: That is the double-edged sword of never feeling good enough. I know for sure that my workaholism comes from that place. I grew up feeling a lot of criticism, so working harder and harder is what I still do so I can feel closer to being good enough. But I don't actually get there all the way, 'cause I'm not yet feeling it, totally, in my heart.

Theo: I always thought of my shame as coming directly from my sexual abuse. I guess I shamed myself by thinking I should have been able to do something different than I did.

Kim: Shame gets its power from secrecy.

Theo: You're only as sick as your secrets, according to the twelve steps.

Kim: When you stay silent, shame becomes pervasive and toxic, and it will go underground. It can sit behind the scenes of all your actions. That is why it is so hard to identify, because it is behind everything really.

Theo: Well, I don't know scientifically what the chemical of shame is, but it's very toxic. Probably the most toxic chemical in our body.

Kim: I don't think we have any idea what the specific shame chemical is either. Yet the minute you speak about the shame, it lessens. It has less punch.

Theo: That certainly is my experience. I see it in all the people I meet who share their story, too.

Kim: When we stay focused on the trauma with relentless positivity, it takes the shame out of shame.

Theo: Yes. I would say that having the opportunity to speak about my experience in a mindful, loving, and caring way has helped me to learn to love myself. I can feel that shame no longer lives in my body the way it used to. When I first came out with all of this stuff in *Playing With Fire* nobody shamed me. Everyone received me and told me I had courage. Even if I wanted to go back to the earlier feelings of shame, I couldn't find them. So in that way I was receiving relentless positivity from the world around me, and when you came around it was just added to in spades, and explained so I could take more of it in. (*smiling*)

Kim: Definitely, the feedback you receive from people around you is overwhelmingly positive.

Theo: Sometimes, I feel guilty about receiving all that love.

Kim: Remember, guilt is different than shame. Sometimes, guilt can be helpful. Like it can keep us humble and mindful. It tells us that what we are thinking of doing, doing now, or did is wrong. It is helpful, because the awareness of it can curb our behaviour. When you get stuck in guilt, it sucks, of course, but without guilt many more hurtful things would likely occur. Shame is way worse, in that it has us believing we are worthless and rotten to the core.

Theo: I think sometimes I still get those two mixed up.

Kim: Many of us get guilt and shame mixed up. I think that guilt can easily trip the shame switch. I know it does for me. My need for perfectionism can have such a grip sometimes that when I feel guilty about something I did, even if it's really minor, I automatically feel like a "bad girl" all over again. It takes less than a millisecond for that to happen in my consciousness, and I have to be mindful to catch it.

Theo: I think that it is very confusing, because it's such a slippery slope. If someone has a better word for shame, let's find it. As soon as you say the word "shame," the look on people's face is disgust.

Kim: Maybe the word could be self-hate? I think some of us are actually addicted to beating ourselves up.

Theo: I used to be one of the worst at beating myself up. But at the end of the day, I know now that I was just sad, that's all, and I could never get to that sadness before we talked about it, right?

Kim: (*nodding*) I think that is why there's a part of you that's actually elated when you hear a "reveal," because you know first-hand what will happen to that person's shame once they speak it. You know it will *at least* start to lighten their load of those self-abusive feelings.

Theo: I've seen people lose the weight of the world off their shoulders from uttering the words, "Me, too." Grown men openly cry from relief when they say out loud that they are amongst the millions who'd previously kept these kinds of poisonous secrets secret. For me, the reveal with *Playing With Fire* was huge; it was a catalyst to begin to look at what it all really meant. Just announcing it didn't make me feel all that much better right away. I think all the supports weren't yet in place, and I really underestimated how many people were going to relate to the issue. I thought if I was just honest and genuine, how could people shame me for that? At the beginning with the media, it was fairly re-traumatizing; but it was a huge learning experience in creating some boundaries for myself. None of this learning, especially the self-awareness, would have happened if I hadn't revealed in the first place.

Kim: Is it critical for everyone to reveal to heal?

Theo: I think so, but not sure. What do you think?

Kim: The minute we can say "this hurts" or "this is hard" and become vulnerable, any shame that's attached to it changes and becomes less slithery, less insidious, less like a snake that could be in the tall grass at the edge of your yard, that could strike if ever threatened. I've thought about it a lot and I don't think a fully public reveal is always necessary though. What I'd certainly say, without any hesitation, is that at least acknowledging it to yourself and one or two trusted people is critical, so that you aren't suffering in silence.

Theo: Maybe the first reveal is like the process when a snake starts to shed its skin? Seeing yourself in a new light.

Kim: Mmhm.

Theo: I know that for so long I was all about justice. I was triggered constantly when the Graham James trial was on. Every time I would see a photo of myself beside a photo of James, I was triggered. I just wanted to wail on someone. I felt so alone and so lost in all the feelings at that time. I think I poured all my energy into "justice," because I didn't know what else to do with my anger.

Kim: That makes perfect sense. Seeking justice from a place of revenge is projected anger, trying desperately to escape all the shame, sadness, loneliness, contempt, and disgust underneath. It is a part of the process, I think, to want justice!

Theo: But I finally realized that getting stuck there in wanting justice wasn't serving me and it held my shame in place. I always say that the shame doesn't belong to me: it belongs to my abuser and it belongs to the justice system.

Kim: I wish shame didn't have to belong to anyone. I have heard you say many times that the "shame" survivors feel is not theirs: it belongs to the abuser. Part of that statement triggers me, I guess. You yourself have said that emotional pain is so bad you wouldn't wish it on your worst enemy. But that is what heaping shame on someone else is doing. It's saying the core of their essence is bad. And it might be. They might be psychopaths or sociopaths who really don't care one iota about other people and exist just to fill their own needs. But I think those situations are in the minority. Most times, it's wounded people acting out, and it's right that they feel *guilty* for what they are doing. But I don't think assigning shame is necessarily helpful.

Theo: So would it be more accurate to say that it's what was done to us that makes us feel ashamed, as if we're all of a sudden bad people?

Kim: I hear you saying that's what happens, and it's understandable, but believing you're a bad person just because something bad happens to you is not accurate.

Theo: Of course not, it's crap. We don't deserve that shame for a second! And since we have nothing to feel guilty about—we didn't do anything wrong—it's the "guilt" that should be squarely with the abuser.

Kim: Yeah. I think that's more appropriate. But you know, there are some people who don't feel any guilt. Some are completely incapable of feeling empathy.

Theo: What type of person wouldn't feel any guilt for being abusive?

Kim: Psychopaths and sometimes sociopaths. When an abuser abuses, we expect them to feel guilty (because they are), but sometimes they do and sometimes they don't. These kinds of people have brains that are actually wired differently from the rest of us.

Theo: What is the difference between a psychopath and a sociopath?

Kim: Psychopaths first. Typically, psychopaths are different even genetically. They are wired up in their brains in a unique way. They are impulsive, fearless, risk-seeking, and unable to understand social norms. They are highly predisposed to violence and enjoy things that would make the rest of us squirm, like seeing an animal in pain.

Theo: How many people are like this?

Kim: Different estimations say between 0.6 percent to 3 percent of our population could be psychopaths. But they're certainly not diagnosed this often, so it's hard to tell.

Theo: People have often referred to me as psycho.

Kim: That term gets thrown around without true understanding. Although you can be impulsive, and risk seeking, you are far too sensitive and empathetic for the term "psychopath" to be attributed to you. When people saw impulsive anger like you were famous for on the ice, it is understandable some might have called that behaviour psycho. It's certainly nothing close to the whole picture though. (*smiling*)

Theo: Whew, relief. One less label for me to worry about.

Kim: True psychopaths tend to be predatory and attack proactively rather than in reaction to confrontation. Think of the character Glenn Close played in *Fatal Attraction* or Heath Ledger's character in *The Dark Knight*.

Theo: Those two definitely don't define me. I was very reactive rather than premeditative with my anger.

Kim: I noticed how you used the past tense there. You are redefining yourself.

Theo: Cool. What about sociopaths?

Kim: Sociopaths also have different brains, but it seems that they aren't necessarily born that way. Most sociopaths have terrible upbringings, and trauma is almost always a part of their history. They can be conniving and deceitful, and despite their charismatic and charming outward appearance, they lack sincerity. They don't lack a moral compass, like psychopaths; it's just that their moral compass is significantly skewed. And they often have very high IQs. They're not always dangerous, but it would be really tough to live with one.

Theo: Makes me think of the character Michael Douglas played in the movie *Wall Street*.

Kim: Yup, there's a sociopath. Also Leonardo DiCaprio in *Wolf of Wall Street*.

Theo: Maybe there's something about Wall Street. (*laughing*)

Kim: Interesting you say that. There is a lot written about the high incidence of successful CEOs and stockbrokers having sociopathic behaviour. Sociopaths do have a sense of right and wrong, but as I said, it's off-kilter, and what's hardest to understand is that sometimes they just don't care, because it's all about them.

Theo: When I think about it, it makes me wonder if Graham James was a sociopath.

Kim: Would it make it easier for you if he were diagnosed that way?

Theo: No, it wouldn't.

Kim: Can you expand on that a little?

Theo: I really don't care less what the fuck he is, because he doesn't have control of my life anymore.

Kim: He certainly doesn't. It's hard to talk about such intense things.

Theo: I lived with the shame of it for so long, that when I talk about it now, the intensity is much less than when it was a secret.

Kim: (*heavy sigh*) It is important for therapists and friend of survivors to remember that when they listen to another person's suffering they need to have some detachment from it. But of course that has to be balanced with empathy. It is a fine line. We don't want to lose the connection, but we don't want to lose ourselves in the other person's pain, either.

Theo: The more we talk about these things, the easier it gets.

Kim: Mmhm. I'm glad it's getting easier. (*smiling gently*)

Theo: Where do pedophiles come into the mix of these predators?

Kim: A pedophile is someone who is sexually attracted to children who have not entered puberty. This is technically identified as a mental illness. And some pedophiles have that disorder by itself, but others have pedophilia combined with being a sociopath or a psychopath.

Theo: I guess the plain old pedophile is less dangerous?

Kim: They're all dangerous. Those who have pedophilia alone, however, may have some possibility for some rehabilitation. The reason for that is they'd be more likely to feel some guilt.

Theo: I've heard the term "ephebophile" used to describe Graham James.

Kim: That is an adult who is sexually attracted to kids who are in their mid-to-late teens. This might be hard to hear, but that is not considered abnormal by mental health standards. That doesn't make it any less wrong or any less child abusive.

Theo: Sick fucks.

Kim: You asked me if I thought Graham James was a sociopath. Why did you pick that one from the possibilities?

Theo: I don't know. He did some nice things for people, but I don't know if that was one hundred percent part of the calculated strategy to lure boys in or not. I know he was guilty of premeditated sexual abuse. I know he manipulated the hell out of a lot of people to get what he wanted. But I might never know the whole story.

Kim: You might never know, and that's where your own work comes in. The more detached you are from feeling ashamed from those events, the better for you. The easier you'll sleep. And the more you can get on with your life.

Theo: I know that, in my case, Graham James was a pedophile, or technically an ephebophile, because there were several of us around that same age that we know about.

Kim: Many adults sexually abuse kids and are not technically classified as pedophiles. It can all be so confusing.

Theo: What do you mean?

Kim: In the mainstream, the word "pedophile" tends to be used to describe all child sexual abuse offenders, but this is problematic for researchers. The difference is that there are exclusive pedophiles (or "true pedophiles" who only get turned on by children) and there are child molesters who are "non-exclusive" sex offenders who hurt children sexually, but who are also attracted to adults.

Theo: Hmm.

Kim: Most of the people who molest children are non-exclusives. But the ones who are exclusives offend more often, have a greater number of victims, and are most likely to re-offend after being in jail.[lxxvi]

Theo: I think Graham James was a true pedophile.

Kim: When pressed, incarcerated non-exclusive child molesters often state that behind their crimes were stress, marital problems, and the unavailability of an adult partner ... not just sexual urges. And incest is a really tough one to get your mind around, 'cause the abusers have close relationships with these kids. And then sometimes, maybe often, power and control can be more of a motivator than any attraction. My stomach is feeling a little sick.

Theo: Whatever the label or definition or what anyone believes is the rationale, it's wrong and the outcome is devastating for the survivor.

Kim: No question. All of this is child abuse, it's all against the law. But from understanding the various intentions and pathologies of the offender, it allows us to consider if there are even remote possibilities for rehabilitation.

Theo: (*big exhale*) When we get abused and feel ashamed of ourselves as human beings, it is never good. It's just wrong and it has to stop.

Kim: I know. It's destructive; it corrodes a person's soul. That's the emotional pain you're talking about. And you're right, the responsibility lies totally with the abuser.

Theo: Yeah.

Kim: You know, I've heard there are self-help groups for true pedophiles or "exclusives." It works like AA in that those who attend try to get support so they don't hurt kids. Their guilt is working for them I guess, as a motivation to try to change or at least curb their behaviour.

Theo: I don't know what to say about that.

Kim: I am glad they're trying. And I hope their conversations and mutual supports do prevent more kids from being hurt.

Theo: Hmm. Do you remember when Bob wrote that blog about compassion for the abuser?[lxxvii]

Kim: Yep.

Theo: The response to that blog was a gong show.

Kim: About ninety percent of the people who responded received the intent, but it definitely triggered a few people who were still suffering! The point of the blog was that working toward compassion is actually helpful to the person who was abused. It wasn't about forgiving the abuser for the pain inflicted. What I got out of people's responses is that there is a lot of confusion between developing compassion and holding the person accountable for their offence.

Theo: It certainly got people talking, and that was the goal.

Kim: One person responded with a statement that I will never forget. She basically said how hell would freeze over before she would have any humane thoughts toward a person who had obviously hurt her, and then said, "'Forgiveness' is for those who forget to put ketchup on your burger."

Theo: I remember responding with the comment, "and so the cycle of abuse continues."

Kim: Your comment came from a place of being triggered, didn't it?

Theo: It did. I reacted.

Kim: What was the trigger?

Theo: I think the fact that she was so critical in her response. It was a personal attack. The intention of the blog discussion was so clearly to help people and she completely missed that. I felt hurt. So I reacted. Hurt people hurt people. I'm sorry if anyone was offended by my response, but I see people who've been hurt throwing out their shit on others quite a lot. I've been there. I recognize it. I don't like it that some of that is still in me. I've obviously got more skin to shed.

Kim: This is how insidious shame is. It can move people from a place of hurt to retaliation. It can happen unknowingly.

Theo: Is retaliation a learned response? I think that it is.

Kim: I think some people internalize their shame and some externalize it. I often say that externalizers "throw up" their shame all over everyone. It's not that they don't care about others; they just have to get it out.

Theo: The world is full of retaliation. We see it on TV every day, at school, from our parents … Think about bullies.

Kim: I was definitely affected by bullies. When I was in grade one, I had this winter coat that my mom had bought for me. I loved that coat: it was black and white fake fur. The first day I wore it to school, a boy called me skunk and threw a slice of tomato at me, staining my coat red. I was six at the time and it devastated me. I totally took it personally. Then in grade two, another boy told me I was fat, hairy, and ugly. It caught on and from that day, I was labelled as ugly. I truly believed it. And based on that experience, when I was around ten years old I consciously decided that I would do my best to be as smart and nice as possible to make up for it.

Theo: But you still felt ugly.

Kim: Of course. The reason I'm sharing this as an example is to show how bullying can affect our long-term self-perception.

Theo: See the damage that bullies cause? You didn't know back then that they were only saying those things because they felt insecure themselves.

Kim: Of course not. I sure know it now. Consciously. But the implicit memory has kind of stuck. It really does speak to why bullying behaviour should be prevented as early as possible. We all deserve to grow up thinking of ourselves as lovable and capable.

Theo: I am with you on that. Bullying is a form of abuse. I was a bully. And it's something that I'm working on. But I'm sure glad I wasn't the guy who called you a skunk. I hope he feels guilty! (*little laugh*)

Kim: I actually "creeped" him on Facebook a little while ago, (I'm obviously still thinking about it), and for profession he put "Porn star"! Oops, just got caught myself retaliating. I do wonder how he turned out though. Sometimes bullies turn out growing up into big softies.

Theo: Porn star! That's something I haven't done. (*sound in between a snort and a chuckle*)

Kim: Would you feel guilty if you had?

Theo: No. Just never got the offer! (*making a goofy face*)

Kim: (*rolling her eyes*) We don't have to do everything in one lifetime.

Theo: (*nodding*) I guess it would help bullies to get some compassion too .... You talk to me about compassion all the time. At first, I think it was hard for me to think about, just like it was for that woman who commented on the blog, but now it is easier to get there.

Kim: Neither compassion nor forgiveness require that you absolve the other person of their wrongdoing. It is necessary to hold them accountable for their behaviour.

Theo: Okay, so what is the real difference between compassion and forgiveness?

Kim: This is a tough topic, especially when it comes to abuse. But here is my go at defining the difference. To me, "forgiveness" means that we must be ready to let go of our anger and resentment toward someone or something. The act of compassion, however, is a mindset. The mindset is having the desire, however small, that all people's suffering be alleviated, even the abuser's. Both in compassion and in forgiveness, we understand that the abusers are fully responsible for their actions. It doesn't mean that we justify their behaviour at all. By being compassionate, we are making space for remembering that we are all human beings. And forgiveness is the letting go of our anger and resentment.

Theo: At the end of the day, this whole therapy process is an inside job. And each of us goes through this process in our own way. We're all trying to get to self-forgiveness first before anything else. But that's not an easy task, because it's so hard-wired into us. I think that relentless positivity stuff is really important.

Kim: How do you start accepting the positives?

Theo: The mindset of willingness has to come first. Then, you shut out all the useless negative noise around you and you go through the layers of the onion, day by day, as they come up.

Kim: Mmhm.

Theo: I think understanding and thinking about the abuser as another hurting person helps with compassion (like you say it's a mindset); whereas, if you ever get to forgiveness it is emotional heart-based work.

Kim: Sometimes you can feel both, or mistake one for the other, and that is why I think people confuse them.

Theo: How do you hold a whole bunch of conflicting feelings inside at the same time? Hatred, shame, love, compassion, forgiveness … It seems like they are not compatible.

Kim: That is what people don't understand; it is possible to feel all of those things at the same time. I remember once I was talking with a therapy friend and it probably sounded like I was complaining about something I was experiencing. I live in Victoria, British Columbia, and we were sitting overlooking the ocean. He stopped me in the middle of my blah, blah, blah, and said, "I want you to look out the window and tell me what you see."

What I saw was the beauty and magnificence of the nature around me. I described that to him and he said, "You see, the negative stuff and the positive stuff coexist all the time. It's what you choose to look at in the moment that dictates how you feel."

That experience was a turning point for me and I try to remember it every time I'm feeling shitty.

Theo: Whenever I'm feeling shitty about myself, I think it's the shame underneath that's coming through, the shame I was trying so hard to annihilate with addiction.

Kim: So what gets you through it now?

Theo: I keep remembering that vulnerability is the antidote to shame. At least it stops me from feeling angry. And I'm hearing what you're talking about, that positives and negatives exist at the same time, together. That's helpful too.

Kim: I agree with you that vulnerability is the key to deflating the power of shame. Vulnerability also helps you feel connected to another person, because you're letting your heart open. Ultimately, shame is the fear of disconnection, rejection, and isolation. Sharing with someone connects you.

Theo: Some shame shit still hangs around and affects my behaviour.

Kim: That's understandable.

Theo: I still hate it when people even wish me, "Happy birthday." When I was young, my mom's religion said birthdays aren't worth celebrating, so I must have really taken that message to heart, like I didn't deserve to have one. At some level, I guess, I still don't think I deserve one. Presents on my actual birthday are tough to receive. Other days, I definitely have less problems with them.

Kim: Right. I remember Bob was sensitive to this when he wanted to give you a Montreal Canadiens golf tee he'd found in his pocket, and he asked if you minded getting a super cool meaningful gift before he gave it. You said sure, 'cause it wasn't your birthday.

Theo: He goes on and on about the fucking Canadiens! (*smiling in jest*)

Kim: Hockey is important to some people. Didn't you know that?

Theo: (*rolling his eyes*)

Kim: When shame is predominant, even close relationships can feel unrewarding. We feel like frauds, waiting to be discovered, believing that anyone who loves us will eventually see how defective we are. "If only they knew." Expecting that the next rejection is waiting just around the corner.

Theo: I think for me, I sabotaged many relationships because of those underlying beliefs you just described.

Kim: I think that is true for all of us, me included. My "bad girl syndrome" still doesn't like having people angry with me, or disappointed in me.

Theo: I think I bought into the idea that I was a "bad boy." But all the "bad" things I did just made me feel more bad about myself. Like a big pile of shit. One of the reasons I liked to hang out with strippers, hookers, and junkies was because we could all relate. But the more I did that stuff, the more I'd hurt the people I cared about, so the more ashamed I felt. I created my own personal cycle of hell, like a hamster on a treadmill. Only I guess hamsters must not feel so bad being stuck there. For humans, it sucks.

Kim: This is the hole that so many of us dig ourselves into! When we damage a close relationship, shame can get in the way of us taking responsibility for our role in that damage. Or, at the other extreme, it can result in us taking all the responsibility for the rupture. Shame interferes with the objectivity of any conflict and it interferes with the potential for true intimacy.

Theo: I am getting better at it, but it used to be so hard for me to say I was sorry. It wasn't that I didn't feel bad about stuff I did; I just didn't know how to express it really.

Kim: What is typical for me is to say, "I'm sorry," even when it isn't my fault.

Theo: Very Canadian of you. (*smiling*)

Kim: Typical for someone who feels like a "bad girl," eh.

Theo: I think I'm better able to stick with my feelings now, so finding the words to say I'm sorry is becoming a bit easier. I didn't always know what I was really sorry for before, because I was just trying to survive and figure out what the truth was. Figuring out my thoughts was hard enough, but explaining my feelings? That made me scared.

Kim: (*nodding*) That's really honest. When you dissociate as a coping strategy, it makes it harder and harder to find your feelings. And you can't really apologize with sincerity unless you connect with your feelings.

Theo: Back in the day when I think I was the hardest to live with, instead of listening to the pain enough to get to the point of apologizing, I would have rather soothed myself with more booze and cocaine. I remember I'd be awake for six or seven days in a row, just shit-faced, and then pass out while still on cocaine, and that was the only real escape. Addiction felt like the only way I could survive without going crazy.

Kim: Do you still have shame about addiction?

Theo: I still have a few addictions that interfere with my path toward wellness. Food, gambling, smoking, and issues around sex continue to stand out.

Kim: Thanks for sharing.

Theo: Reminds me of that movie.

Kim: Yep. *Thanks for Sharing* was the name of the movie on sex addiction we saw when you were visiting us in Victoria. Have you anything to say about that topic?

Theo: Got a while? On second thought, let me go have a dart [a cigarette].

Kim: Ha. I'll wait.

Theo: (*having two puffs outside and coming right back*)

Kim: Sure you want to talk about it?

Theo: Well, drugs and alcohol, they don't have an allure for me anymore.

I see them for what they are. I'll always be an alcoholic, because I'm made that way, but I know one hundred times over I am better off without it, and have enough support around me that avoiding them isn't the huge deal it used to be.

Kim: But sex?

Theo: Well, it's sex. I don't think we ever lose our interest in that. Hope not. (*smiling*)

Kim: Sex is curious. When would you say a sex addiction is different from a sex drive?

Theo: When it becomes something that negatively interferes with your life, and you can't seem to control it. When there are negative consequences. Like all addictions, that's when it's probably an issue.

Kim: When sex becomes more of a priority than friends and family and work, it's said the compulsion is out of control. The full spectrum of sex addiction includes the need to "compulsively" engage in masturbation, sexual relationships, pornography, prostitution, exhibitionism, voyeurism, indecent phone calls, or cybersex, and in severe cases, it can extend to child molesting, incest, and rape.

Theo: I do not do all of those. (*looking serious*) I think there's also an opposite extreme though too—people who are sexually anorexic. Those are people who avoid sex completely, just like people who starve themselves.

Kim: I've heard of that. When you deprive yourself of sex with that level of fierce control, it can help you to feel defended from more hurt. But any extremes aren't healthy. Just like addictions, extreme behaviours are coping strategies.

Theo: All these behaviours seem to have shame attached.

Kim: Why do you think our society so often associates shame with sex?

Theo: Just look at the church. I think anyone over forty can remember hearing masturbation will make you go blind and give you hairy palms. There is a complete contradiction between the church and evolution. One is telling us that sex needs to be monogamous in an exclusive, loving, caring relationship; but we are still animals! Herein lies the struggle we all have with spirituality, because sex is a spiritual experience when you are connected to somebody. The church has flipped it around and made it bad.

Kim: That reminds me of a story my amazing Irish friend told me. What a great spirit she has! Anyway, she grew up in Ireland when the schools were all run by the Catholic Church. Before she told this story she said she'd prefer to have a drink in her hand to tell it, because there are some things she's very shy about. But she braved it anyway and told me what the nuns had told them in their sex education class. Which she said was very, very limited. In her thick Irish accent (*imitating her friend's Irish accent*) she said, "It didn't look like they knew a whole lot about it themselves."

Theo: That's a great accent!

Kim: Do you want to hear what those nuns told them?

Theo: Of course! (*laughing*)

Kim: (*back in her Irish accent*) "Anyway, we were told that if we girls were ever to touch ourselves in private places, as in masturbation, we would end up smelling like rotten fish. Needless to say I asked my parents who said that this was not true. But in the meantime, the boys who also had a very naïve sex education class were told that if they were to touch themselves in private places they would go blind. So one day the boys and the girls were put into a big room and we were all allowed to ask any questions from either the priest or the nun. It was asked again if it was really true, that the boys would go blind and the girls would smell like rotten fish if they touched themselves in private places. And the nun and the priest both agreed that yes it was true, and all the boys and girls were quietly aghast ... But one of the boys in the back raised his hand and asked the sister, 'But sure, Sister, isn't that alright? Even if the boy goes blind, if the girl smells like rotten fish, he'd still be able to find her.'"

Theo: What a shit disturber! (*big laugh*)

Kim: And she added, "And that was the end of that class, for a long time."

Theo: Wild what shit the Church got away with telling us, eh. Think it's linked to the amount of alcohol the Irish drink today?

Kim: No idea. But when I asked my friend if I could share her story to make a point, she said over her dead body can I mention what county she's from or the shit disturber boy's name, 'cause that event forty-five years ago is still a case for embarrassment. Shame sticks around a long time.

Theo: Well, thank her for her courage to let you tell it at all, and for allowing you to borrow her excellent accent!

Kim: Yessiree, shaming and sex go way back.

Theo: That shit disturber had a lot of courage!

Kim: (*grinning*) I have a very honest friend who once said that when he was a little boy he used to play his penis like a guitar. His mom noticed him once in the bath and told him, "It's yours; you can play with it if you want. Just don't play that guitar in public," as if it wasn't such a big deal. He claims that attitude saved him years of worry.

Theo: Ha. That is fucking hilarious. (*laughing*)

Kim: So how about you? At your home growing up, did you ever talk about that kind of thing?

Theo: Are you kidding? I'm from Russell, Manitoba. No one touches themselves on the prairies … Or at least no one talks about it.

Kim: I know it. I am from the prairies too.

Theo: Just saying. We're all a product of our upbringing.

Kim: But masturbation, ages ago, was accepted as normal. Pictures of men masturbating are found on prehistoric rock paintings all around the world. Wikipedia has tons of information about this stuff. I remember it mentioned that Ancient Egyptians believed the universe was created by one of their gods—Atum—when he masturbated to ejaculation. And that the heights of the ebbs and flows of the Nile river are dependent on how often he does it. The Indian Hindu text the Kama Sutra teaches best practices …

Theo: How do you know this shit?

Kim: When it comes to shame, I want to know what's at the bottom of it, and you can find a lot on the Internet.

Theo: Well thinking of people in history who had lots of orgies, I can think of the Greeks and the Romans. It's pretty common knowledge they were all over it. (*smiling*)

Kim: But in more modern history the guilt trips about masturbation were really widespread throughout our culture; it wasn't just the church. Even before the Victorian Age, people really believed that doing it would make you very sick. Doctors were sure masturbation caused a whole slew of diseases, including acne, blindness, epilepsy, definitely insanity, and even suicide … Prominent thinkers like Immanuel Kant and Voltaire openly warned against it. One theory was that if people ate less red meat or other foods that were "suspected" to make them sexually aroused, and only ate really bland foods, that it would decrease their urges to masturbate.

Theo: What?

Kim: Here's the weird thing, that theory was promoted by two outspoken masturbation haters, Dr. John Harvey Kellogg and Reverend Sylvester Graham.

Theo: And?

Kim: Those are the inventors of Corn Flakes and Graham Crackers.

Theo: No shit?

Kim: I really investigated this. Now you can think about that every time you eat breakfast and have S'Mores. (*smiling*)

Theo: Thanks. Good reason to change diets.

Kim: Can I say more about this, or is it upsetting your stomach at all?

Theo: I'm tough, but I don't talk about this every day.

Kim: I learned Dr. Kellogg was a legitimate enemy of masturbation; he didn't just invent cornflakes to make money. As a doctor, he wrote about how masturbation could actually kill you, and if not physically, then morally. To "help" patients who "suffered" from it a lot (according to who, I don't know), he prescribed acid on clitorises, and the suturing of the ends of penises with wire so they couldn't get erect.

Theo: Jesus!

Kim: Awful to think about, eh. Hey, do you know why circumcision was so widely adopted in the US and the UK? At least part of it was because of its "believed" preventative effect against masturbation. And those chastity belts? They were made for both women and men, and not only to protect the users from other people.

Theo: To protect them from touching themselves? This is crazy shit you're talking about.

Kim: There's way more. The earliest Boy Scout manual from 1914 specifically warned boys against the dangers of masturbation, and the Girl Guides book did too! Good girls don't touch there, that kind of thing.

Theo: Lady Baden Powell specifically told them not to masturbate in a Girl Guides manual? That's unbelievable. I gotta look that up. (*getting out his iPhone*) I'll just google it: "girl guides ... masturbation." (*waiting five seconds*) Holy shit! Seems like shame must be decreasing a little since then ... there's at least a hundred sites that are now teaching them how to do it!

Kim: That's a good point. The people who associate masturbation with shame the most, aside from the stricter religions, are middle-aged to older people who bought into these former beliefs. Today, there are at least two government-run health agencies in Europe that are actually openly promoting it to teenagers for mental health reasons. One of the slogans I read all over the Internet especially the UK is, "An orgasm a day keeps the doctor away."

Theo: (*laughing*) Are you recommending it?

Kim: I wasn't saying that. (*a little embarrassed*) Just noticing the changing of attitudes. Professionally, what I know is that masturbation is normal and what I believe is that it's definitely not healthy to associate shame with it.

Theo: I haven't talked this much about masturbation in my whole life.

Kim: Not many people have. What do you think helps us get past some of the shame around sex?

Theo: I'm not ashamed about it.

Kim: Really? I have to say I'm not so comfortable with the topic; it ties perfectly into my "bad girl" thing. So back to the topic of sex addiction. What about it is a recurring problem in your life?

Theo: Well, when you put it like that ... Well, I like it. So I feel I need to have it.

Kim: And ... that sounds like most people, at least at some points in their lives. (*laughing*) Maybe not all menopausal women, perhaps; sex drive for everyone is really variable and complex and depends a lot on changes in hormones. But what you say sounds like a lot of people a lot of the time ...

Theo: There is a sexual component to almost everything. My first sexual experience was with a pedophile. What does that tell you? That should say a lot. Most people's first sexual experience is horrible.

Kim: Say more.

Theo: It certainly explains a lot of the experimentation after the fact. The shame attached to it is overwhelming.

Kim: I notice you're not even including the word abuse just there. The omission suggests a degree of shame.

Theo: I'm thinking back to my longest-term relationships ...

Kim: Would you say it's accurate that a loving connection was the goal behind almost all of your actions, at the beginning of all your long-term relationships?

Theo: I'm not sure I have always used sex to express my connection in the healthiest way. I sometimes did it 'cause I felt I needed to, not always because the woman I was with was in a healthy relationship with me.

Kim: Wow. When do you feel most connected to people? To those who are closest to you?

Theo: What's sad, and we've been talking about this, is that sometimes I feel most connected with my significant other when I'm verbally fighting. Not a good habit, eh. In past relationships with old girlfriends or wives—I'm embarrassed to say—when we weren't in conflict or having sex, there didn't always seem like there was much of a relationship.

Kim: Wow, that's honesty. People who come from dysfunctional backgrounds are vulnerable to seduction, so they might enter into relationships quickly, without discernment. Because it's important to differentiate between someone saying, "I admire you," meaning they respect your essence on the inside, and "I admire you," meaning they want to sleep with you. When you're feeling unlovable, it's easy to misinterpret flattery and kindness as true love.

Theo: It wasn't just me coming from dysfunctional families. All of my exes had their traumas too. And having those experiences in common, even if we didn't talk about them, explains a lot about why we got together, right?

Kim: Yep. Sometimes it takes a while to recognize those patterns.

Theo: I am now trying to think of sex as a spiritual connection with another person. I think that's beautiful, and way better than feeling shame in it. It takes some undoing of my original beliefs, though—about how you have to be married to one person your whole life and *only* be doing it to have kids—to have a guilt-free sexual connection. How rare is that?

Kim: Spiritual connection is great, but based on what I know about you neurochemically, I'm wondering if you are not also craving the intensity aspect that can come with sex.

Theo: Hmm.

Kim: When you come from a family where there is insecure attachment and you meet someone and have a lot of feelings, all of a sudden, it's easy to confuse intensity with intimacy. Aside from the physical arousal, if there is accompanying high drama, betrayal, and passionate make-up sessions, this is not what intimacy is about, but it is intensity. Intensity can be addictive.

Theo: Ooph. (*exhaling*) You nailed it. I think a lot of people in dysfunctional relationships, especially those who've been in sexual abuse situations, can relate to this.

Kim: The intensity is higher when there's betrayal.

Theo: 'Cause you know it's wrong.

Kim: When trust is breached, you're left feeling abandoned. Abandonment is at the heart of addictions. This is partly why sexual abuse is so damaging, because it often involves a deep level of betrayal.

Theo: Graham James was a mind fuck. He was in charge of taking care of me and the abuse was definitely a betrayal.

Kim: And then add in the sexual component and it totally messes with your mind.

Theo: Because I had orgasms, and I hadn't been with girls in that way, it's only logical I'd worry I was part gay back then. That part made me sick. And it was never a question with attraction, I certainly to God never found him attractive. That thought disgusts me. I love women.

Kim: I understand that.

Theo: I know there are some people who think most of the child molesters do it because they are gay. I gotta say that is bullshit. Child molesters do it because they are sick. I know homosexual men are not any more likely to abuse children than heterosexual men are. Just want to be clear. Homosexuals in our society have faced enough trauma; let's not make it worse by believing their gender preference makes them hurt children. That belief is out there, but I don't buy it. I think it's been made up by anti-gay activists to make heterosexuality look like more of a healthier choice—as if it's a choice ...

Kim: I'm really glad you brought up that myth. 'Cause you're right. Statistically, homosexual men are not any more likely to sexually abuse children than heterosexual men. This position is fully backed up by the American Psychological Association and many other objective sources. As I have said before, there are two kinds of child molesters out there. True pedophiles are only attracted to children, and it's often irrespective of the child's gender. According to the literature, non-exclusive child molesters also find adults attractive; they claim they primarily abuse children only when confronted with stressful situations. Of these non-exclusive pedophiles, though, a higher percentage of them are actually heterosexual in their adult relationships.

Theo: Interesting how what's real and what's myth is often reversed, eh.

Kim: Yep. Moral of that story, according to statistics, is that the highest percentage of child molesters know the children they abuse quite well. The range I've found is that between 80 and 95 percent of childhood sexual abuse happens with people who are already well known to the family. So it's important to talk with our kids about boundaries and feeling safe to tell an adult they trust if anything happens that makes them uncomfortable.

Theo: Absolutely. It just shouldn't ever happen.

Kim: Well, I know something to make it easier to talk about sex.

Theo: What's that?

Kim: Talking about the physiology of the sexual response. The physiology of sex has a profound impact on anyone's psyche, but using scientific terms helps to take the emotion out of the conversation.

Theo: Okay, tell me about sex on the brain. What's goes on up there? (*pointing to his head*) when something's going on down there? (*catching himself and not pointing*)

Kim: Ha! Well, sex is pleasure! It has to be, to ensure that our species survives. If we didn't experience pleasure when having sex, procreation wouldn't continue as easily. So at a very basic level, the chemistry of the sexual arousal response is dopamine—the "I gotta have it!" neurochemical.

Theo: I get the "I gotta have it" part.

Kim: The next chemical involved in the sexual response is oxytocin. This is the same chemistry that is released when parents and babies gleam and beam at each other. Oxytocin surges briefly after climax, even if you don't like the person you're having sex with. Oxytocin is part of the chemistry of bonding.

Theo: I've heard some monkeys do it with all the other monkeys around them to bond as a big group.

Kim: Yep. But as humans we wouldn't get away with that. (*rolling her eyes and shaking her head*)

Theo: The point of what you're saying is that when you orgasm, you bond yourself to the person you're with, right?

Kim: So to speak. Chemically, but not necessarily emotionally. If orgasm tightly bonded lovers, we would never see any one-night stands. If lovers wish to strengthen their emotional bonds, they are likely to make more progress with daily skin-to-skin contact, gentle stroking, and gentle intercourse. This kind of affectionate, generous contact produces way more oxytocin and soothes the regions of the brain that need to relax in order for us to bond more deeply.

Theo: Hmm.

Kim: The occasional blast of oxytocin at orgasm, which drops soon afterward (along with the dopamine), probably isn't as reliable a bonding mechanism. When dopamine drops, you register your mate as less rewarding, even if your emotional brain is still being dowsed with oxytocin. We need the right levels of both dopamine and oxytocin for that loving feeling to create sustained intimacy.

Theo: Would that love chemistry be very different from the chemistry during sexual abuse?

Kim: That's a loaded question. I guess at some level, chemically, whoever you have an orgasm with does share a small dopamine/oxytocin hit with you, even if that isn't at all what you wanted. That's why it can leave some people really confused.

Theo: (*starting to move in his chair with discomfort*) It is so interesting how I'm connecting to feelings of shame even as we talk about this. A perfect example of someone who has it right is the chick from *Sex and the City*.

Kim: As in Kim Cattrall? What was it about her that makes you say she's got it right?

Theo: She doesn't seem to associate sex with shame at all. The rest of us always listen to the noise, because we don't feel good enough or lovable. It is us, I mean me, that keeps the cycle of shame alive in my own mind. I've gotta change my beliefs about sex being so shameful. This isn't how I want to feel. I am forty-six years old and I want to have deeper connections in my relationships.

Kim: Just verbalizing that intention helps the old patterns of belief to change.

Theo: I agree.

Kim: You asked about the neurochemical effect of sexual abuse. I had to think about that, but I've got a start on it now. The chemistry in each person's brain is likely different in every individual case of abuse. It would be affected by the nature of their relationship with the abuser, the intensity of the sexual response, the age of the child or teenager, the amount of violence, secrecy, dissociation, lots of things.

Theo: Well, for me the experience was terrifying. I would dissociate for the majority of the time and then orgasm.

Kim: In my understanding, that kind of experience would wire together terror with pleasure. That is very intense.

Theo: We've talked many times about my addiction to intensity. You know, in the last year, I went to speak at and participate in a healing circle for men who'd been sexually abused. That kind of thing doesn't happen all that much, and it was powerful. All these men were openly sharing and asking questions; trying to understand what the hell had happened to them. And there were a lot of tears, too.

One guy, toward the end, asked me a question that stopped everyone in their tracks. He said, "Why is it that the orgasms when you're being abused feel so much more intense?"

You could have heard a pin drop, and probably twenty guys in the room thought, "Oh, fuck, why the hell did he have to ask that?"

I didn't know what to say, but now I'm thinking it has a lot to do with what you're talking about. When you're over-the-top terrified and all your senses are alert, when you know it's wrong and a secret, and it's still physically arousing, maybe the whole thing is just super intense from every perspective, according to your nervous system? Does that make sense?

Kim: Wow. For sure. That it's an incredible insight you just had. Dissociation is the highest form of terror possible. The same intensity seeking that you crave in other addictions can also be a component of your sexual addiction. If someone repeatedly wires their early sexual pleasure with fear, it could easily leave them feeling potentially sexually dissatisfied if that same intensity wasn't always available. Fear and sex can definitely get wired together in the brain.

Theo: (*shaking his head*) That is such an aha for me. It explains why I have been attracted to the same high-risk patterns and types of partners over and over again.

Kim: When there is a sexual relationship that involves hierarchies of power and betrayal, the intensity can be even more enhanced. All of this together, especially if it happens over and over, may make you want to find other ways to match that intensity. Not necessarily that specific activity, but that extremely high level of intensity. Intensity of that kind seems like a barrier to real intimacy though. What do you think?

Theo: I think this is all overwhelming. But it explains a lot about my sexual escapades. Alcohol, cocaine, and sex mixed together was what I went after. Then I'd hit the repeat button, over and over again. The sex was the chase and the danger. The intensity of the sex mixed together with the alcohol and cocaine was insane. Cocaine gave me focus, alcohol made me emotionally available, and dangerous sex was the intensity. What a mixture. Fucking dangerous game to play.

Kim: Even the snakes would prefer to go hide under a rock.

Theo: I am starting to see these compulsive-addictive trends in my relationships, not just in my addictions to booze and drugs. I never before thought of myself as being addicted to intense relationships.

Kim: When we get into relationships that replicate the qualities of an earlier abusive relationship, these are called trauma bonds. It is a common outcome of childhood abuse that, again, is driven by implicit memory and triggered unconsciously.

Theo: This is common with women who are always attracted to abusive men, right? Their friends go nuts watching them make these choices over and over again.

Kim: Yep. Another uncomfortable topic to think about is how some people can actually grow closer to their abuser in the face of trauma. That in and of itself creates such tremendous confusion for the survivor.

Theo: I guess that would be especially difficult if you loved your abuser. That is why I think incest would be so bad.

Kim: Yes, I would expect that the closer the relationship, the greater the inner conflict a person would experience. I read somewhere that 60 percent of all sex addicts were sexually abused as children. Sex addicts seem to confuse sex with love, but love rarely, if ever, has anything to do with the addiction.

Theo: That must be difficult to understand when you don't have a different reference point in your experience.

Kim: For sure, especially for little kids who wouldn't have a clue what's appropriate and what's not. And then later in life, it is difficult for them to be attracted to someone who is not familiar at least in some way.

Theo: Ugh. (*wrinkling up his nose and squinting his eyes in disgust*)

Kim: Sometimes we don't always remember sexual abuse events. Especially if they happened in infancy. I had a client who was sexually abused as an infant. She had no clear recall memories, but had enough convincing clues from implicit memory that still got triggered as an adult. She was bothered by different sensations, textures, and specific smells. She didn't seem to associate her sexual abuse with terror (she wouldn't have had any clue what was going on). But what she seems to have picked up on the most was the deep guilt experienced by her abuser. She was pretty sure he was a family member, and it's easy to speculate he'd have shown tremendous nervousness and guilt about what he was doing. She likely picked up on all his nonverbal communication and encoded it into her implicit memory. So as an infant, she likely associated sexual pleasure with the overarching feeling that was in the room at the time: intense anxiety and shame. Little wonder she grew up to feel uncomfortable with sex, even though it felt good physically. Totally different experience from yours, but similar in that what happened years and years ago still affects her adult relationships today.

Theo: It's all fucked up, isn't it?

Kim: She's done a lot of work around it. Happy to say she ended up finding someone awesome who loves her for the whole picture of who she is.

Theo: (*exhaling*) Recovery from trauma can happen.

Kim: It certainly doesn't always end up that way, eh. Sometimes an abused child's needs for love, nurturance, affection, and attention may never be met. As a survival strategy, some children learn to engage sexually in an attempt to meet their basic needs. Some continue to behave in a seductive manner in an attempt to gain favours. They may also become promiscuous or indiscriminate in their choice of sexual partners just because it's what they know.

Theo: I've seen that quite a bit. It sounds a bit like me.

Kim: Many children experience pain, numbness, and dissociation at the time of the abuse. But research is showing that children are physiologically capable of experiencing sensations of arousal and orgasm. So it's natural to experience sensations of arousal when one is sexually stimulated, even when it's not consensual. What I'm hoping to convey is that the physiological responses we have to pleasure don't get turned off just because it's in a traumatizing context. And I hope that hearing this can somehow reduce confusion and shame.

Theo: You'd mentioned even super young children experience sexual pleasure. I didn't know that was physiologically possible.

Kim: I was shocked too. But, according to my research, even babies can feel some amount of pleasure from genital touching; it is wired into us. Four-dimensional ultrasound shows that baby boys experience erections as early as seventeen weeks after conception. Our sexual responses are natural, and our body is designed to be a source of pleasure. As I've said, what becomes confusing is when a baby connects those feelings of pleasure together with shame, abandonment, disgust, or pain. These unnatural combinations will wire together as an experience into implicit memory. This could potentially create layers of confusion during future sexual activity.

Theo: Ah, man. (*rubbing his face*) I know you're watching me rub my face, but I'm staying with you though.

Kim: Awesome attunement. It's important to note that the natural sensual pleasures experienced by babies and young children are self-generated, created by touching themselves. What is not natural is when these sensations are intentionally created by others. So when pleasure of that kind is received in the context of an interaction with an abuser, that would be a developmentally foreign experience to the baby.

Theo: That stuff's just hard to even think about.

But for me, like all addictions, adult-to-adult sex can just be about escaping pain. There is some aspect of the sexual act that you become addicted to and the acting out can become an obsession. After sexual abuse, I had flashbacks and re-experienced the trauma. I had trouble sleeping at night, because I was abused in a dark room. I didn't become a perpetrator, but I did act out sexually. I'd play hockey and get off the ice, and the first thought would be, "Let's go get drunk." The next thought was, "Who can I pick up?" Because the chase, the game, the manipulation was all stimulating. It wasn't about the relationship, or "Can I marry you?" It was all about, "Can I fuck you?" By then I'd be so drunk that I'd have to use cocaine to get a hard on and then the sex would be wild. Crazy, spontaneous, but I wasn't present to any of it. I couldn't tell you an eighth of the women I've slept with. I'm beginning to work through the shame I feel about that now. Cocaine induces an incredible amount of conversation. You talk nonstop and that alone increases connection.

Kim: (*holding the space*) That was an intense reveal. That's the first time I've heard you talk about your sexual addiction with such clarity and linked to the sexual abuse.

Theo: Vulnerability is the true self. I can feel my true self when I am vulnerable. But I am checking out a lot during this conversation. This is very hard work for me.

Kim: Similar to the sexual anorexics that we talked about before, many of my clients experience the opposite of what you have described with your intensity-seeking addiction. They become averse to their sexuality and may completely shut down from starting relationships. Others go numb or experience very little pleasure or satisfaction through sexual interaction. It's because they are reminded of the initial trauma if any relationship gets too close. For some, it's the fear of the physical act of sex, and for others it's the fear of being intimate with anyone.

Theo: I think you flipped to that description, because it is one that would be easier for you to relate to.

Kim: You could be right. Relatively speaking, I think withdrawal would be more of my response.

Theo: Hmm.

Kim: Some survivors of sexual trauma feel that all they are good for is sex, and they often find themselves being used sexually in their relationships. Boundaries are very difficult for these individuals and they typically comply with the needs and demands of others. They may repeat having sex against their will as a pattern that perpetuates the feeling of the initial abuse. This would be very common of an avoidant A strategy individual who needs to avoid intimacy.

Theo: So someone might have tons of one-night stands to avoid the closeness of a real relationship?

Kim: Yep. Like my favourite actor Jake Gyllenhaal in the movie *Love and Other Drugs*. He tried his hardest not to fall in love specifically to avoid intimacy.

Theo: You can become either a seeker or an avoider of sexual activity in response to sexual abuse, right?

Kim: Yup, but in both responses to sexual abuse, for both sex-seekers and sex-avoiders, the shame can eat away at you. Sexual abuse can also be linked to food issues. Many survivors of sexual abuse gain weight as a means of protecting themselves from unwanted attention or sexual advances, or alternately starve themselves.

Theo: I can relate to having food issues, but not that I specifically wanted myself to be unattractive.

Kim: With food addiction, the craving for food is beyond the need for comfort food, and not all food addicts have been sexually abused. As you yourself said, you know your abuse was not your only underlying issue.

Theo: What I am wanting now in my life is to connect love with sex. That cuddle sex. Intimacy from cuddling, holding hands, in combination with loving the other person's heart, mind, and soul. Think it's possible?

Kim: In your words, Theo, "Anything is possible." (*nodding*)

Theo: Kim, how much energy are you wasting by carrying around shame related to sex?

Kim: What we all need to remember is that everyone carries some developmental trauma that leads to feelings of abandonment, rejection, and worthlessness.

Theo: Notice the "distancing language" that you used just there talking in generalities instead of your own personal experience. Keeps you safe, eh.

Kim: It's getting better, but sex is still a hard topic for me, because I grew up in a home where we didn't talk about it. At all. My sister and I weren't even given words for our vulvas and vaginas. Sounds a bit crazy maybe, but we referred to that whole area as our bums.

Theo: (*surprised*) What?

Kim: It's embarrassing to talk about. I don't know what my mom was thinking. But I still love her. (*smiling*) Theo, I appreciate how you know when to wait when I can be a little vulnerable, too. This helps to increase the trust between us.

Theo: (*reflecting*) I realize that I have some unfinished business about the whole Graham James thing. It's about not protecting myself during the time I was sexually abused. I was a teenager and I think many people think I should have been able to do something to stop the abuse. Different from if you are a young child.

Kim: In my opinion, it is about the relationship with the person that is the mind fuck. Master manipulator, as you say. Sometimes we don't totally hate our abusers, and sometimes there are things about them we totally admire. The emotional feelings that we have about the person can create tremendous inner turmoil, at the same time that we know the abuse is sickening.

Theo: I can feel my feelings now. Something is not right in my body. I think it is initially anxiety and then it goes right to anger. Fight or flight, and I usually pick fight, right?

Kim: It's gonna be okay. I think Graham James had a tremendous amount of power over you that you couldn't control.

Theo: If you mean the NHL, yes, and no. He scouted me, was my coach, and had the NHL connections, and that is a lot of power to a kid. Despite my certainty of my talent and work ethic, I had a definite fear of not making the NHL, and he would have seen that. But I'm coming to realize that a big part of the "relationship," with him, aside from the fear of not making the NHL, which was admittedly the biggest one, was that he was my primary source of approval and consistent attachment figure at the time. He controlled not only my ice-time, but my finances, and if he liked me, I'd be okay (in some ways). And you and I have established that I use a people-pleasing A type attachment strategy to feel emotionally secure. So that means I was probably more compliant than I should have been had I known other strategies back then. So, there was confusion, yes.

Kim: You were doing the best you could with the tools you had at the time. Remember, compliance is a strategy intended to keep other people happy, so you can be safe from danger. You were doing the best you could with what you had.

Theo: What was warped is that even after I started dating my first girlfriend, who I was totally attracted to, I'd still go see Graham once in a while and expose myself to that routine of tortured dysfunction. I'm ashamed I accepted to go with him and Sheldon to Disneyland when I was sixteen, knowing at some level what a sick fuck Graham was. Goes to show you how young teenagers make stupid decisions, based on what they think their "approval status" needs to be. That's why parents need to stay involved in their kids' lives.

Kim: You know he's never going to hurt you again.

Theo: He can't. And he isn't highest on the list of people who could even possibly hurt me. I'm still at the top of that list.

Kim: Nice awareness!

Theo: Speaking of Graham, just to get him out of my head right now, if I had the wherewithal and the self-confidence back then that I have today, I would have punched him firmly in the mouth, told an adult what he tried, and that would have been the end of it. I still would have made the NHL. I was that good a player. Some might think he made me angry so I'd be more motivated every day to be tougher, but I was already motivated more than anyone I knew. In hindsight, all that energy wasted on him and my lack of sleep—that was such a waste. If anything, he held me back as a player. People need to know childhood sexual abuse is never okay.

Kim: That is for sure. (*exhaling*) I've got a question for you. You've said you're still working on trying to trust men in general, especially ones in positions of power, and that is understandable. Do you ever think you give women too much credit?

Theo: Hmm. Nope. But I got a story for you. (*grinning*) Do you mind if it's a little X-rated?

Kim: I can handle it. (*smiling*)

Theo: So Little Johnny's out in the front yard, playing with Mary, right? Johnny pulls out his penis and says, "Ha, ha, I got one of these!" And she drops her knickers and shows what she's got and says, "Well, I got one of these, so I can get one of those, anytime I want." (*laughing*)

Kim: You think women really have that much power over men?

Theo: Big time! No question. Why do you think men chase it so much?

Kim: Really? That is foreign to me. When you say "chase it so much," do you mean chase the power or chase the vagina?

Theo: Both! And it's not just about the vagina; it's about the chase.

Kim: Hmm. Speaking of lack of power, some men tell me their penis size is their biggest source of shame. Seems crazy to women, but is there really truth to that?

Theo: Well, I would have missed out on tons of amazing moments if I had connected anymore to my own feeling of being ashamed of my penis size. All those showers after games, hot tubs, saunas with the team. I just trained myself to put it out of my mind. And you know what they say: "It isn't the size of the ship in the sea. It's the motion in the ocean." (*laughing*)

Kim: I always thought it was the person it was attached to.

Theo: Really?

Kim: Yeah. Men don't truly believe their penises have different personalities from themselves do they?

Theo: Of course they do.

Kim: Wow. I'm trying to internalize this. So for all the women out there, we really shouldn't judge penis size or make jokes about it?

Theo: You are a therapist with a world of sensitivity expertise, and you are asking me that?

Kim: (*laughing*) I know I shouldn't be laughing.

Theo: (*rolling his eyes, shaking his head, and talking softly to himself*) Thank God, I didn't play basketball.

Kim: (*changing the topic*) We haven't really talked about your relationship with women. You said you feel emotionally safer with them than with men, and I know you've been with a ton of them sexually. I guess the question is, when you confuse sex with love, how much does that get in the way of common sense for you?

Theo: Sex is not always about love.

Kim: It really is for me.

Theo: I get that. (*respectfully*) But it hasn't been my experience, often.

Kim: I feel so vulnerable with sex; I couldn't do it if it weren't in the context of a loving relationship. But I don't want that to come across as judgmental.

Theo: I think everyone wants that.

Kim: And that's why Bob is so keen about the topic of his next book, to do with intimacy as we mature. I agree that sexual connection as we get older is full of fascination and very powerful.

Theo: And we shouldn't feel ashamed of it?

Kim: No, Theo. We can afford ourselves the luxury of not feeling ashamed of it.

Theo: (*jumping up*) Well, Hallelujah! I'm cured! Front page news! Tell everyone! (*laughing*)

Kim: Sex and shame will continue to be connected, especially as long as abuse stays silent. And pain from shame will persist until we learn to safely connect with the uncomfortable feelings that hold us back.

Theo: Ah, there's the point.

9

Learning To Sit With Your Shit

"Lightbulb moments, through mindfulness, rewire my brain."
Theo Fleury's thought that came in a moment of shit-sitting reflection

Kim: Our early conversations didn't start with any of the hardest personal stuff.

Theo: No, they didn't, did they.

Kim: They began with generic information that you could digest and reflect upon, and then come back to me with questions about.

Theo: But that seems like a long time ago. Now, what I've learned is that I have to feel uncomfortable, sometimes, to change.

Kim: When you have spent your life numbing out through addictions, it is difficult at first to even know what your feelings are, never mind tolerate them and deal with them.

Theo: Remember when I told you about when I came back sober from the treatment centre in Tucson, while playing in New York, and the only feeling I had all the time was anxiety? Because I couldn't stand it, I started using again. I didn't have enough new skills to do it differently. I was still playing well, but I walked around feeling nervous and out of control. Couldn't even name any of the feelings back then; all I could sense was anxiety and panic.

Kim: I too have had black periods of time in my life. I call them the "dark nights of the soul," where I felt like my emotions were going to swallow me up and I'd never crawl out. I remember what it's like to feel emotionally hopeless.

Theo: I never want to return to that level of blackness again.

Kim: Getting through those, I realized that feelings are just pieces of information that help us to connect with and understand our lives.

Theo: I've heard that emotions are the language of the soul. They speak to us, if we are listening.

Kim: I like to think of emotion as energy in motion. When emotions are overwhelming, it is helpful to remember that they are going to pass. In *Macbeth*—one of Shakespeare's gems—is the statement, "Come what may, time and the hour runs through the roughest day."

Theo: Very eloquently put. (*smiling*)

Kim: But it makes sense, right? The more experience we have at feeling our feelings, the more we learn to trust that they are not going to take over our lives.

Theo: Right. When I'm overwhelmed, I always tell myself, "This isn't my first rodeo." I have experience with so much shit, and survived; I can draw from those survival successes and feel encouraged that I will be okay.

Kim: Cool. Emotions are the stuff that tells us that something in our life has changed, for good or bad. No matter how many times you repress an emotion, it will come back. No matter how many times you try to drug, meditate, pray, or wrestle an uncomfortable emotion into submission with just your intellect, it will come back. Until you dare to look at it and feel it. But it always moves, and we will never be stuck in a single emotion forever.

Theo: Well, there is one emotion I am really good at feeling—anger. I was in a counselling session one time with my ex-wife. In truth, we should have done that more often. But in this session, she was criticizing, blaming, and dismissing me. She wanted me to take responsibility for every single piece of shit in our relationship. I was immediately enraged; I felt dismissed, disrespected, and hurt. The counsellor we had at the time did something really wise. He interrupted my tirade and asked me to talk to my anger as if it were a separate entity. He invited me to have a conversation with my anger, to ask it what purpose it served. So I did that, and had a conversation with my anger.

Kim: Wow.

Theo: My anger told me that it was there to protect me, to help me get the love that I need. Before too long, I found I was in fucking tears. The therapist asked me to thank the anger for doing its job, and to tell it that it had served me well. He asked me to tell the anger that now I could protect myself, and that I no longer needed it to defend me. (*exhaling*) I felt so empowered by that exercise.

Kim: (*smiling*) What an exceptional example of learning to be able to speak the language of our emotions. It doesn't help to be angry at anger. That just keeps it stuck in place. When you reached underneath that anger and felt the sadness, the anger just dissolved. Once you've had this kind of experience, you will always remember it.

Theo: That's for sure; I will remember it. It helps me every time now when I am about to move into rage.

Kim: Good for that counsellor!

Theo: Yeah. You know, I'm learning to trust them more and more. (*smiling*)

Kim: One tool I've used to deal with anger is a baseball bat. It's something we call baseball bat therapy. When I was feeling incensed about something, I would take a baseball bat and hit something that wouldn't break, like a tree or the ground. I was amazed at how much power I had in my arms.

Theo: I feel sorry for the tree. At the Life Healing Center of Santa Fe, we would hit pillows. I would beat the crap out of the pillows with my fists and it scared the shit out of everybody around me.

Kim: I can imagine that intensity. I've also used sturdy plastic bats on pillows; that can be fun, too. Better for the pillows to receive all that energy than the alternative. When I first started baseball bat therapy, it felt a bit contrived, but as I got going, it actually felt great.

Theo: I always felt better afterwards.

Kim: Anger is a powerful energy. Directing it at something rather than at another person is healthier, but it can't be a stand-alone intervention without accompanying emotional work. Otherwise, it is simply a form of releasing anger without the necessary understanding of why the anger was there in the first place.

Theo: When I was directed to attend anger management classes, I always thought of the concept of controlling my anger as being the same as suppressing my anger. Another way to suck it up so to speak.

Kim: Lots of people who attend anger management classes think that they just have to hold in their feelings more. But imagine what that anger does when it turns inward! There is a distinct difference between controlling your anger and the healthy expression of angry feelings. But even the concept of being able to express anger in a healthy way is foreign to most people.

Theo: I know it was to me.

Kim: Most of us are afraid of being the recipient of someone else's anger. One of the most common phrases I remember hearing in my house growing up was, "Don't be mad." No one showed anger overtly; it was all underground. "Passive aggressive," so to speak. Lots of resentment.

Theo: Anger and conflict were totally prevalent in my house, and as I said, my mom cried a lot. I interpreted those tears as manipulation. (*thinking*) Wonder if I got that right?

Kim: I've had a couple of boyfriends who felt the same way when I would cry; they felt like they were being manipulated. How we learn to respond to emotions is so dependent on what we learn to do with them in our family of origin.

Theo: I'll help you with anger, if you help me with sadness.

Kim: Whew, that will require vulnerability on both sides. I know that I am mindful of the potential intensity of your anger. When you speak sternly at times, I have to regulate myself and hold the space. It's been great practice for me to stay present with you while you are angry. I've witnessed this intensity, but you didn't eat me up and I never felt like I had to leave the room.

Theo: I don't think you could make me angry.

Kim: I'm sure I could, perhaps unintentionally. But even when you are angry about something else that doesn't involve me, the intensity is big. I still have to regulate myself so I don't become overwhelmed.

Theo: I am sorry.

Kim: Don't be sorry. This is part of my being vulnerable. It is hard to talk about these things. I want to be able to be present to your anger. Part of what a secure attachment does is allow you to feel safe with all your emotions. If I can't feel safe when you are angry, then you are likely to feel dysregulated and disconnected too. You might escalate to rage or dissociate if I'm not present while you are triggered.

Theo: I don't like my anger and I don't like when I have to talk about it.

Kim: Ah, so you are comfortable *feeling* anger, but it's hard to talk about it? Anger has equal value as any other emotion. All the emotions are equally important.

Theo: Ah, okay, but I still don't like talking about it, at all. (*getting a little angry*)

Kim: I understand. What I hear in the rattling of your rattlesnake tail is a defensive signal that tells me not to push right now. But I want you to know there is no shame in having anger.

Theo: Yeah, yeah.

Kim: You mentioned your addictions were like a hamburger with hockey and healing being the buns. Well, I think of emotions like layers within a sandwich. They are stacked on top of each other. Sometimes, you can't even see what's plastered closest to the bottom piece of bread. When someone defaults to anger all the time, what he or she really typically feels is a great deal of sadness that they can't get to. For you, this was definitely true.

You would easily escalate and ignite into anger and irritation as an automatic protective response without thinking.

Theo: I remember when I was working with a therapist I liked in Chicago by the name of Jonah, and we did this therapy activity with emotion cards. She would describe to me a hypothetical situation and ask me to choose how I would feel in that situation. The only emotions she gave me to choose between in this exercise were Angry or Sad. In the stack I picked, angry cards were piled knee high, and there were no sad cards whatsoever. We ran out of angry cards! I remember she asked me if I had any insights into that. It was pretty easy, I recognized that I was "stacked with anger."

Kim: The surface layer emotion is always the easiest one to connect with, but often the unexpressed emotion is the true feeling about the situation.

Theo: I have a great deal of difficulty connecting to my sadness, even in private. Wow, an aha! (*getting a dopamine hit in his brain*) For the past while, I think connecting with sadness onstage has been easier to do than talking about it at home. Shit.

Kim: But you can get to anger anywhere, right?

Theo: Sure. No problem.

Kim: Feeling anger tells us that a boundary has been crossed, and that's how it's a form of protection. But if you get stuck in anger and don't look at the sadness or disappointment underneath, you won't know what you are longing for. It's sadness that tells you what you are missing in your life.

Theo: I used to have so much difficulty crying. I just couldn't get there.

Kim: I remember the first time when you openly cried in my presence.

Theo: I remember it, too. Surprised myself there. We were just sitting at my kitchen table watching *Fat, Sick & Nearly Dead*. It was Phil, the American truck driver, that brought the tears out. He started his process of healing from being an obese, sick, depressed man and through his connection to juicing, he began to feel healthier. He had such hope to get better! And through that hope he healed himself and inspired so many people. I could really relate to him and watching him triggered me.

Kim: That's a cool example of how a trigger can bring out a positive emotion and not just a negative one. In Phil's eyes, you could see yourself as being an inspiring motivator, also spreading hope to many people. His turnaround was a great mirror for you. It was very appropriate to have tears of joy about those qualities in him and in you. You see in others what you see in yourself, eh.

Theo: I remember you cried too.

Kim: A whole bunch of mirrors in that example, but in different ways. It was watching you get teary that brought tears to my eyes. That was the first time I'd seen that emotion. I guess you could call it self-love, in you. (*looking at Theo*) A good emotional cry is restorative and cleansing. It's been shown in experiments that *emotionally* induced tears contain opiates and oxytocin, so they turn on the natural relaxation response in the body. This means that a good cry releases and flushes the toxic stress hormones (cortisol) right out of the body.[lxxviii]

Theo: Why do we hold it back so much?

Kim: I think it's because we fear being exposed or looking weak and vulnerable. For me, I don't want the other person to see me cry, 'cause if they're the one who's triggered my reaction, I don't want them to have the satisfaction of seeing how they've upset me.

Theo: When the other person is vulnerable along with you, it makes it easier.

Kim: No question. (*reflecting*) Hey, what do you think of this concept of sitting with your feelings—or "shit"—when they're negative feelings?

Theo: Well, like just about everything we're talking about, you introduced it to me as a concept first, before I had to try it. You didn't push me into this process. So that made it easier. Your knowing when to act and when to wait is helpful. You have lots of patience.

Kim: Sometimes, I just ask you. It doesn't have to be complicated. When you bring up something difficult, do you notice I check in sometimes and ask "Do you want me to listen, or to fix it?" We do this at home, too, 'cause the natural response—especially I've found with men—is to rush in and try to fix stuff, when often all we need is for someone to listen.

Theo: Just listening is generally the harder option, I'd say. I must be male. (*making a face*)

Kim: You know how many of us get into trouble? We give advice before it's asked for.

Theo: Ya think?

Kim: Well of course, many of us like to give advice, and there are different reasons for that. Most often it's 'cause we can't stand it when the other person is upset. Or, we want to help so that we feel needed. I think it's pretty natural to want to help. But to protect myself I figured out a way so I won't get in trouble for putting my nose into other people's business.

Theo: Yeah, I've seen it when overhelping can be worse than not helping at all.

Kim: Right, it can be intrusive. No one wants their stuff meddled with, or micro-managed. So, to prevent this, I made up a rule, and it especially works with family members (when we remember it). Here it is: don't give anyone advice unless they ask for it three times. That often means we do more listening first, before jumping into action. It's not easy. (*smiling*) Because listening is not the same thing as waiting to speak. Listening is being present to the other and feeling what you're feeling at the same time.

Theo: I know I have resistance to sitting with my emotions. Way easier to do just about anything else.

Kim: When you "sit with an emotion," it's like you're becoming an observer of your feelings. When I do it, I think of it like there's a cartoon bubble coming out of my head that's making declarative statements about my behaviour as if I were talking about someone else. "There she goes feeling angry again," or "Boy, that comment was sure loaded with sadness."

Theo: I can see you with a cartoon bubble over your head. (*smiling*) It's saying "I just made a good point and I'm proud of myself in this moment." (*laughing*)

Kim: (*smirking*) Are you making fun of me, Theo Fleury? (*trying to regain the seriousness of the topic*) But when I do this observing of my emotional state, it creates a bit of distance between me and the intensity of the emotion I'm experiencing. So it makes the emotion a bit easier to tolerate. It is a self-regulation strategy, but it does take practice to become good at this skill.

Theo: I have had so many triggers. I am not sure what emotion I should be sitting with first.

Kim: "Sitting with an emotion" is kind of like pressing the pause button and slowing down our reactivity. It gives us time to think and discover what it is that our reactions are trying to tell us.

Theo: I remember the time I was triggered with your friend Marie when we were talking about religion; I was able to slow it down that time. But I could do it because she was so present and safe, and didn't respond with anger in return. And you were also there, holding the space, helping us keep it together. Once I calmed myself a little, I felt the sadness underneath and it allowed me to see what I was longing for, as you would say.

Kim: And what was it that you were missing?

Theo: Since my early religious experiences were mixed with fear and loss, what I think I was longing for was deeper connection and safety.

Kim: (*smiling*) There is an example of the power of going deeper when you can sit with it.

Theo: It's an inside job.

Kim: Triggers give us lots to work with. They happen during conversations, watching movies, observing the actions of others ... I think this is why I love watching movies so much—I see them all as personal growth opportunities.

Theo: (*sarcastically*) Wouldn't you be fun to watch a movie with.

Kim: The ones we've watched together have all been intense! But I do like to reflect on things intentionally. Going to an emotionally evocative movie is like going to a meditation retreat where I get to contemplate ideas and see how they relate to my experiences.

Theo: Lots of times, triggers just come at me out of the blue, like fucking shrapnel in the trenches in WWI. No, that's not the best example, 'cause in that case, you'd be expecting something to hit you. It's more like swimming blind into a jellyfish, or being hit with a golf ball without anyone yelling, "Fore." Hey, it happens.

I was playing at the Inglewood Golf course in Calgary and I got hit right in the chest. It knocked me on my ass. And I didn't kill the guy! He apologized, and said he'd just hit the longest golf shot of his life. I was fuckin' mad, but what can you do? Shit does happen.

Kim: That is often when triggers are the most powerful: when they are unexpected. When a trigger sneaks up on us and we have an intense emotional response, the potential to glean wisdom from those feelings is also intensified.

Theo: One trigger that I have is when the people I care about feel hurt. When we were at a group retreat a few months back and the facilitator led us through a guided meditation, it was hard for me to watch you when you got stuck in some of your stuff.

Kim: Yeah.

Theo: I really didn't know what to say or do to help you move out of your space. It reminded me of my mother when she would get into those places and I would try to help her. Your sadness was difficult for me. When I see something that is clearly not true, and the other person can't see it, it frustrates me. When the other person is stuck, I want to shake them and say, "Why can't you see what I see?" It's frustration, helplessness, and all those things mixed together. I just want everyone to be happy, right? When they're not, and I can't seem to do anything to fix it, typically I want to leave that kind of stressful situation entirely.

What surprised me that time was my ability to stay with it, and to stay relatively nearby your physical space while you were clearly stuck.

Kim: What were you thinking about that helped you stay present without doing anything?

Theo: Instead of trying to rescue you, which was my first instinct, I remembered that all this personal work is an inside job. You had to figure it out and there wasn't a lot I could do other than hold the space. Maybe I realized that I am good enough to just be; I don't have to fix everything. I think I realized for the first time that holding the space for somebody is enough. You just have to be there; you don't really need to say a whole lot. That is a really cool feeling.

Kim: I had a hard time staying with my stuck feelings myself that day. Partly 'cause the issue itself—in this case my body image stuff—is such an old one that I think I should have been able to deal with it by now; I was embarrassed at being so vulnerable. It was a big step for both of us. This conversation is a good example, right here, of being able to sit with your shit and process it. When you can recognize how you feel and share it, greater depths of connection are created.

Theo: I remember telling you to, "Let it go."

Kim: I remember wanting to tell you to "fuck off" when you said that. I've been trying to let it go for over forty years.

Theo: Why didn't you just say that to me?

Kim: Because I was sitting with my shit. I was really trying to work it through. And I knew you were just trying to help.

Theo: Shame revisits, doesn't it?

Kim: We can only work on so many issues in one lifetime. I remember when the facilitator asked me a "why" question related to my feelings. Oddly a "why" question, when I am stuck in a feeling, is a big trigger for me. It makes me furious. In moments when I'm feeling overwhelmed and I'm not thinking clearly, a question like that feels like I'm being pressured to come up with an answer. When I can't find the answer right away, I immediately feel "not good enough." It is so connected to my perfectionism. These are the layers of awareness that arise when you can sit with something long enough. You find out what is at the heart of the matter.

Theo: The whole experience you were having was about not being good enough.

Kim: Sure. Our core issues snake their ways into so many aspects of our behaviours.

Theo: Look at how long it has taken me to even realize that my past is what triggers me. Now when I get triggered, I have to work to stay here in the present and figure it out. To work through it.

Kim: You have come a long way, very quickly.

Theo: Long way to go! Another trigger we started talking about was free give-away schemes on the Internet that really just make you pay later. When someone said I should do those as part of my own marketing, I immediately responded with anger and defensiveness. 'Cause if anyone's giving away stuff for free that means they don't believe they've got any inherent value, and thinking like that just triggers my not-good-enough stuff. And I've been ripped off by so many fucking Internet schemes, I don't trust any of them. So why would I ever want anyone else to ever have to second-guess that kind of shit? (*reflecting*) I guess I'll have to work through all this before I'd really consider doing anything like that. See, once you start to connect to the anger, and understand there's a reason for it, then the situation no longer trips you up, and you can actually think rationally.

Kim: That kind of awareness will allow you to say something next time like, "That hasn't worked for me in the past, so let me think about it and get back to you." And there would be no edge of irritation in your voice. You would experience the anger, understand the anger, and move into a place of ease with your communication. That's controlling your anger.

Theo: It's all about regulating yourself.

Kim: Or not. You can just choose to skip over a trigger. It's actually very hard to always look at it in the moment. Eventually, you have to make the space and time to reflect; otherwise, it'll just come up again.

Theo: I think this whole process for me is about moving through the layers of my anger.

Kim: Being able to feel a feeling and express it without being out of control helps to develop greater degrees of intimacy and authenticity in relationships. Here's an example. Being able to say, "I don't feel safe right now" is an alternative to snapping into rage that creates distance and disconnection.

Theo: Having a script like that is so helpful when you feel like you're gonna explode and you don't want to do more damage than you've already done.

Kim: A struggle for me is that I expect myself to be able to notice every trigger, change my response to them all, and know how to communicate the emotion attached to them all from a place of clarity *now*.

Theo: I didn't know there was a "Trigger Bible" that says we have to do it all, right now. Maybe we don't have the tools yet. Way too high an expectation.

Kim: (*smiling*) Ha. The way you said that already helps me to soften the shame around my imperfection of not being able to do this process perfectly all the time.

Theo: Now the process of personal growth has become another layer of perfectionism for you to work on. No rest for you, eh!

Kim: (*laughing at herself*) Perfectionism in personal growth. How ridiculous is that concept, eh!

Theo: We sure need patience. And self-compassion. Progress, yes. (*in New York accent*) Perfection, forgeddaboudit! I think all of us who have suffered trauma are looking for perfection though. We wanna feel fully better. But we need to remind ourselves what we really need is just to put one foot in front of the other.

Kim: Not all triggers are lightning bolts. Some of them are very subtle and require that you're paying attention so you notice them. When other people do things that bug us, that don't directly affect us, we can still explore why it's bugging us. For example, when we see people being impatient in line, it could be we're feeling the same way, but just controlling ourselves better. Noticing what we're feeling is the goal. That's what it means to be connected to yourself and awake.

Theo: You have to celebrate all the baby steps along the way.

Kim: Every piece of self-awareness that we have helps us to connect to what we're experiencing. So each recognition is a success. Even small achievements are achievements. When I work with caregivers of multi-handicapped children—and some of these kids are nonverbal, limited in mobility, visually impaired, and the list goes on—it's really important for caregivers to acknowledge every minor miracle, every day, no matter how small.

Theo: Why aren't we all doing that? Remember we're all special needs in some ways, right? (*little smirk*)

Kim: You know it.

Theo: My biggest handicap is that my brain doesn't produce enough dopamine.

Kim: I think that it's amazing how you understand the impact of that on your life. What I've found is that a lot of the strategies I use in working with special needs people are helpful in effective communication and teaching with absolutely everyone. It's just that people who work with the special needs population all the time need a lot of patience, so sometimes celebrating the baby steps is as helpful to the caregivers as it is for their clients. It allows them to see that some progress is being made even when it doesn't always feel like it.

Theo: Must be hard to have that much patience. Think they all go home and drink after work?

Kim: It's no different from teachers or counsellors or therapists, or anyone else in the helping professions. When you work with people, you need patience and compassion. But you do need outlets to relieve your own stresses, that's for sure. (*little giggle*) Can I tell you one secret coping strategy that I have to help me with my perfectionism?

Theo: (*grinning*) Why the hell not?

Kim: I work very mindfully at being nonjudgmental, compassionate, and being nice, right?

Theo: You're exceptionally good at it. Especially with me.

Kim: But to be that mindful and cautious *all* the time is exhausting! So I learned this trick from a good friend. And she's one of the genuinely nicest people I know. She started an "I hate people club." It's not a club, and she doesn't hate people at all; it's just a funny name she gave it. It's something that she does by herself for about five minutes a month, when she goes through a mall or somewhere where there are lots of people. No one around her knows it, but she actively allows herself, in her own mind, to criticize them all randomly.

Theo: That's hysterical!

Kim: Every person she sees, she just looks for their imperfections and doesn't feel one bit of guilt about it. It's hilarious. I find myself doing this in airports when I'm noticing I'm a bit stressed. I think things like, "Why would she wear that?" or "Gee, that haircut's unfortunate" or …

Theo: "What a fat ass on that one … ?"

Kim: Theo! (*laughing*) And after a few moments of unedited and, thank God, unverbalized criticism, believe it or not, I'm feeling less stressed. Because I'm laughing at myself for even doing this.

Theo: Laughing at yourself is awesome! (*smiling*)

Kim: By choosing to do it so consciously, though, it really does help me to not take myself so seriously. That's the point of this! It reminds me I'm not needing to be perfect either, 'cause no one is. I guess I have to keep reminding myself of that.

Theo: You really do have a drive to be perfect, don't you? What is that about?

Kim: Perfectionism's about people pleasing, or more specifically, avoiding the pain from blame, judgment, and shame. It's thinking you should be something other than who you are. And it's a self-destructive, addictive thought.

Theo: So for people, like me, who have issues with not feeling good enough, are you saying your "good enough" is only being met when you are being perfect? 'Cause that's not cutting yourself a lot of slack.

Kim: It's not, is it? I'm working on that all the time. Not so I'll have to get perfect at it though. (*laughing*) That wouldn't be realistic, or necessary. So you see, I'm certainly not wishing ill will toward any of the people around me. I'm just laughing at myself for feeling the waste-of-energy need to be more perfect myself. Cutting myself some slack, I guess. It is a stress reliever, though.

Theo: (*smiling*) Speaking of humour, I think humour is very important as a part of tolerating painful feelings. If you can't laugh at yourself, you're in a tough position. One of my favourite comedians is a First Nations guy, Don Burnstick. Fucking hilarious. He gets it. And there's another guy, Steven Wright. I just have no idea how he comes up with that kind of stuff! (*laughing*) But if I'm ever in the long-term care unit of a faceless hospital with cardboard food, I'd really appreciate a visit from Patch Adams. Gotta laugh. (*pausing*) So sad to hear about Robin Williams passing …

Kim: God, yeah. A huge loss. He was one of the guys who would have been able to tell us that chemically, laughter releases endorphins and eases pain. Guess he didn't find enough laughter himself. Really sad.

Theo: We gotta keep going, and trying. (*with emotion*)

Kim: We do.

Theo: What we have to do is carry on with his best qualities—his making us laugh, and making us think.

Kim: He was good at both.

Theo: I'm remembering oxytocin and endorphins and dopamine and wondering what to do to feel a bit happier right now … So hugging, laughing, crying, and yawning all at the same time is like the healthiest thing we can do? (*little chuckle*) Should we add farting to the list? Has anyone ever done them all at once?

Kim: You're funny. Are you making fun of me? So when was the last time you had a full-on belly laugh? When your whole body was just shaking with laughter?

Theo: You were there! It was on Bowen Island when we heard music by the docks and walked over and were generously invited to help crash a guy's fiftieth birthday party. Live music, everyone was super happy, but the birthday boy hadn't arrived. He'd missed his ferry coming from Vancouver. So when we knew his boat was coming in—and by this time Bob seemed to know everyone on the island—all these people go out to meet him. Of course, Bob is right in the middle of it, bright orange shirt … and when birthday boy Tim (who's the cable guy on the island) comes over, Bob just prances toward him along with a few others and Tim had this look on his face like, "Do I even know this guy? Not a chance … Oh, what the hell! It's my birthday!" and they shared a full-on joyful body hug! What was funny was that I saw it coming. And it's something I'd never *ever* do! I was practically busting a gut watching, 'cause it was so predictable, but fucking hilarious!

Kim: I was hiding my face and laughing at the same time. And yes, Bob can be so social, you could say he's outstanding at fitting in. He's a pretty full-on happy person sometimes, and I love him for it. (*smiling*)

Theo: I'm *way* more shy. That was one of my reflections from that evening. But watching Bob was hilarious though. Good dancing, too. Even Bob was surprised he could have so much fun being perfectly sober.

Kim: True. How many people can really let loose, sincerely, without alcohol?

Theo: I'm learning ... So what about you? When was the last time you really busted a gut laughing?

Kim: (*thinking*) I think it was in writing this book! You know when we're talking about all the ways to use the word "fuck"? Bob and I were going over it reading out loud, and we decided to mix it up and he read my part sounding like Mrs. Doubtfire, and I read your stuff sounding all tough and manly. We were both on the floor in hysterics.

Theo: I can see that.

Kim: Gotta laugh, eh. Certainly can't sit with our shit too long. Gotta laugh.

Theo: 'Cause all you have is this moment. You can get thrown by a trigger from any direction at any time. So when something funny comes along, it's good to embrace it. Hey, that thought reminds me of something I saw on *Oprah*.

Kim: You watch *Oprah*?

Theo: Yeah, used to. She's awesome. Inspires a lot of people.

Kim: What did she say?

Theo: Something about reminding ourselves that this very moment is the only one we know we'll have for sure ...

Kim: You really work at living in the moment. So might as well enjoy it.

Theo: When we can, yep! (*smiling*) 'Cause I never know what's around the corner. Something'll happen or something'll be said that I recognize as a trigger (often it's when I get pissed off) and then I'll have to ask myself, "Am I going to get real here or am I going to use my same old strategies?" Living in the moment means getting real.

Kim: Honesty with yourself helps you learn to tolerate your discomfort. Giving airtime to your negative feelings actually helps to diminish them.

Theo: One of the hardest things for me to sit with is confusion. I want to move into action.

Kim: Mmhm, I can relate to that. We often move into action when we can't stand the discomfort of the confusion. Not because the action is deep down helpful, but just because it gets us out of the immediate discomfort. One of the most difficult things to do is nothing.

Theo: Tell me about it. (*nodding*)

Kim: But that's essentially what it means to sit with it. To wait and see what happens, rather than to push through and make decisions based only on your triggers. Like kids who get mad and want to take their toys and go home. Adults act like that too when they don't sit and think a bit.

Theo: Patience. It takes patience, goddammit.

Kim: We can't grow any faster than we're ready to grow, because you can't truly grow without some experience. Take a new helpful habit and repeat it, wire the productive pattern together through practice, and have patience.

Theo: Fuck, I am forty-six years old and I want to be able to respond to things like a grownup more consistently.

Kim: When you have clarity, you'll know it, because there is very little emotion attached to the situation. You just know what the right thing to do is. There is neither an urgency to get away from something, nor an urgency to move toward something. When you're in the flow, everything just unfolds easily.

Theo: Sometimes I think I mistake my impulsivity with my intuition. I think that I am following my instincts, but really I am just being impulsive.

Kim: Like I said, you'll know it's your intuition when there's a sense of ease, and there is no urgency to it at all.

Theo: (*thinking*) I think I've often sold myself out. I'm realizing I've entered into relationships out of fear of being by myself, rather than because the relationship was really the right one for me.

Kim: Interesting insight. It is hard to sacrifice "good enough" to wait for "even better," when in the meantime you have to be alone. Instant gratification is what many of us choose.

Theo: I guess the other extreme of this is that some people sit with their shit for years.

Kim: Some of us overidentify with our shit.

Theo: That is so common with the First Nations community, for example. It is easier to be a victim than to be a victor. I really applaud those who are standing up for themselves with real pride. There's a chief in the Osoyoos region of British Columbia, Clarence Louie, who constantly reminds the youth in his community that none of their ancestors were unemployed. "Want a job? Create one!" This attitude is so healthy. They are doing great things.

Kim: And of course, success brings success and is contagious! But at the other extreme, many people are attracted to each other just based on their shared wounds. We can wear our wounds like a badge. It's understandable, but sometimes we feel reinforced when we go on and on and on about the drama of our trauma. And then there are other people who sit in it without talking about it! It's both of these types of over-indulgences in pain that will keep us stuck. This is exactly what happens when we sit with our shit for too long.

Theo: It's really hard, this emotional work. Because often our survival doesn't depend on it—we're getting enough of our basic needs met to stay alive. It's very easy not to bother doing the emotional work at all. It's a voluntary action, and it requires inner motivation.

Kim: It has a lot to do with your tolerance of emotional pain. Emotional pain motivates us to try to change. (*thinking*) I guess the decision to change happens only when the discomfort of the emotional pain is felt (first of all), and then also when the pain exceeds whatever secondary benefits any of us might think we're getting from feeling like a victim.

Theo: Did you ever feel like a victim?

Kim: Um, nothing as pervasive as what can happen on an entire cultural level, but sure. Enough so that I know the effects are debilitating.

Theo: When?

Kim: Well, I had an experience with a relationship many years ago that was traumatic for me. I had a serious boyfriend, who I thought I really loved. We'd been making all kinds of plans for the future, and it seemed we were both on the same page and ready for a happy life together. Then one Christmas morning he basically woke up, rolled over, and announced that he no longer wanted to be with me. Didn't love me anymore. I was blindsided, devastated. My mind struggled with every strategy I had to try to understand "Why?" I was all in my head, thinking what did I do wrong, what could I have done differently? I didn't want to feel the pain of the rejection at any cost, so I stayed in my head going round in circles, but of course it didn't help. I wasn't eating, I couldn't work. Took me a while to talk about it at all, and even then it took months and months. I spent many nights curled up in a ball on the floor in pain. Physical pain and emotional pain. It didn't seem rational that this loss would shatter me to the core of my being the way it did. At the depth of it, I really thought I might die. But when I came out on the other side, it was good. I think that was the first time I really explored the concept of rejection at that level of depth, so something came out of it. My friends were very patient. But I think I may have sounded a bit like a "poor me" after the third or fourth month.

Theo: I bet that guy didn't feel good enough for you, and just didn't know any other way of saying it.

Kim: Hmm. Are you a psychic?

Theo: You know I am. (*smiling*) But I gotta say I don't like whining.

Kim: Neither do I. I don't like that victim position. Makes me feel yucky.

Theo: So why do people do it then? For attention? Connection? They must get something out of whining; otherwise, they wouldn't do it.

Kim: Right. But in my case, I totally felt victimized, and at this point I can finally say that I know I sat with that particular shit for far too long. I have come a long way in the past twenty-five years.

Theo: Many times, the pain we have is better than the unknown, and that can keep us stuck for a long time.

Kim: Well, sure. If you don't feel lovable and you've just been dumped, the unknown is "Will anyone ever love me?" That feeling just sucks.

Theo: I know. I went to my addictions to numb my pain.

Kim: Yeah. But aside from not eating and being deeply depressed, there are many other forms of self-abuse that people express emotional pain through; other ways that really just contribute to keeping them stuck in their shit. Some of my clients will self-harm: cutting themselves, burning their skin, banging their head against the wall repeatedly, hitting themselves, self-mutilating ...

Theo: I guess we all hurt ourselves in different ways. But why the deliberate infliction of physical pain? I don't get that.

Kim: Each person who self-harms does it for a different reason. Often, it is to override emotional pain; sometimes, it's to punish yourself or to counter feelings of numbness ... All these behaviours can be interpreted as masks for deeper levels of "shit" lying underneath. When someone's cutting—and this happens a lot more than we know—the core problem is not the behaviour; there is always something beneath it that needs to be explored with compassion. If not, and even if the cutting stops, the emotional pain underneath will very likely present itself in another form of self-abuse.

Theo: I certainly know physical pain, but I have never inflicted it upon myself.

Kim: Self-harm is often very difficult for others to understand. The way I explain it in workshops is that people self-harm either to up-regulate (getting more chemistry in their brain) or to down regulate and calm themselves. In order to figure out the treatment, you have to find out how they are processing the sensations from their bodies, and their feelings about what they're doing. Whatever the reason they do it—and it's like being a detective to figure it out—it's a behaviour that frightens people around them.

Theo: It must be crazy hard for parents to see their kids doing this to themselves. Are anorexia and bulimia forms of self-harm too?

Kim: Definitely.

Theo: Lots of people look so good on the outside but are dying on the inside. I know that has been true for me many times in my life.

Kim: Yeah. And that's why sitting with your shit is so important.

Theo: To stop the feeling of dying on the inside?

Kim: That, without question. But also to help our insides and our outsides match, so we're able to live more authentically.

Theo: Authenticity is great, but pretty rare, no? Before we get there, what do you think of the saying that we've got to fake it until we make it?

Kim: I'm not sure how I feel about that. If we're faking happiness when we're sad underneath—I'm not sure how healthy that is. But if it helps someone with confidence while they're actively doing the work at the same time, that's okay. Like if a guy's at work on the first day of his new job, feeling like he's in way over his head, but he's got a new suit on, maybe it'll help. Having confidence is really important for self-esteem, so I wouldn't discourage anyone from trying to make themselves appear more awesome.

Theo: Ah, so where's the line with authenticity when it comes to things like boob implants, cosmetic surgery, hair implants ... ?

Kim: I don't have the answer for that. It's all a personal choice.

Theo: Good answer.

Kim: But I could add, if cosmetic surgery seems to become an addiction, and we've all seen famous people who seem to have overdone it a bit, I'd suggest they'd do well to look at themselves a little deeper on the inside and find a really good friend to talk with.

Theo: That's a nice way to say they're nuts! (*laughing*)

Kim: No judgment. We all have our own stories and reasons for why we do what we do.

Theo: You're right.

Kim: You like fake boobs though, don't you?

Theo: I don't really care if the breasts are authentic or man-made. I like them all, especially the nice ones. (*smiling*)

Kim: (*with a wry smile*) Funny you should mention authenticity … when we hear about people who are all talk and no action, inauthentic, those are the ones who might benefit more from sitting with their shit a little longer. There is a big difference between understanding a concept that relates to an issue, and owning your relationship with that issue. When you sit with your shit, it allows you to act from a position of clarity, and you don't have to talk all around the topic. Yet when you simply analyze an issue (*pronouncing "analyze" with emphasis on the "anal"*), it's not as sincere. It's that clarity that I suggest we aim for. When we embody an issue and when our actions become effortless, it's because we own them.

Theo: What's an example of someone who owns their actions, and has clearly sat in his shit to get there? And give me an example of someone who could really use some shit-sitting time.

Kim: Of course, I don't want to get into trouble. But if George W. Bush had really looked at the deeper reasons for why he pushed for the Iraq War, I wonder if it would have happened the way it did? Or maybe he was just a pawn in the big scheme of things; who knows. But you know what? I've heard that since his last term as president, he's done quite a lot of painting, which at least some have considered to be art therapy. I'm happy for him if he's consciously making the time to get any emotional support.

Theo: Hmm. And whose actions seem effortless? Who has sat with their shit well?

Kim: I like Ellen, you know, Ellen DeGeneres. Not 'cause she's necessarily got a lot of shit; she just seems really comfortable in her own skin. And out of people I've met, I respect Pema Chödrön for this quality. She's a Buddhist nun living in Cape Breton, Nova Scotia. And my friend Joe Connolly, who passed away. (*remembering him with a smile*)

What about you? Who do you see as having an inside and an outside that match?

Theo: Well, in hockey, that's easy. Some guys are so genuine you can see it a mile away. Wayne Gretzky is like that. Mario Lemieux, Joe Sakic, Steve Yzerman. Quality people.

Kim: (*smiling*) You're gonna be so proud of me!

Theo: Why?

Kim: I recognize those names!

Theo: My God! (*rolling his eyes*)

Kim: (*totally proud of herself*) Aren't they like the best hockey players of our generation?

Theo: Absolutely.

Kim: But you're talking about them as being excellent people, their characters, nothing to do with ice time. What does that say about nice guys finishing last?

Theo: You're right.

Kim: I think that saying "nice guys finish last" is a bit off. 'Cause it's not about being nice that matters anyway, is it? It's about being genuine.

Theo: True. Sometimes being nice can be an act, and other times it can come at your own expense. But being genuine doesn't have a downside.

Kim: Who else comes to mind who's like this?

Theo: Outside hockey, I'm thinking I'm most happy for Grandma Ruth. She's come so far back to herself that the word to describe her is "serene." She used to sleep in the homeless shelter in Winnipeg and now she's a spiritual leader. I'm aiming to get to that level of feeling comfortable in my own skin, as you put it. No rush, no desperation; but that's where I'm heading.

Kim: I'm also happy for people who are aligned with themselves. It's easy to tell when people are genuine, eh. You know to get there, sometimes the transition from awareness to action is instantaneous, and other times, it takes years.

Theo: When we don't sit with our shit, we tend to act out, badly. Our actions can be so hurtful toward others. And we know that hurt people hurt people. (*reflecting*) Okay, I'll say that a bit more clearly, and own it. When I don't sit with my shit, I act out more, and then I regret it. I don't want to hurt anyone anymore.

Kim: Wow. Good ownership. Your point shows why the concept of sitting with our shit can't be ignored. It's a way for us to take responsibility for our own feelings and actions. And you know what? It is absolutely critical in stopping the cycle of abuse.

Theo: But we don't want anyone to be shamed into looking at themselves ... 'cause we know how well that works. (*making a face*) Might as well tell another hundred addicts to meditate on command the day they get into a rehab clinic! I'm still reflecting on how unrealistic that expectation was!

Kim: So, Mr. Theo Fleury, how does someone get to the point of *wanting* to sit with their shit?

Theo: That's the billion-dollar question. If it were easy I'd still be playing hockey. Well, maybe not, but you know what I mean ...

Kim: (*waiting patiently for his answer*)

Theo: It's gotta be from within supportive relationships. Just safe conversations. Step by step. 'Cause once someone starts getting those lightbulb moments, they'll want to keep going 'cause it feels so good to feel better about yourself.

Kim: And I just thought of another motivator, too. Our health! Negative emotions or "shit" lives in our bodies, not just in the chemicals in our brains. Our bodies carry the impact of both the positive and the painful events of our lives. Our muscles, heart, nervous system, respiratory system, digestive organs, and other physical structures develop fixed patterns that continue to speak to our brains about old traumatic and developmental wounds. Some people would say that the body has its own wisdom, and that may be. But it definitely has its own sense of memory. Again, this is being proven by science all the time.

Theo: So how would memory in my body affect me and my health today?

Kim: Good question. Let's look at that. When there is trauma, like sexual abuse, we frequently don't have the ability to complete the actions that our fight-or-flight systems would like to initiate.

Perhaps during the trauma we were physically immobilized, or frozen with fear. That was the case for you in the context of your sexual abuse. So because this happened repeatedly, I'd suggest that you've got some negative stress built up in the areas of your body that hold on to that shit. Places like our necks, shoulders, low backs, guts ...

Theo: That totally makes me think about the gut pain from my Crohn's disease, and where the hell that might have come from. You know, I am getting to the point of being sick of that kind of pain in my body.

Kim: No question. And you're working hard to get rid of it. The stuff you're doing by looking at your relationship with food is a huge part of that solution. How did you even get to the awareness that this was important? I think part of it is that you've been investing time sitting with your emotional shit. Because part of that process inevitably means listening to the feelings in your body.

Theo: That's one of the pains of this self-awareness stuff. When we pay attention to how everything's feeling inside, we don't always like the answers we get. So what am I supposed to get out of feeling the pain in my gut at this point?

Kim: Just take it as a message to do something about it. And you're already doing that. My theory is that when we don't connect with our emotional pain, it will eventually come out as physical pain, in ways that are unique to each of us, depending on where our physical vulnerabilities lie. For Bob, he feels it in his lower back; for me it's my effing shingles and eczema; for you, I'd say it's your Crohn's. Do you notice that the physical pain will act up more frequently when you're suppressing something emotional, or in times of relative stress?

Theo: Sure. Yeah. That makes sense. I have never been one to take a pill when I am in pain.

Kim: I've seen that. With physical pain, your strategy is to suffer. Some people have a very limited tolerance for suffering and will take a pill at any inkling of pain.

Theo: But that's physical pain. How do I tolerate sitting in my shit (the emotional pain) without escaping or indulging? That's what I want to know more about.

Kim: The most powerful way that I know to cope with emotional discomfort is to have a healing conversation with a safe person. It's the co-regulation in that kind of conversation that can calm us down and make us feel better. I'm not just talking about venting or gossiping to another person, that's not helpful, but about having a mutual conversation that is attuned, with self-awareness and compassion. When we look at the face of a calm and caring person, the amygdala in our brain—where we process stress—immediately calms down. And so does our stress.

Theo: I think that relationship can only take you so far, though, because eventually you have to be able to tolerate these feelings by yourself.

Kim: No question. But it's very familiar in neurodevelopmental science that the more we all practise interacting with well-regulated people, the more our own brains learn to calm and soothe themselves. In any case it's a way to start.

Part of this is learning to trust your instincts. And speaking of your gut, your "gut feelings" are important. When your spider sense is tingling and something doesn't feel right, a high percentage of the time it isn't. So when I'm considering escaping or indulging in some way, I ask myself, "How does this idea feel in my body?" I check in with myself and if I'm feeling good, then good. If there's some physical awkwardness anywhere, then that's a signal I gotta dig deeper to resist making an impulsive decision or action.

Theo: Hmm. So you ask your gut if it feels okay about you having a doughnut? Sounds like a conflict of interest.

Kim: I don't just ask one part of my body anything. I ask the whole thing.

Theo: Another example of how men can learn from women. (*with a smile*)

Kim: I have a saying when I'm trying to make an important decision: "When in doubt, throw it out." In other words, if I'm in doubt, I do nothing. So, I wait, consciously, until there is some level of certainty and calmness in my body before I act. If there is a doubt, I either wait until some new information presents itself or I just say no. Does that sound wacko to you?

Theo: Probably smarter than just rolling the dice. (*laughing*)

Kim: It speaks to the body's wisdom maybe. Ever wonder how Yoda did it? How he used the force?

Theo: No. (*then laughing*) I'm just shitting you. Of course, I think Yoda is awesome. But are you saying we can all be like Luke and learn to lift fighter space ships out of swamps?

Kim: Sound's a little far-fetched, eh. (*smiling*) But I do believe there is a lot of untapped potential in us all, every one of us. Where the limit to it is? I don't know.

Theo: In the past, I felt like I was supposed to have it all figured out on my own, but you know what? Not quite there yet. This is something that has become increasingly better over the past couple years.

Kim: (*smiling at Theo*)

Theo: What I was getting at is the realization, the acknowledgement, that I don't have to have it all figured out on my own. That I'm not alone. Aha. There's the difference. I think in the past when the bus I was driving was always crashing, I didn't care as much. Now I do. So I'm accepting help.

Kim: Good on you for that aha. What kind of help are you still looking for?

Theo: It's still the question of how can I sit with my shit on my own, without being overwhelmed by it or totalling ignoring it.

Kim: Aside from healthy conversations, we can self-regulate. Just a reminder about how you can use more of your body to calm yourself down when you feel agitated—we talked about yawning—but taking a couple of deep breaths works the same way. Both of those simple things naturally calm our fight-or-flight response, and the calming directly helps us tolerate sitting with discomfort. Slower, regulated breathing decreases the metabolic activity in different parts of the brain and specifically allows our frontal lobes to calm down so that we can think better. And be more rational.

Before and during a time when you're giving a speech, when most speech givers are incredibly stressed, that's a great time to consciously slow down your breathing. People listen better when you talk more slowly as well.

Theo: When I'm anxious, I think I hold my breath.

Kim: I know you hold your shoulders up around your ears sometimes, which is often a body signal of breath holding.

Theo: I always have pain in my shoulders and in my neck. Makes sense.

Kim: Most people do. That's why those massage chairs are popping up at all the big airports; they know it's very often all about the neck and shoulders.

Theo: Many times you've told me you notice when I soothe myself by touching my face or putting my hand on my chest. I don't even notice I'm doing it.

Kim: We talked about this a little bit before. But it really helps to know what simple and free tools are out there that help you relax a bit when you're uncomfortable. When you rub your skin, especially on your face, your chest, or any midline structure on your body, you release the neurochemical serotonin, which is specifically there to help calm you down. It is a fantastic strategy for self-soothing, 'cause you can do it just about anywhere. You were doing it just a while ago—rubbing your nose—and probably didn't even know how much it was helping you.

Theo: And you told me how yawning helps release tension. I know I've started doing that a bit more. Just not in front of people when we're talking, because they'd think they were boring the snot out of me when it could be the opposite.

Kim: Good reminder. Anything we do affects the other people around us. Have you ever heard of Gregg Braden?

Theo: Can't say that I have.

Kim: He's the scientist with great hair who's gone around the world learning from mostly indigenous cultures and remote monasteries what our western science has been missing.[lxxix]

Theo: And what have we been missing?

Kim: That the empty space between us really isn't empty at all. That everything we do and think and feel affects everything else around us. Modern science is catching on to this, and the study of quantum physics is fascinating beyond compare. I think in a hundred years we'll understand how interconnected and inter-dependent we all are on each other, and that'll make the 2010s look like the stone age.

Theo: But, until all this stuff becomes mainstream knowledge, we just gotta get through, right? Take care of ourselves and each other.

Kim: That's all we can ever do. But by taking care of ourselves and each other, it'll be the same outcome as when we know how it works.

Theo: Before we have proof that we all matter to each other, we just gotta have faith. 'Cause living life thinking we don't matter to each other is pretty empty.

Kim: In moments when something is tough, being able to regulate your-self is the key to both internal health and healthy relationships.

Theo: I try to tell my mind to keep calm, keep calm.

Kim: But remember, trying to use your mind to calm yourself down is okay, but the fastest way to self-soothe really is through the body. That's why hugging an infant to calm them down works way better than just about anything else.

Theo: That's interesting. What about smoking? Chemically, it's inhal-ing poison—we all know that—but is it doing any good on any level?

Kim: Smoking is not recommended for health reasons to anyone, and watching my dad die from complications made worse by smok-ing reinforces that more than a thousand times over.

But to answer your question, I know you smoke as a form of self-soothing and self-regulation. I used to chuckle, because we'd be in the middle of a conversation and all of a sudden you'd disappear. Bloody vanishing act. Fifteen seconds later, you would be back. It wasn't even long enough to have a quick pee. Then I found out what you were really doing. I discovered you'd go outside alone, take two little puffs of a smoke, put the whole thing out, and come back inside.

Theo: Many creative thoughts are born while having those two little puffs.

Kim: Well, it makes sense to me in that the act of sucking produces endorphins and serotonin, just like a baby sucking his thumb. And I know two puffs aren't as bad as smoking the whole thing. I think you do it for the endorphins and serotonin, more than for the nicotine though. Wonder where else you could get those helpful chemicals from instead of the cigarette.

Theo: We just learned from Sherry Strong—food philosopher—that when we eat cheese we get a natural opiate hit. Everyone's got some habits to keep them going, right?

Kim: When I heard that, I thought, "No wonder I like cheese!" I often go grab a piece of cheese when I'm stressed. Those opiates affect the brain just like endorphins, giving us a natural high.

Theo: I definitely eat to self-soothe. Sherry helped us understand what foods are better for us than others. There are so many different opinions out there about diet that we've all become confused about what to believe. Her basic explanation is that foods that are easier to get from nature are better for our bodies than foods that are hard or impossible to get from the wild. I know my Crohn's felt way better after eating her stuff for a couple days. But putting that mindful eating into practice for myself isn't easy. Especially when I am on the road. I'm working at it though.

Kim: It's a start. Practise, practise, practise. What I learned from her is that I've been using certain foods to comfort myself rather than to nourish myself. With food it's best we consider the nourishment aspect; comfort we can get from other sources.

Theo: Other than relationships and the self-soothing techniques you've mentioned, what other comfort sources are there?

Kim: There are some basic ways to calm ourselves that most people might not know about. Deep pressure touch also releases serotonin. In my profession of occupational therapy, we have a saying whenever we want to help a client stay calm and regulated: "When you don't know what to do, use deep pressure." It's so easy and effective. We wrap people up in sheets of Lycra, use weighted blankets, have them wear fitted Lycra clothing, or, when they can tolerate it, give them a deep pressure massage. It makes people feel connected to themselves and relaxed.

Temple Grandin, who is a magnificent ambassador for Autism Spectrum Disorder, was associated with the Ayres Clinic in Los Angeles when I was a student therapist back in the early Eighties. When I was just beginning to learn all about sensory processing, she was developing her famous hug machine that she invented for her own self-soothing. The hug machine was inspired by her observation of how cattle would calm when they entered the squeeze chute before they were slaughtered. Amazing lady, she ended up getting her PhD in Animal Science and has helped the world over understand what autism is like from the inside out. We have spoken at lots of the same conferences and she continues to inspire me.

Theo: Another person we could invite over for a conversation at the kitchen table! Kim, I remember seeing those Lycra play structures that you have for your clients. I want one of those in my home.

Kim: You mean the Lycra sandwich frame, where several sheets of strong Lycra are layered on top of each other and attached at four corners to a frame?

Theo: Yup, that thing, I really need help to relax.

Kim: You can lie in it like a hammock and the Lycra provides resistance to your body, kind of snuggling you in. I imagine it's a bit like being back in the womb. Clients have them in their houses all the time. We can figure out a way to have one made for you.

Theo: Right on. Tell me your weighted blanket story again.

Kim: Well, I had a client who was a young man with mild autism. He was experiencing tremendous anxiety and received high doses of anti-anxiety medication. He attended college, and this medication seemed to help him to cope and maintain his function at school, until his liver started responding negatively to the medication. Then he worried about how he was going to cope with anxiety without his meds, and it was at that point when I was asked to become involved.

From talking with him and his roommates, I heard he liked to crawl between his box spring and the mattress to feel the pressure against his body. When I asked him about this, he said it helped him feel calm and safe. But it wasn't easy for him to do; it's a bit awkward to be moving mattresses around.

So I decided to try a weighted blanket. I guessed he'd need something heavy, but how heavy? So I decided to sit on him and he said to me like, "Are you sitting on me yet?" That was the best compliment I'd ever received from a client!

The point is he was unable to really perceive my one hundred and x pounds, so we added more weight. His roommate was a two hundred-pound guy, and when he sat on him, that's when my client was in bliss. So I went down to the beach, got some British Columbia sand, and sewed maybe a hundred little pockets filled with that sand and made a two hundred pound weighted blanket. Then, we had to figure out a way to make sure people wouldn't suffocate under these things; but we worked out the logistics, it did the trick. He'd spend a bit of time under there every day and was able to cope with his life without the use of the anxiety medication.

Theo: That is the coolest story. I want a weighted blanket too. Next time I feel anxious, I can lie underneath a weighted blanket instead of having a smoke.

Kim: Perfect! Not sure that would always be the most practical solution when you're on the road, but you obviously get the idea.

Theo: What I take from it is that the body plays a big role in self-regulation.

Kim: Yep, it does. To be clear, the mind, the body, the spirit, and the emotions are all involved in self-regulation.

This reminds me of a guy in Seattle. I was speaking at a trauma conference, and there was a security guard in the conference hall. During my presentation, I noticed he kept coming into the room and was checking under the chairs and tables. I thought he might have been looking for a bomb. His coming in and out of the room was actually making me a little neurotic. So, at the first break, I went out and talked with him, to find out if everything was okay.

He totally surprised me and said, "Oh yeah, everything is more than okay."

So I asked, "Then what's going on?"

He replied by asking me if I had ever seen the movie *The Hurt Locker*. And then said, "The main character in that movie was me. I was a bomb defuser in Iraq, and now that I'm back here in the US, I can't function. I'm going out of my mind."

He explained that he'd been making up reasons to keep coming into the presentation room so he could listen to what I was saying about trauma. He hadn't bought a ticket and wasn't sure if he'd be allowed to be in there if he wasn't looking like he was working. He told me that all the things I was saying about how you can soothe trauma through the body were making so much sense to him. He then explained that the only time he felt sane was when he did his daily intense morning combat trainings in the park.

I explained to him how heavy physical work—like moving your body against resistance and deep pressure touch—is by far the fastest way to regulate your nervous system without using drugs. With his workouts, he'd intuitively found a way to heal himself.

Theo: Hearing this, I'm really glad I had hockey.

Kim: For sure. What was so cool was that that guy kept in touch with me, and about eight months after that conference, he emailed me to say he'd found a way to get a modest grant from the US army to help vets with PTSD, by leading intense physical exercise programs combined with meditation and support groups. How cool is that?

Theo: Totally.

Kim: And this is catching on. If you look at many of the progressive police, fire, and paramedic stations, they now have standing desks, treadmills, stationary bikes, and moving chairs to help their employees regulate the stress of their intense jobs by moving and using their bodies, instead of just sitting the old-fashioned way.

Theo: When I think of stress, I think I'm still too much in my mind. I bet I'm over-relying on my thoughts to get me out of it. So when I'm trying to tolerate my discomfort going forward, I'll try to remember that going through the body is actually the faster way to relax. (*reflecting*)

Kim: What are you thinking about?

Theo: I'm thinking of golf. It's just a way to have fun, but I think golf is actually a huge form of self-regulation for me.

Kim: Could be. Say more about why you think that.

Theo: It gets me away from all the noise in my head, where I can get out in the fresh air and find success without having to think too much. It's really rewarding when I can just do something well without any stress attached.

Kim: Maybe golf is a form of meditation for you. Although we know it's not so easy, meditation is an excellent source of self-regulation and self-soothing. Most anxious people who find a way to get into it (when they're not being pressured) find that the more they do it, the calmer they are.

Theo: There's gotta be a way to make it easier, aside from the sa ta na ma, sa ta na ma's. Can't get much easier than that one. Are there any others?

Kim: There is a video game *Journey to Wild Divine* that promotes stress management through the use of breathing, meditation, and relaxation exercises. The player has biofeedback finger sensors that measure heart rate as a signal for when they are getting stressed or excited. Unlike most video games, this one is actually designed to help keep you calm. So when playing the game, if you get too excited, the game will suspend itself until you calm yourself down again. It gives you inherent motivation to want to calm yourself so you can excel at the game.

Theo: That sounds like a cool mind-over-matter activity. Never got into video games much, except for on-line poker. Which brings my excitement up, not down.

Kim: I find that the game of *Journey to Wild Divine* is best suited for kids with very high distractibility issues. It seems to really keep them focused, but regulated as well. One client I saw had been in eighteen foster homes. He was only eight years old, and he literally couldn't sit still for a second. When he tried that game, it was the first time anyone remembered seeing him being still, except for when he'd been sleeping. I've seen it work for adults, too.

Theo: Hmm. Makes you think, eh. About whatever else is out there that could help regulate us without drugs. Or forced meditation! (*making a face*)

Kim: You know, prevention is often the most efficient way to save energy with all this. If you don't have to feel anxious to begin with, how much easier would that be?

Theo: What do you mean?

Kim: Well, once we practise sitting with emotions, we're better able to develop our sense of boundaries, right? And clear boundaries are what keep us emotionally safer going forward.

Theo: I definitely didn't learn about setting boundaries in my family.

Kim: Did you know that one of the functions of anger is to restore the boundaries that you lost during abuse and trauma? Your anger is very functional, to a point.

Theo: Anger definitely keeps people away.

Kim: Did you know that you can be angry and still be lovable? Those two are not exclusive of each other.

Theo: My NHL coaches loved me even though they saw my anger. The good ones knew which buttons to press to get me to perform, and it wasn't from telling me nice things about myself. I saw my parents fight all the time and I think what I did early on was define that kind of chaos as love. You know, thinking about it, I'm not sure I understand yet where the difference is between chaos and love.

Kim: Interesting. I do think you're learning that difference though. (*reflecting*) For me, I think I just figured out my own anger/lovable thing! It's that feeling like a "bad girl" again! Growing up, I saw anger as "bad," so I thought I wouldn't be loved if I were seen to be angry. And anger is related to boundaries, 'cause you get angry when they are crossed. So if I couldn't show any anger, then my boundaries would have easily been compromised, for sure.

Theo: Wow. No expressions of anger at all? You could have got walked all over! You know, there were no unwritten rules like that in my house. We just did whatever and had no sense of consistency.

Kim: So what happens when you have rules now?

Theo: Well, I did learn about rules, from outside my family, by being a part of a team.

Kim: Rules are how boundaries become internalized, so they are kind of interrelated. Want to hear some questions I ask myself when

I'm considering how my own boundaries are doing today?

Theo: Sure.

Kim: "Am I able to say no in this moment? Am I asking for what I really need right now? Am I compulsively people pleasing by what I'm doing? Is the reason I'm feeling upset just because others around me are unhappy?" If I can answer these honestly to myself, it will tell me a lot about how I'm doing with my boundaries.

Theo: Hmm. I'm guessing both of us still have some work to do with these questions.

Kim: I think all of us need to be mindful of our boundaries, and other people's too.

Theo: I am way better at setting boundaries than I ever was in the past. I had nowhere to go but up.

Kim: I saw an excellent example of you having boundaries the other evening, when a woman was somewhat forward with you in a seductive way. You were able to keep your boundaries in such a mature and kind way. You were clear and managed to not leave her feeling ashamed or embarrassed. It was a really good example of boundary setting. I think you said something like, "Thanks for your generous offer and I'm sure it would be fun, but I'm just not looking for any extracurricular activity." Whatever exact words it was, it was impressive. I was actually surprised at how happy I was that you let her down *in a classy way*.

Theo: Thanks for saying that. It's hard when all the women in the world want to be with me! (*laughing*) But the truth is I no longer get hooked by seduction as easily as I used to. But who am I kidding with this talk about flirting? I don't need the fucking drama! Enough extracurricular already!

Kim: When I first started learning that I need to keep communicating even when I'm feeling uncomfortable, I decided I needed a few scripts. I know my thinking brain isn't as available to me in those moments, so I needed some pre-planned lines I could refer to. Like an elevator speech when people invariably ask, "And what do you do?" So I prepared little statements to help me get through potentially unsettling moments. I use the lines, "This is hard for me" or "I am uncomfortable right now" or "I don't feel safe in this conversation" or "I need to think about that, and we can talk again ... " These are some tools I have in my toolbox whenever I get triggered. I think I use "This is hard for me" the most. It's really easy to remember, and almost always makes the other person back off just enough.

Theo: I remember when one of our colleagues asked us how she could calm down her neighbour to get her to stop screaming and yelling at her. I loved what you said. "You have to be calm yourself."

Kim: You cannot regulate another person unless you regulate yourself. You have to validate them, support them, and see the fear in them, instead of the outer presentation they are showing you.

And remember, each person we encounter is a reflection of ourselves. It's always best to be mindful about your own role in any dynamic when people are screaming ...

Theo: And you said before that when you're screaming, the other person isn't really able to listen anyway, right?

Kim: Yep. So the simple answer to her question is, if you want to calm someone down, you definitely can't be yelling yourself.

Theo: Seems so fucking obvious, but how many times did I do the exact opposite? "You calm down! No, YOU calm down. NO! YOU CALM DOWN!" What a waste of breath, eh!

Kim: People get upset …We need to try and not judge them when they are. I like to think they're doing the best they can with what they've got. (*reflecting*) You know, I believe that learning to sit with our shit helps us, but I'm not sure if we ever really "let go" of all the tough stuff. Mindfulness helps us notice the shit as it comes up, and acknowledging our resistance to it helps it to soften and fade over time. But I'm not sure it totally ever goes away.

Theo: I think it's like grief. When we lose someone close, or even something close, I think the loss is still always a little bit with us.

Kim: Yeah. I miss my dad every day.

Theo: When I think of missing someone, I think of my buddy Chuck who died in a plane crash. Fucking sad.

Kim: I think what helps is when we have these feelings, which are part of us, we can learn to become an observer of them, rather than becoming engulfed by them. Easier said than done, I know. But when we feel angry, sad, or afraid, learning to "sit with these emotions" serves at least to turn down their volume.

Theo: Yeah. And whenever I remember to pause before reacting, I'm thankful for it. Every time.

Kim: When you learn to sit with your shit, whether it's in the moment of a conversation and it just helps you pause to think, like you just said, or whether it's deep reflection when you give an issue some real airtime, it leads you to good things.

Theo: Like what? What would you say is the best product that comes out of all this mindfulness, and all this effort? (*leaning forward with anticipation*)

Kim: I think all of this is the key to healing yourself. And the greatest bonus of that? That's what builds healthy relationships!

Theo: (*huge smile, like he's ready to go out and hug Tim the cable guy*) Imagine what it would be like if we all were doing it!

10

Helping is Healing

"Demasiada cordura puede ser la peor de las locuras, ver la vida como es y no como deberia de ser." (Too much sanity may be madness. And maddest of all, to see life as it is and not as it should be.)
Miguel de Cervantes Saavedra, Don Quixote

Theo: You know what, Kim?

Kim: What?

Theo: I've messed up a lot of relationships.

Kim: I know.

Theo: It's my biggest regret.

Kim: (*holding the space, not rushing a response*)

Theo: I'm working hard to change every day, but when I really think about it, there's still guilt. Especially when I think about my kids. I know at the end of the day they are forgiving me, but the fact is I wasn't always available for them. Hardly at all when they were little. Shannon was right in that HBO documentary—she did all the emotional work as a parent for Josh.[lxxx] And Beaux and Tatym didn't have me as anything close to a decent dad until they were just about hitting the double digits. Skylah's with me more often, but I'm not even close to perfect with her. Fuck. Parenting isn't easy. If I can change any outcome, it's these relationships that matter the most to me.

Kim: When you connect to that regret, that is part of sitting with your shit. It is helpful when you connect to feelings of guilt, as motivation, to make things better. But it's not where you want to get stuck. Remember emotions move; change is inevitable. Your real intentions are setting your course, right now.

Theo: I guess it really is one day at a time.

Kim: With relationships, it's never too late for repair. And I know this with certainty. If both people want it, it's never too late for repair, until you stop breathing.

Theo: Repair, you mean like apologizing?

Kim: It could be an apology, or a forgiveness, or something else. But whatever form repair takes, it's about restoring a bond. Reconnecting, after there's been some sort of disruption in closeness.

Theo: That's why I wanna get better, and keep getting better. For me, part of the agony of my developmental trauma and sexual abuse is knowing that, although I did nothing wrong and it wasn't my fault, I often hurt and neglected others throughout my life. I know it's in part because of my pain and shame, and this is why the epidemic of trauma absolutely has to stop, to stop this cycle. I know intuitively that our end goal is that we repair as needed and develop strong relationships. I know that's the goal. So what more do you think I gotta do?

Kim: You don't want to be told what to do.

Theo: (*little snort*) You're right about that. I hate being told what to do.

Kim: I notice a habit in you when you suspect people will just end up telling you what to do, or judging you—you sometimes omit telling them the whole story, to protect yourself.

Theo: That could be. Do you see that in me, because it's in you? (*laughing*)

Kim: In the past, it used to be a very strong pattern. But you know, I'm not gonna tell you what to do, unless you ask three times, and I'm not going to judge. So neither of these are the case here. (*smiling gently*) In repairing these relationships, or any relationships with the people you care about, what do you think you have left to do?

Theo: Well, I don't think I can go around saying sorry to everyone I might have hurt, unless I've truly forgiven myself first. That's the hardest part. And I think that's where most people do get stuck. So I think that's where you have to start. And it's gonna take a while, 'cause all this internal work is just beginning to make me realize the affect that people had on me. So naturally, I'm just beginning to realize the affect I might have had on others.

Kim: That's phenomenal insight. If you're just beginning to realize the impact your behaviour's had on others, apologies you make now will have so much more depth to them than they would have had ten years ago, won't they?

Theo: Of course! Saying sorry was never easy for me. Getting honest means looking that fucking rattlesnake in the eye. I know I have more work to do; good thing I have my whole life to keep it going.

Kim: As do we all. Repair is not easy when you're still hurting. Both for you and for the other person. Talking about apologies …

what's really behind them? Meaning, do you think that when it's genuine, saying sorry is an expression of remorse, or is it a request for forgiveness?

Theo: Hmm. I have to think about that. For me, it's not just admitting guilt, though, it's more than that.

Kim: As I'm reflecting on this, I'm having an aha right now. When I've hurt someone, I feel such a sense of urgency to receive forgiveness, I can barely tolerate it. I think I feel so bad that I fear what I did wrong will sever the relationship. I always hope that the apology will result in a repair and a restoration of that connection. The challenge for me is that I sometimes feel the need to apologize, even when I haven't done anything wrong. So maybe for me it's more of a request for forgiveness.

Theo: I don't say sorry easily. So I think I say it when I feel it, when I'm feeling badly, and wishing other people were feeling better. I do think there's some truth that I'd only be saying it if I wanted them to like me ... but I wouldn't say it if I didn't feel it.

Kim: I notice that when you do say sorry, it's when you're feeling some level of emotional safety.

Theo: 'Cause I don't always trust people that they won't be manipulating me somehow.

Kim: That's honest.

Theo: (*exhaling*) And when other people say sorry to me, their sorries have often sounded empty. I guess there are still some trust issues out there.

Kim: One of the things I've noticed is when parents are really quick to tell their kids, "Say sorry," when their children have hurt someone else's feelings. It's positive to help your kid learn that what they do affects others. But seldom does a child really understand what they've done to be offensive. There's no learning in that. It's as if the saying of "sorry" magically makes everything okay.

Theo: Like saying confession in church and then going out and repeating the behaviour.

Kim: Ooph. That's an even stronger example …

Theo: I'm sorry. (*laughing*) No I'm not.

Kim: I know what you're saying. Neither of those processes really encourage people to feel their remorse and sit with their shit, do they?

Theo: Not all that many processes in our society do. We all just want to feel better immediately. Band-Aid this, Tylenol that, "Little Johnny, say sorry just so you can relieve my guilt as a parent in this moment." (*laughing*) "So I can get on with buying more Band-Aids and Tylenol …"

Kim: That's funny.

But there are some ways to look at yourself deeper. Before you got fully sober, you went all the way through the Twelve Steps, right?

Theo: (*nodding*)

Kim: Can you tell me more about how that process went for you?

Theo: Sure. There was a lot of good to it. The bulk of it happened years ago when I was following the Twelve Steps word for word, when I first went to Santa Fe. I totally bought into the system and I'm pretty sure I set the record for the number of AA meetings I attended. I went to three a day for months.

Kim: What was at the crux of your motivation for that?

Theo: I had let down the people in New York and that felt like shit. Doing the Twelve Steps was the first time I saw an actual plan to get better. Although I don't like being told what to do, I actually like having a plan, if I buy into it. And it was the only option in front of me at the time, and there were many others doing it too. That's what makes the difference. It's the other people that keep you motivated and in line; well, most of the time anyway.

Kim: So how do the Twelve Steps help with the repair of relationships?

Theo: Steps Eight and Nine are both related to "Making Amends." Step Eight is to make a list of all the people we've harmed throughout our addiction. It is recommended that we reflect carefully upon each situation and categorize them all: which ones should we approach directly; which ones should we tread cautiously with; and which ones should we stay away from for fear of creating more damage? After we've figured that all out as best we can, then Step Nine is to go around and make amends with as many of those people as possible.

Kim: Wow. Tough choices.

Theo: I know that you know that I know that I wouldn't even be able to remember all of the people who should be on a list like that. Especially when I was so out of it from drugs. When I was in survival mode, I did things to get me through and I certainly didn't have the ability to be mindful about who I might have been hurting in the moment. I did make a list though, many years ago now, of the ones I knew.

Kim: I would think that just making that list would be hard work.

Theo: Yeah. It means we're asking ourselves which relationships we think can be saved and which ones are done forever.

Kim: Hmm. Is that where the famous serenity prayer comes in?

Theo: It applies with this, sure. And with a lot of things. Beautiful thoughts. It always helps me to say it again. (*quoting from memory*) "God, grant me the serenity to accept the things I cannot change, the courage to change the things I can, and the wisdom to know the difference."[lxxxi]

Kim: Well, I can see how if you misjudge the situation, someone might be traumatized by the attempt at an apology. I've heard it's often profoundly healing for both the apologizer and the one who gets the surprise visit, but I imagine if the person who was offended was still in deep pain, the experience could be extremely stressful.

Theo: All the Twelve Step programs that I've been through, like Alcoholics Anonymous, they are sensitive to that possibility. They teach us that if we suspect it could be a highly emotional event, we need to really think it through very carefully before we move to making amends.

Kim: That's good to hear. That's a great example of sitting with your shit before acting!

Theo: In truth, my initial response to this task was to rush out and try to do them all quickly, and with the toughest ones, not to do them at all.

Kim: That's honest of you. I think that many recovering addicts would initially need to try to resolve their guilt as fast as possible. They wouldn't have the tools in their toolbox, as you would say, to tolerate the pain of their guilt and shame at first. And it's important not to make an apology solely for self-serving purposes. A byproduct of the suffering that people around alcoholics go through is that they've learned from experience not to trust; so apologies might not be so easy to accept.

Theo: For sure.

I've received apologies, too. Time helps.

Kim: It does. It takes wisdom to know when to act and when to wait. There are some on the receiving ends of apologies who have so many of their own unresolved personal issues that it renders them incapable of finding any compassion. It's good to consider the whole situation before rushing to fix things.

Theo: That's for sure. But if we don't directly try to make things better, what else is there to do? Some people desperately want to make things better.

Kim: Mmhm. I think saying sorry and making amends is positive whenever it can be received. And from what I've been learning about the science of compassion, I think there are Buddhist concepts that complement the Twelve Step process. These concepts of compassion promote the idea that the genuine intention of loving kindness is just as powerful as an outward gesture. Instead of pushing, it's like allowing. Instead of swimming feet first upstream, perhaps it is best to go with the current.

Theo: (*making a bit of a face*) Or just stay out of the water. (*thinking*) Not doing anything concrete would probably be harder though. The inside stuff always is.

Kim: Takes practice. Wanna send some loving kindness to your ex-wives right now?

Theo: You are a troublemaker. You know, one thing we learned is to keep our hearts open in case any of the people we've hurt ever choose to come to us …

Kim: That's important! Relationships work both ways. (*reflecting*) And repair doesn't always mean allowing someone back into your life, either. It can be about awareness and boundaries and inner forgiveness.

Theo: I never really thought much about forgiving others. Sometimes, I'm probably too quick to forgive. And sometimes I know I hold on.

Kim: Comes back to boundaries. You can forgive someone without allowing them back into your life.

Theo: Hmm.

Kim: When you talk about making amends, that's different from simply apologizing, isn't it?

Theo: It is, it's much more profound. Say you borrow $40 from someone to buy a bottle and five years later you go to them and say, "Sorry I never paid you back." That's what it is, saying sorry. Might help a little, might help a lot, might not help at all and actually make it worse. But if you want to make amends, then you'll give them back the $40.

Kim: I like that.

Theo: And then there's "living amends." That's even better. It's when we actually choose and succeed at living differently. When there is a genuinely consistent behavioural change that stops us from hurting people going forward, that's how we can regain trust. It can be small changes, like from being chronically unreliable at picking up the kids from soccer practice to being punctual every single time. Changing behaviour patterns for the better is an awesome way to say sorry.

Kim: And how was that whole formal amends process for you, emotionally, when you first did it?

Theo: Sometimes it was amazing. A huge relief for me. A few times, a lot of tears, on both sides. A couple times, it was re-traumatizing though, like you said. But I don't know if I'd really been ready. I mean, was the list of people a really full and complete list? No. Did I manage to fully repair everything I wanted to? No. Is it going to be a much longer process than I originally thought? Maybe. No. Yeah, it will be for sure! Because I don't want to be promoting Band-Aids. Other than for boo-boos, of course.

Kim: That's awesome commitment. It's important that, when you set out to repair, you remember not to be attached to the outcome.

Theo: What do you mean by that?

Kim: When you're attached to an outcome, your main emotion is fear that it won't work out. If you're not attached to an outcome, you're letting go of the need to control, which is a big piece of the puzzle in how we can be happy.

Theo: I guess we can't ever control how others are going to react to things, can we?

Kim: Obviously not, but it's funny how some of us try anyway, isn't it! I think of it as counterproductive when anyone feels responsible for other people's choices and actions. What other people choose to do is not your fault. And when people suffer in silence for things that aren't their fault, it's sad, eh?

Theo: I don't expect any of this relationship repair stuff to be simple. And I know no one owes me anything.

Kim: Don't be too hard on yourself, though. (*knowingly*) Some people weren't always nice to you.

Theo: That's fucking true. And they know who they are.

Kim: (*waiting to see if he wants to vent*)

Theo: A certain businessman who screwed our concrete business into bankruptcy got what he deserved, even if we didn't get our money back. He was arrested with fraud one hundred times over and is sitting in jail.

Kim: He never came to you and tried to make amends?

Theo: Fuck, no. And I don't ever expect him to. But I believe in karma. (*exhaling*) And I know holding on to that resentment isn't healthy for my body.

Kim: Sure.

Theo: So, before they try it, how does anybody who's hurt someone know how sensitive or even how dangerous it's gonna be?

Kim: What do you think?

Theo: Well, why do you think I've waited as long as I have in some cases? I don't know. No one wants to get their head chopped off. And I know myself a little—if someone responds to me being there by yelling, I haven't always been so good at being mindful and holding the space for them. My natural reaction to being attacked is just like a fucking venomous rattlesnake. When I'm feeling attacked, I strike. Not 'cause I want to hurt, but because I am feeling attacked. My attacks are just about always in defense.

Kim: Funny, I thought you were a forward. (*making a funny face*)

Theo: Sometimes, the best defense is a good offence.

Kim: You are very insightful.

Theo: Well, I actually got that line from the Oilers, back in the day. But it explains my anger; it's not like I'm going around aiming to hurt people. My level of passion, how I compete, that might have looked like angry aggression, but that's just 'cause I wanna win. My anger is a whole other thing. You see, it's like my anger is sitting back at the blue line, with vigilance—right?—waiting for anyone to dare to try to cross it. And if I felt my line was ever crossed, and they didn't even know where that line was, then Bam! See? My anger was actually playing defense. So the Oilers were good for something! They helped with self-reflection. (*laughing*)

Kim: The Oilers, that was Gretzky's team, wasn't it?

Theo: You're bullshitting, right? You knew that, right?

Kim: Are they from Ottawa? (*pausing for effect*) Of course, I know they're from Edmonton! I can pull your leg too. (*grinning*)

Theo: My God, you scared me. Sometimes, it seems like you don't think hockey matters in this country. (*pulling out his hair*)

Kim: I guess that's one of the ways I'm special needs. (*little laugh*)

Theo: (*shaking his head*) I'll try and have compassion for you. I'm thinking about that snake analogy. Snakes can change. They have to, to grow. Ever seen them change their skin?

Kim: Not in person. You?

Theo: (*nodding*) They do the whole thing. Once they get started, they go all the way. They take it all off. All in. Nothing half-assed. I like that.

Kim: Every time they change their skin, do you think they're getting better and better?

Theo: I don't think they're thinking about it. That's why we're different. We can think about it. We know we are capable of changing, and we can set the intentions.

Kim: Sometimes you say pretty smart things. (*thinking*) We've been talking here about the amends process from the AA perspective, but lots of people have relationships that need serious mending, even if alcohol isn't an issue. And when there's been early childhood trauma and those kids are predisposed to having challenging relationships later on, that also doesn't always include addiction.

Theo: That's true! I've known sober people to be messed up too! Interesting how we can get stuck thinking of things only one way. I guess I still identify myself as an "addict" and continue to minimize the depth of impact of my family-of-origin stuff.

Kim: Getting back to attachment theory, I've heard Dan Siegel say that the best predictor of how healthy our kids will be in their relationships depends on how well we, as parents, make sense of our own childhood traumas. To them, what happened to us wasn't as important as how we dealt with it, understood it, and shared it with them. What kind of stories did your parents share with you about their childhoods?

Theo: Well, I know I was scared shitless of my grandma, my dad's mom, so Dad couldn't have had it easy. And I'm sure something must have happened to my mom when she was little, too, but I don't know what it was. Neither of them talked about their childhoods.

Kim: If either or both of them experienced childhood trauma, it may be a part of their implicit memory. They may not directly remember any specific events, or talking about it might just be too hard for them. Do you think it would help you if you knew their stories?

Theo: Like you said, if they could make sense of their stories and shared them with me, it follows that I'd have more of a clue as to what happened to them. Then, maybe it would help me make more sense of my own story. Which would help my kids make sense of their own stories. Wow. What a lot of intergenerational stuff.

Kim: Yep. And it probably goes back further than that. You know that many First Nations say that whatever happens, seven generations are affected into the future. Should make a lot of us stop and think, eh.

Theo: I've heard that and believe that.

Kim: Attachment therapists know that when parents have had a rough childhood and are unable to make sense of what happened to them, they are more likely to pass on their dysfunctional patterns to their children. And their children are at risk for unconsciously passing them along again, to their children. And their children, in turn, to their children.

Theo: My parents abandoned me and I did the same to my kids. I am trying to repair that with my kids now.

Kim: What do you mean when you say that you abandoned your kids? When you say that, it sounds a little harsh. You didn't leave them on the street.

Theo: Certainly not. They've never wanted for anything, in that way. But emotionally, that's another story. Plus, they also had to listen to their mothers tell them what a shit I was all those years. A lot of it was likely true, but it was probably doubly traumatizing to the kids. And it was a lot of my fault that those relationships didn't work out. I feel guilty about all that. Especially not being present for the times when they were just little and needed stability. This was especially true of my relationship with Josh. Josh is the one who called me when I was suicidal. The way I remember it, he helped save my life …

Kim: What's your relationship with Josh like today?

Theo: Josh is an adult now. We get together whenever he wants, really. I love spending time with him. We've come a long way.

Kim: Is that an example of a living amends? Are you able to show him that you're not repeating the same old patterns?

Theo: That's one reason why I'm still working at all this. I want to be an example of a living amends. Can you still develop secure attachment with your kids even when they are adults?

Kim: You definitely can. Being emotionally available, being consistent, and setting boundaries with support are all good patterns when developing secure attachment at any age.

Theo: Right on. That gives me hope.

Kim: What does it tell you?

Theo: Well, I'm just thinking this through … So it's not my fault that my parents were messed up before they made me, and it's not my fault they were messed up when I was a kid, and it's not my fault Graham James was a sick person who took advantage of the kind of kid I was. And assigning blame to any one of them isn't helping me to begin with. Because deciding whose fault it is doesn't make me cured. I used to be so effing angry and needing justice from the court system. I still think the "injustice" system has a long way to go before the perpetrators of sexual abuse get what they deserve. But if my own healing is dependent on that outcome, I would likely never get healed. What I am responsible for is owning my part in keeping relationships around me healthy, and trying to repair the relationships I contributed to damaging along the way. And I can do that.

Kim: That is a great declaration. Being in alignment with what is and doing the best we can with what we've got.

Theo: Yeah, and moving forward.

Kim: So how do you think we really truly heal? What is it that makes you feel happy to be in your own skin?

Theo: I've travelled all across our amazing country. I've seen a lot of amazing people. Just because you and I are talking publicly about childhood trauma, I've seen a lot of them who are in pain. Either in the middle of their journeys or just at the beginning, and I've come up with the most basic of basic truths.

Kim: What's that?

Theo: That helping is healing. Sure as hell seems to be working for me.

Kim: Mmhm. (*smiling*)

Theo: What I'm finding is that when I'm able to give back, it's making a difference. And that's giving me more than just dopamine hits.

Kim: Let's explore that concept! Helping is healing. What do you mean by healing in this case?

Theo: When you inspire someone, you ignite their self-healing switch. Their inspiration becomes your inspiration and that immediately affects you. What is healing, in your mind?

Kim: We mentioned that many people think of healing as curing. But I define healing as being in alignment with what is. That means connecting to the experience with your feelings, feeling all the shit, and moving into alignment with it. Notice how I don't use the word "acceptance." That word sounds like resignment to most people. Hopelessness is often associated with acceptance and being resigned to something. Feeling like we don't have any choice but to accept our fate and suck up our feelings is not what I mean at all. You know you've had a breakthrough in healing when you feel a shift in your emotional state, when triggers no longer affect you in the same way. It's as if you can experience the situation with a new perspective, new eyes, and a new physical response. So, healing, to me, means going through all the stages of your emotions about the situation and coming into a state of neutral detachment from your experience, where the emotional charge is no longer there.

Theo: Wow, that sounds really hard.

Kim: Yeah, but it's worth it. Let me give you an example. It's ultimately how I got through my experience with that boyfriend who broke up with me on Christmas morning. Remember I'd spent months looking at it backwards and forwards, from every angle I could think of, especially from the perspective of, "What could I have done better?" But I stayed stuck for far too long, because I was always looking at it from a mental perspective. I was all in my head, spinning and spinning, getting nowhere. I am sure you can relate to this crazy inner dialogue that comes with rejection?

Theo: Terribly. I can feel the pain as you talk about it.

Kim: At the time, I was voraciously reading self-help books and trying to do my "spiritual work." I read that forgiveness was a part of the healing process. So I prayed to forgive him. At that time, I equated forgiveness with freedom from my pain. So one night, I was meditating on forgiveness, but I found myself just getting madder and madder. I was so pissed off. Pissed off at the situation, pissed off at his cowardice, pissed off at his inability to work it out, pissed off at his unwillingness to work on himself. The list went on. Then I started to laugh. I realized the impossibility of my desire to get to forgiveness without connecting with all the underlying feelings along the way. I actually needed to be mad. Part of the healing for me was to really feel the anger, instead of bypassing it as I'd been doing for so long! What a weird idea. That's what I needed at the time, though.

Theo: I feel mad easily.

Kim: As I've said before, usually the feelings that surface most easily are not the ones we find the most painful. For me, I learned I'd been so stuck in the sadness I couldn't reach the anger. I don't think I felt safe enough to be angry. When I finally allowed myself to feel it though, the sadness just dissipated. Although he'd said, "You're probably going to hate me for the rest of your life," you know what? I don't hate him anymore. I just had to connect with that emotion of anger, and that was enough. Only took me about ten years to get there ... Wow! Had I ever been stuck in sadness.

Theo: (*exhaling*) You know I am completely the opposite, right? When I'm upset I get stuck in anger as a cover-up for all my sadness. I know it's a defense, but it's pretty close to the surface.

Kim: We learn from our earliest experiences that certain emotions make us more vulnerable. Then we avoid them like the plague. I must have learned from my family that anger was the most dangerous. That it could hurt people. Given that we were expected to care about other people's feelings way before our own, expressing anger was not tolerated. So we had an anger-free home as I'd mentioned, but in hindsight, our insides and outsides didn't always match.

Theo: I must have learned in my family that if you show sadness, people will take advantage of you. I always interpreted crying and sadness as manipulation. Didn't understand it as being valuable.

Kim: When we try to skip right to forgiveness or actively seek a cure from our pain without being connected to each step along the way, we are bypassing the healing process and are in fact keeping ourselves mired in it longer.

Theo: So what does forgiveness have to do with healing?

Kim: I don't think you have to forgive to heal necessarily, but it definitely lightens the emotional burden. Remember, real forgiveness does not make excuses for the other person's hurtful behaviour. Forgiveness is a decision that you make with your whole self after you have done your emotional work. It is a conscious process.

Theo: I think you probably have more than one go around with forgiveness, no?

Kim: Very few of us are able to let go, all in one shot.

Theo: I want to make a conscious choice to move beyond feeling sorry for myself. (*thinking*)

Kim: You're talking about forgiving yourself, right?

Theo: Of course. I mean, I gotta ask myself, how happy do I want to be? How much more loving do I want to be? (*quick reflection*) Listen to me. Guys didn't use to say this shit. You know, Kim, I think we're part of a new movement where the days of only being tough are over. Tough love does a lot of damage. Ripping you to shreds to get you to perform, to get you to comply! Strip you down bare and then slowly build you back up. That is what I learned in the old-school hockey world. Maybe it works sometimes, but that doesn't mean it's good for our spirits.

Kim: What about forgiving others? How are you doing with that? I remember you said at one point you'd be willing to meet Graham James. What would that be good for?

Theo: Just to see and show that he can't hurt me anymore. I don't think I need to say, "I forgive you." But if he'd have the courage to see me, I'm not afraid to talk with him. It might help to ask him what the hell he'd been thinking, but it wouldn't be out of hatred the way it would have been a couple of years ago. Maybe it would help put an ending to it. He doesn't deserve to live in my brain.

Kim: How far you've come, eh.

Theo: Well, we've been talking about this stuff for a long time, and whenever we've brought a bunch of people together, just to talk, every time, it really reinforces that abuse has to end. The cycle, if there is a cycle, just has to end … I'm not sure how offenders can change. I think that there are some offenders who probably can't. But I cannot imagine for a second that the injustice system is the only answer. It's critical to lock people up if there's danger of more abuse. But if change is possible, and I'm seeing it is at least with me, then who am I if I don't feel something for people who are wanting to get past their own demons?

Kim: You know this represents a huge shift in the way people know you. You were the guy who always said, "Lock them up and throw away the key. There can never be enough jail time for these monsters."

Theo: I was really angry. And there are offences that happen out there that still trigger me to want to punch these child molesters in the mouth, or much worse. But it's not black and white. It's more like that book all the middle-aged women read, *Fifty Shades of Grey*.[lxxxii]

Kim: So that guy in Nanaimo who shared with everyone at our Forum that he was both abused and became a violent offender, do you think he was helped in any way by his sharing?

Theo: Absolutely. Years and tons of shame came right off him. Couldn't count the number of people who came up to him right away and thanked him for being so willing to seek help. And for having the courage to show vulnerability. If nothing else, what he got from it was that not everyone sees him as a monster. The behaviour was monstrous, yes—and he's the first to say it's inexcusable—but not the person.

Kim: And you witnessing this—helping to facilitate this—helped you?

Theo: Yes. Every time I think about it. From him, I got the reflection on my own anger about abusers and then was amazed at the depth of my own compassion for someone who'd been an abuser. No past justifies hurting another person, but it did make me wonder what hell Graham James quite possibly went through to get as messed up as he was.

Kim: You often say, "Don't let anyone live in your brain rent-free." That means you're encouraging others to think for themselves, right?

Theo: There will always be hundreds of people wanting to manipulate you. Don't let them.

Kim: Good to see you've obviously clarified your own boundaries in that regard.

Theo: Now, I see what you mean. You have to participate in your life in order to heal! Any form of disconnecting from our emotions just interferes with the healing process.

How is helping other people helpful to us, in your therapy and science lingo?

Kim: Lots of ways. Maybe spiritually most of all. One famous spiritual writer, Joseph Dispenza—not the author Dr. Joe Dispenza I mentioned earlier—says that the proof of a healthy spiritual life is the extent to which we make ourselves available to the needs of others.[lxxxiii] I also believe that helping is spiritual.

Theo: It definitely is for me. I know I am on my spiritual path when I'm doing something that's not directly for myself.

Kim: What does helping look like to you?

Theo: I used to be chirpy and judgmental. To get people off their game, right? It worked; I could piss people off so they didn't perform at the top of their game. That helped my team, but didn't help the other guys. But now that I'm not playing hockey, I realize there's no one else to be playing *against*. And that I do better myself by helping people get on their game. To do that I've had to become more mindful and supportive.

Can you imagine if I would walk into a grocery store and tell the cashier she's got her makeup on so bad she reminds me of my uncle Harry when he dressed up for *The Rocky Horror Picture Show*? (*laughing*) I might succeed in encouraging her to key in the wrong numbers on the cash or drop something, maybe, but it wouldn't help her feel decent about herself, or honestly make myself feel good, would it?

Kim: (*laughing*) Theoren Fleury, don't you ever do that!

Theo: It's not rocket science. I can still be judgmental. I just don't think it's useful for me to say out loud that someone's a "fat fuck," even if they are. Hell, I'm not a saint. But let's think about it. Even if I were thinking of myself first and what's in my own interest, does it feel better to kick someone when they're down or does it feel better to extend a hand when they're looking to get up? You know the answer.

Kim: Ah, here's where the science kicks in. Did you know that by helping others you can make your brain work better and your body become healthier? This is being proven. Especially when you experience anxiety, depression, or stress, helping others not only makes you feel good, it also strengthens the structure of your DNA.

Theo: You keep talking about DNA, but how does that really work?

Kim: Well, remember when I talked about how sperm is affected by exposure to alcohol? That was an example of epigenetics, how genes interact with the environment. But your genes are not only exposed to bad things: they can bathe in good chemicals too, which will affect the function of your DNA.

Theo: I guess helping others is one of those good things you are talking about.

Kim: Yes. In order to appreciate how that works, it'll need a bit of an explanation. Are you sure you wanna hear about it?

Theo: Absolutely. I want to be as healthy as possible.

Kim: Okay. Well, remember that DNA is the code within your cells that makes you who you are and unique from everybody else. Every time a cell in your body divides and makes a new cell (which is happening all day long), your DNA is exposed to all the chemistry inside your body. When the replicating strands of DNA are chronically exposed to stress and anxiety chemicals, your DNA gets worn down. This wear and tear makes it harder for you to cope with life's challenges and increases your body's potential to develop disease over time. On the other hand, when you engage in helping, feel-good chemicals like dopamine and oxytocin float around in your bloodstream. These chemicals turn on all the parts of your DNA that help you to become resilient, healthier, and better able to cope with stress. Although it might seem like doing nice things for others is only altruistic, ultimately we are helping ourselves greatly in the process.

Theo: I know it feels good to help, so I really am getting dopamine hits by helping!

Kim: It's more than just that though. There is this really important piece on the end of our DNA strands that protects them from damage over time, and keeps us healthy longer as we get older. This little piece is like a shoelace tip and it is called a telomere. There is an enzyme (a kind of chemical) that helps to keep these shoelace tips healthy and it's called telomerase. Low levels of telomerase and short shoelace tips result in accelerated aging in the face of unremitting stress.

Theo: I must not have any shoelace tips left.

Kim: There is very cool research that shows when you practise mindfulness and when you help others, your telomerase goes up in quantity, which helps to grow your shoelace tips back. You are definitely growing yours back!

Theo: People who look happy and genuinely go around helping do look younger, or am I imagining that?

Kim: No, I think you're right. They did a study on moms, and those who reported they were overwhelmed and stressed had significantly shorter telomeres than those who were relatively relaxed.[lxxxiv] Among the moms in the study, those who had children with disabilities had genetically aged about ten years in comparison with the women who didn't have those constant caregiving responsibilities.

Theo: Holy shit. You're telling me that stress is not only bad for your brain, but bad for your genes, too? Fuck, so that's how stress makes us older and more susceptible to diseases.

Kim: Yes, that's one way. But there is good news. When you connect with others in a truly helpful way, you can grow those protective shoelace tips back.

Theo: Can't we just help our telomeres by eating more nutritiously and exercising?

Kim: Anything that reduces your level of stress, or your perception of stress, will help. What that study suggests, though, is that the stressed women were able to repair their telomeres after joining support groups. Similar results were found with men who joined a comprehensive support group after going through the stress of being diagnosed with prostate cancer.[lxxxv] In their cases, a significant increase in telomere length was recorded.

Theo: Cool. It's great to hear that the rationale for being part of support groups is backed by science!

Kim: For sure. There is actually a Center for Compassion and Altruism Research and Education in California that studies this kind of stuff. One of the scientists who specializes in this, Stephen Post, talks about how helping others reduces our stress, which naturally boosts our immune system. He emphasizes the value of peer support for all kinds of healing, and believes the more we engage with others altruistically to overcome obstacles, the healthier we'll all be.[lxxxvi]

Theo: Altruism is when we do nice things for other people, right?

Kim: True altruism is perhaps a little different than simply helping. A helpful action or intent is considered to be altruistic when you don't expect anything back in return. Altruism is a truly unselfish concern for the welfare of others. It's the oxytocin chemical that we have in our bodies that gives us the ability to be altruistic, and when we are altruistic, our oxytocin levels go up.

Theo: Like when so many Calgarians stepped up for each other during the flood of June 2013.

Kim: Exactly! Despite the damage and the loss, the volunteers would have been unknowingly improving their own health with their intensive rescue, comfort, and repair efforts.

I read an article in *Psychology Today* that talked about how scientists have found that antibody levels (the armies that fight infection and disease in your body) immediately increase and are sustained whenever we engage in a generous act. Or even if we witness one![lxxxvii] Other researchers had a group of students watch a film about Mother Teresa's work with the sick and poor in Calcutta (Kolkata), India. In the people who watched the Mother Teresa movie, compared to students who simply watched a neutral film, there was a significant increase in the protective antibodies found in their saliva.[lxxxviii] That means their immune systems got stronger just from watching.

Theo: So this is like those mirror-neurons at work; when we watch people help, it's as if we are doing the helping ourselves. And we get physiological benefits from that?

Kim: Sure. It's like when people watch hockey, they can feel the game in their own bodies. They don't get the cardio-workout, or the injuries, but they can sensorially feel like they are playing themselves. After watching an intense Canadiens game, Bob often says, "Whew, I skated hard tonight!" That may sound ridiculous 'cause he was on the couch, but deep in his brain, it's real. Fans everywhere get adrenaline, dopamine, and probably cortisol when their team's in trouble …

Theo: Hockey does matter, Kim!

Kim: The mirror-neuron phenomenon also happens when elite athletes visualize a movement over and over before they do it for real. At a neurological level, they are getting their system primed for performance. And in rehabilitation, there's something called "virtual reality therapy" for spinal cord injuries that helps these patients improve their movements just by watching others do the movement they are trying to learn. Mirror-neurons give us a shared experience, and are known as the cells of empathy.

Theo: I totally relate to visualizing as an athlete. We'd go over plays on the chalkboard so we could see ourselves doing it in our heads, and then we'd go out and execute it perfectly. It's wild to think we can benefit from watching others doing good things though.

Kim: It does speak to the importance of hanging out with positive people—doesn't it?—when we understand that we resonate with the people we are with. That's another benefit of volunteering. Often, it's other positive people who are also doing it. And they're having fun together. When we engage in helping behaviours, it's proven to turn up the volume on that oxytocin again, which naturally relieves stress. And perhaps most interesting to you, our giving-back behaviours connect to the reward system of the brain that releases dopamine and endorphins. They call it the helper's high.

Theo: And it's free?

Kim: No money involved!

Theo: Maybe some people get addicted to volunteering? (*smirking*) Hey, is there a Twelve Step program for that? No, that's not right, that's a good addiction.

Kim: As long as there's some altruism involved, it's awesome. Can I brag for a second?

Theo: Sure. (*smiling*)

Kim: I have an amazing daughter. (*sitting up straight*) Lista's volunteered with me, helping special needs kids at camps and such since she was eight years old. She just graduated from high school and went through the process of deciding what to do next. In some ways, it's hard for kids these days as there are so many options. So after some soul searching, she made her decision to take a gap year before university, and next month she's off to live in a remote community in eastern India. It's called Jhamste Gatsal, which means "garden of love and compassion." It's like an orphanage, but the whole community is basically children; apparently, it's a really special place. Once she gets there she'll figure out how to help however she can, and she's so excited. I'm only bringing this up because I know her helping others absolutely contributes to her own self-esteem and happiness!

Theo: Lista is an outstanding kid!

Kim: It has been researched and well established that volunteering in adolescence and young adulthood enhances social competence and confidence, decreases the risk of substance abuse, and increases academic performance. But as a mom, I just know it makes her happier, and that's the bottom line.

Theo: And more humble, eh. Giving sometimes reminds us we've actually had it pretty good.

Kim: Yeah. There's always someone who has more challenges than us.

Theo: The ones who've really lived through crap and come out the other side are the ones who inspire me. And even the ones who are managing to hold on even though they haven't found their way yet. I find that extra effort very powerful. You know when they dig real deep and find that extra ounce of tenacity to keep on trying … The human spirit is strong, eh.

Kim: We all find different ways to be resilient. That's what impresses me! Every single person has their own story.

Theo: We're sure learning that!

Kim: What about your kids? What are some of the things they're happiest about?

Theo: I'm glad that they've each found a talent they can be good at, whatever it is they choose. They all seem to have a way to excel in whatever they really put their minds to. Beaux's right into soccer and getting really good at golf. Taytm's super talented at horse jumping. Skylah's got her gymnastics, and Josh is a hard working kid, with lots of good friends.

Kim: You still call Josh a kid?

Theo: For sure.

Kim: They all seem to have got some of the good genetics, eh?

Theo: You know, at the end of the day, what I hope they get from me is to know how to work hard. And put in a lot of effort. I hope that's what they get from me.

Kim: I think that they are. (*smiling*)

Theo: I'm just glad they're active, you know, focusing on the good stuff.

Kim: Totally. Makes me think of what happens to us as we get older and naturally begin to have a lot more time on our hands. Not yet in our cases, we have a lot more super-active years.

But it comes back to this "helping is healing" idea. What about the dynamic of older people who've lived a full life and now have a lot of time on their hands. We're learning that the more people sit by themselves and maybe watch their TVs, the faster and further their health degenerates, both physically and mentally. But these same studies show that the more they retain purpose and meaning in their lives, the healthier they stay! So I'm really thankful to all those people who make the time to volunteer in their communities, who consciously get out there and get involved. However they do it, even if they're only minor acts of kindness, it really does make a difference.

Theo: Totally agree.

Kim: I wonder what the stats are on volunteerism in Canada. (*whipping out her iPhone seconds before Theo does*) Aha! Stats on the Internet about Canadians show that 47 percent of us volunteer in our communities, the youngest age group represents the highest percentage of volunteers (58 percent), and the population over 65 donates the largest number of hours.[lxxxix]

Theo: (*a little slower on the draw*) It says 84 percent of us donate money to charities. And the provinces that have the highest volunteer rates? Can you guess? Saskatchewan and PEI.[xc] One thing I know is that the reason small towns survive and thrive is all about volunteering! You could never have paid those parent coaches what they were worth. Never.

Kim: That's beautiful. (*smiling*)

Theo: You know what? I love being one of those people out there who encourages other people to get the help they need. I know I'm getting healthier the more I do this.

Kim: There was a time when you couldn't, eh. I know this from common sense, but also from scientific research, that whenever anyone is in their own survival mode, and/or actively in an addictive state, their brains put the brakes on their ability to help others. It's a survival mechanism. Our brains make a choice and when we have to become more concerned about ourselves, our altruism or capacity to help others shuts off. For addicts, their need for rewards through addiction competes with their ability to help others.

Theo: You are definitely self-absorbed when you are in the throes of addiction.

Kim: To turn this around, helping others would take people out of their self-absorption, because when you're helping others, you have to be thinking of them, at least a little. I think this is a key benefit of twelve-step programs and self-help groups. And when you can see yourself helping, you get dopamine, so it lessens the perceived need for the addictive source of dopamine.

Theo: I like this idea. Doesn't seem at all easy when you're right in the middle of it though.

Kim: No. I'm not suggesting it is. To suggest that would be setting people up for failure. Hardly anything we're talking about is easy. But by pointing things out, hopefully we're at least clarifying options. And remember, staying stuck in pain isn't easy either.

Theo: No.

Kim: I've got another example of when helping is good for the helper, and it's something else you're already doing. You know all that fundraising for charity that you do? Well, according to a survey overseen by researchers from Harvard University, those who gave contributions of either time or money were 42 percent more likely to be happy compared with those who didn't give anything.[xci]

Theo: Hmm. That's great. You'd think just knowing that would help people choose to give more of themselves, right? Maybe it will! (*reflecting*) You do a bunch, too. I noticed you're also spending a lot of time helping people learn about cerebral palsy in Asia ...

Kim: What do I say: it feels good. And there's a bottomless pit of need out there, too.

Other research that inspires me is the work done by Dr. Richie Davidson of the University of Madison in Wisconsin. He talks about the effects of compassion on the brain. I love that guy. To do this research he used MRI scans to study the brains of Buddhist monks meditating on compassion.[xcii]

The scans revealed that the parts of their brains that plan productive action were firing on all cylinders, even though they weren't doing any "direct" helping; they were sitting still! This was an unexpected finding, and one interpretation of this is that when we see suffering and feel compassion, it is natural to want to do something in response.

Theo: So meditation's for more than calming?

Kim That's what this research is saying. Especially when we're in a situation that requires us to help support someone else. In these circumstances, our brains not only experience compassion but the desire to act on it is ignited. We are literally moved toward action by our brain.

Theo: So the more I connect to the stories that people tell me, because I'm feeling compassion, the more my own brain is encouraging me to want to help, which continues the dopamine cycle. That is fucking awesome.

Kim: Even more exciting is that during compassion meditation (if I were able to do it), the activity in the regions of my brain that keep track of what is "me" and what is "you" becomes quieter. It's as if, during this experience, I'm literally opening my heart and mind to others, without my ego-self getting in the way.[xciii]

Theo: I think that is what helps spiritual connection.

Kim: Neat thought. You know, if we think about it like this, then helping doesn't have to feel like a burden, and it doesn't have to be energy draining, which it can become if we ever feel resentful.

Theo: I know that I always feel pumped when I have made someone else feel good.

Kim: You know we get a little dopamine hit every time we smile? (*smiling*)

Theo: (*smiling back*)

Kim: Feels good, eh? (*laughing*) In case you're not already convinced, I've got one more brain concept for you. The more we have positive thoughts about others and offer positive actions to others, the more we develop the left side of our brains, the happy positive side. This reduces the control of the dominant negative right side of our brains. What brain researchers are suggesting this means is that positivity makes it easier for us to be engaged in helping during a conflict, rather than just avoiding a situation altogether.[xciv]

Theo: So thinking positively makes us be more open-hearted?

Kim: It helps us step forward instead of back when we feel threatened.

Theo: Cool. 'Cause sometimes I'm shy, and I'd like to help more than I'm helping.

Kim: Me, too. I'm not at all an extrovert.

Theo: Think the old rattlesnake could actually move out of his defense position?

Kim: I do. When you're in a positive helping mode, I think that rattlesnake is able to relax enough to be able to sleep on a hammock instead of under a rock. Your threat system naturally relaxes when your positive left brain is in action.

Theo: No wonder I love our Forums so much. Hey, thinking about Forums, the fans in that old hockey shrine in Montreal—the

Forum—were sure into those games, back in the day. It was like everyone in the building was engaged in the whole experience. (*sitting forward in his seat*) Life's awesome when we're more involved in it, eh?

Kim: (*smiling*) I guess calling our events "Forums" is appropriate in more ways than one … But I know that you speak about healing to thousands across Canada and beyond. At all the events I've seen you at, I know you reach out and speak directly and compassionately with absolutely every person who shows up. You make time for everyone who wants to say hello or share something personal. It's like you're a spokesperson for speaking out …

Here's a question: By making yourself available to inspire and support others as they go through their healing journeys, how does being in that position help *you*?

Theo: We're all here for a purpose. I used to think it was to play hockey. Now I know different.

Kim: What aspect of this role do you love?

Theo: Seeing and feeling that it's making a difference. The people who stood up at the "Conversations With a Rattlesnake" Forums and spoke from their hearts on stuff that they'd been carrying, some of them for their whole lives, just releasing the shame—it was a series of miracles, one after the other.

Kim: It was. And we didn't set the Forums up with that clear intention; it just happened naturally when people felt safe enough to say what was really on their minds.

Theo: Some of them I'll never forget as long as I live.

Kim: Which ones really stand out for you?

Theo: The woman who shared that she'd been with so many partners they all just became a numb blur. You and I talked about it already, but did I ever relate. (*looking down*)

Kim: You really checked out on that one, just dissociated before coming back to the group. Where did you go?

Theo: Right to my own shame. She mirrored to me what I'd lived and kind of forgot about. Like I forgot about forgetting. The crux of my shame is that I related perfectly to her story. I realized there are many women out there who I slept with, and I have no idea who they are. I could bump into most of them in a library returning books and not have a clue I'd been intimate with them. Remember their names? Not even close. Numbers, I couldn't guess. I am not proud of this at all. The opposite. I don't even know how many people whose feelings I may have hurt, and I've got no way to say sorry if they were expecting a call the next day or whatever else they might have been thinking. I was so lost in my own sadness I didn't care about them, and I realize that's sick. I feel a bit like that man who said he was a violent offender. I didn't use violence and I didn't molest children, but it stands to reason I probably hurt a lot of people's feelings, not to mention the feelings of the people I was cheating on.

Kim: That's shame. How can we get past that?

Theo: Acknowledge it. Say sorry in our minds.

Kim: You are brilliant.

Theo: I say I'm ashamed and you say I'm brilliant. Am I missing something?

Kim: Not at all. You are brilliant, because you just verbalized the answer to getting rid of so much of our shame. Everyone carries some. By reducing her shame with your compassion, through the mirror-neuron phenomenon, you were also reducing your own. And by connecting to the remorse in relation to the women you don't remember, you're not only helping yourself (as we've discussed), but subtly helping them through the force of quantum physics.

Theo: I am brilliant then.

What are you talking about? (*thinking about what she just said*)

Kim: Stuff that ancient mystics have thought about for thousands of years, which is now being proven in quantum physics, because of the scientific advancements of recent years, and because we're asking the questions. We're finding that all things are made up of energy, they all interact with one another, and ultimately, we're all connected. And our thoughts are part of this energy.

Theo: Okay?

Kim: Stay with me now. Quantum entanglement is the phenomenon that says there is a web called the quantum field that connects all life, energy, matter, and existence to a single system. And that everything we experience has a single interconnected source.

Theo: Wow, that's spiritual.

Kim: And scientific. Interestingly, the Dalai Lama is one of the biggest sponsors and proponents of both quantum physics and brain science. It's like religion and science are getting along very well by proving each other's existence, or trying anyway. (*smiling*) But what I mean to get out of this is the point that we are connected to each other, and therefore we affect each other, way more than we know.

Theo: There's a lot we don't know.

Kim: Shakespeare had a great line. May I?

Theo: Go ahead.

Kim: It was Hamlet, who said, "There are more things in heaven and earth, Horatio, Than are dreamt of in your philosophy."[xcv]

Theo: Why do you like Shakespeare so much?

Kim: He just has a way of bringing up thoughts that make sense and says them in ways that are memorable. Like this one that means there's a hell of a lot going on, in the big picture, that we really don't understand.

Theo: Fair enough. (*smiling*) Thinking back to our Forums, who else from the audience helped you to learn something?

Kim: (*trying to remember*) Maybe the most dramatic event for me was from the perspective of something I'd never been exposed to before, from the incredibly vulnerable and brave gentleman who revealed his involvement in gangs, from when he was just a kid right up to being a much-feared leader. What I learned from his tragic and emotional story is that one abuse event of a child can lead that child—when they grow up—to so much anger and destruction, even outright killing. And then, that it's never too late for repair when surrounded by support.

Theo: Man! Could he write a good book. What a turnaround! Remember how he had the opportunity to have his abuser taken out? And he chose not to? Fucking incredible mercy. Made me think a lot.

Kim: And that young boy in Calgary. My heart just melted. I'm so glad he came to the Forum.

Theo: His courage affected everyone in the room. He'd been sexually assaulted over and over by an uncle, and although he was only going into grade seven, he managed to bring it into the open, 'cause he knew it was wrong.

Kim: Phenomenal. Remember how clearly he spoke, and that he wanted to come right up on stage with us? When someone asked him what made him come forward and be able to talk about it, he said, "I just didn't want him to touch my penis. So I told my Grandma." Sounds so straightforward, but some people in the audience said that if they'd just been able to do that they would have saved fifty years of shame and countless years of dysfunction.

Theo: The message for me in his story is that I really admire courage, and his example inspires me to go further when my own courage is tested.

Kim: Which other stories helped you to clarify your own stories or thoughts?

Theo: The angry lady in Barrie who wanted justice so badly. Unfortunately, she projected her anger onto the group who she seemed to perceive as not fighting hard enough against the injustice system. For me, it reinforced my belief that if you think the justice system is going to give you closure, it's not going to happen. At its worst, the justice system is the Disneyland for pedophiles. So, affect the things you can change.

Kim: Yeah, she was in pain. How she helped me is by reminding me, again, that hurt people hurt people, even unintentionally. I don't think she was aware of how her own behaviour was blaming and verbally abusive. I feel for her, because had her trauma event not happened I'm sure she wouldn't be carrying the anger she is.

Theo: What that reinforced in me is the concept that it doesn't really work to enforce our wills on others; most people don't like to be told what to do. It's okay to allow, but don't push.

Kim: Wow, by organizing days for healing conversation, we're sure helping ourselves with all these insights, eh?

Theo: The funniest was the man at the back in Barrie who said how ironic it was that after struggling for years and years, he'd never felt as good as he did that day, and how it's all because of a "fucking hockey player" of all people. (*laughing*)

Kim: Reminds me you never know where your next support will come, so stay open for the unexpected.

Theo: Just knowing I had an effect certainly made my day!

Kim: But after having all those lightbulb moments, there sure is a period of extreme fatigue afterwards.

Theo: I think it must be chemical. We couldn't do that every day. Once a month would probably be about right.

Kim: What happens is that when you interrupt an old neural network, or brain pathway, to think in different ways, you're letting go of a lot of compressed energy. And when you let that go, what sits underneath all the contained pressure is exhaustion.

Theo: But it is so worth it, because of the one guy in line who first told me, "Me, too." I had no idea that the common denominator between so many of us, maybe eight million in Canada alone, is trauma and attachment. It took one person, the guy in the line in Toronto, to bring it all together.

Kim: So these conversations, even the quick ones, help, eh? I've seen countless·times that people feel more secure from meeting you and connecting. How do these brief moments of connection affect you?

Theo: When I can help others, and all it takes is one to get this feeling, I feel the opposite of worthless and ashamed. And then there's the value of reflection. By hearing their story, and not just the content but the feelings, there is a pile of material to work with. Is listening and helping others self-serving in some ways? Absolutely. Nothing wrong with that.

Kim: The Dalai Lama says it's in our own interest to be good to people, because it increases the odds other people will be nice to us. Do unto others as you would have them do unto you. Karma.

Theo: Can't help everyone though, Kim. Not realistic. And not sure saints had all that much fun! (*making a funny face*)

Kim: Ah, yes, we are all imperfect. If anyone believes we always do everything we talk about, they are mistaken! (*big smile*) Remember when I said that to a group of therapists in Fort MacLeod?

Theo: Yep. A lady stood up and said you were adorable! (*laughing*) I think a lot of people think you're close to saintly …

Kim: (*ignoring the compliment*) You know, Theo Fleury, I was thinking again of that rattlesnake analogy. You were saying you were really playing defense all those years. I didn't quite understand what you meant by that.

Theo: Snakes attack for two reasons. To eat and to defend. I've never needed to kill anyone to get a meal, and I'm not with the mafia nor am I a cannibal. Thankfully, I don't need to hurt people to make a living. But when I feel attacked, I can be vicious. Hurt me, my friend, you're gonna pay. Trigger me with rejection, or any of my key issues, I can still make you wish you weren't anywhere near me. Especially those closest to me, the ones I might hurt the most; they know I can emotionally rip them apart. I can still scare myself. Knowing that, scares me. And this is why all this effort is so critical. I care about the people I care about. Even the ones I don't know. Because I am beginning to care about my own heart more. Hurting people either with words or neglect is something I really want to be only part of my past. I know I've come a long way these past two years.

Kim: (*smiling at him*)

Theo: I'm still crazy (*grinning*) you know, but it's waaaaaay more manageable.

Kim: What would you say, Theo, to someone who is just beginning their healing process? What advice would you give them?

Theo: I wish I knew then what I know now. I would have saved myself a lot of pain. I would have repaired a lot of relationships. I was so desperate. I delayed my own process of healing with all my resistance. I knew somewhere inside of me that I didn't want to die and that I didn't want my pain to define me. I didn't want to be a victim, so I'm not.

Timing and knowledge were key factors in the readiness. This is why I want to talk about healing *now*. It is my intent to help others feel safe so that they can take the leap sooner.

Even when I was completely wasted, I would have moments of clarity when I would think to myself, "What has my life come to?" Even though I was an addict in pain, I still had those moments of clarity. It was just that I was out of control all the time around those moments.

(*thinking*) Maybe there's someone else out there who can relate? There's gotta be.

(*leaning in*) If I could give anyone advice, I'd say, "Feel free to learn from my mistakes. Please do. Take comfort that you are not alone, and begin."

I'd tell them their story matters, 'cause it does.

11

Walk With Thousands

"We're all just walking each other home."
Ram Dass

Kim: I was just re-reading the parts in *Playing With Fire* that described your time in Santa Fe and especially the out-of-control behaviour with Stephanie when you trashed your house, went to jail, and then right back to drugs. The image of you standing alone in the desert as the cop cars beamed their lights toward you on the horizon is heart-chilling. What struck me when reading it again, though, is not how that story was so legendarily dramatic (even though it is), but that the person sitting here with me today, you, and that wild character back in the book, are not even remotely the same person.

Theo: Thanks. (*emotional*) I've been working hard to get myself back. The person in that book wasn't really me you know. My core is back in Russell, Manitoba, wanting more than anything to play hockey and baseball with my amazing athlete friends. I was a decent, friendly kid and I think my old buddies and their parents (some who were the coaches) still remember me as that.

Kim: (*tearing up*) You're making me cry.

Theo: I forget how far I've come.

Kim: What makes me emotional is not how far you've come since, but how close you are to that kid who was trying so hard to excel. You're all about that now, doing everything you can to get healthy, and helping others to get healthy. I bet you're putting in as much energy into these ventures as you were in taking slapshots against the garage door, dreaming of playing professional hockey.

Theo: You know, I don't do anything half-speed. (*reflecting*) What makes the difference for this level of motivation and commitment? I know—it's feeling like I'm on a team again.

Kim: (*smiling*)

Theo: The best feeling in the world is being in the locker room with the team and doing something as well as humanly possible, often against the odds, with people you care about, who have your back and are having just as much fun as you. That's what this is. I've been really busy surrounding myself with the best people in the world at the things we need to do to make a difference. You help me with the emotional stuff, your husband Bob Spensley adds some common sense, Julie Salisbury makes sure the books are available, Amber Craig helps with technical marketing, Phil Deschambault and Patty Phillips are my musical cohorts, and (*smiling*) Dawn Roberts my bookkeeper/manager is like my God.

All of the people who have worked on this book have been changed forever. It's impossible not to change. Because when you're having conversations at the level we are, you will change, automatically, even if you don't come up with the answers. 'Cause if we're in therapy for the rest of our lives and we're not having these kinds of conversations, why are we going? We're going through the whole gamut of emotions in our conversations. What do I feel? That's the question. Well, in writing this book, we all felt all of our emotions.

We're all in this mission to heal and help together. Very different experiences and strengths, but all working toward the same goal.

Kim: The common denominator is what?

Theo: Trust. We all know we could show up at 6:00 a.m. any morning and have the other person to go for a walk with.

Kim: That's true.

Theo: It feels amazing.

Kim: Comparing that ugly face on the cover of your last book with how you're doing today, I wonder if people out there even know all that you're up to now.

Theo: I don't know. I'm glad I've got a lot of contact with people through Twitter and Facebook; it feels good to be able to connect at least a bit in those ways. But people will always think what they want to think. All I can do is affect the things I can control, like myself, at least as much as I can.

Kim: I'm thinking of things you're doing like the Victor Walk. And country music, and getting your doctorate, and London …

Theo: And our Forums!

Kim: Right!

Theo: It would be good to talk about this stuff, because they are connected and it really is a movement going on. People all over are waking up to the realities of the damage that abuse and trauma can cause, and what we can all do to prevent it, and, of course, help others deal with it.

Kim: And bring more mindfulness and compassion into the equation. I think this is all helped by the knowledge that we aren't at all alone when thinking about abuse. The Victor Walk is a great outlet for participants to remember and internalize this fact.

Theo: I hope so; that's the intention! It started out in May of 2013 with the 450-kilometre walk from Toronto to Ottawa, and we had some political messaging as part of it. I think we succeeded in raising awareness of childhood trauma, and more people were definitely seeing that orange is the colour of courage. But, like all things, it's been transforming in shape, and next time it will be a bit different.

Kim: I remember when we were on the steps of Parliament Hill in Ottawa at the conclusion of the Victor Walk, with maybe twelve hundred people who came out to support one another that day. A female survivor who was with her brother approached you and shared her story with you. I watched it from a distance and will never forget it. As she shared her story, her eyes were lowered, her hair covered her face, and her hands were folded together in front of her. She couldn't even look up. Her feelings of shame were palpable. You were present and open and, as she began to cry, you gave her a hug and she sobbed uncontrollably in your arms. You stood there and held this stranger and she was "seen" and "accepted." She allowed you to comfort her and after several moments, her body relaxed and she looked you in the eye and said, "Thank you."

Theo: I remember her. It was just instinctual, natural. We're human beings here on this planet to care for each other. This kind of connection happens all over when we're talking about these things, because we understand each other without any formalities. Someone who has lived through abuse knows what it is and instantly relates to another who's gone through it, and has compassion. We have to understand this. We are not alone and all it takes sometimes is for us to get together and look at each other to know that we are all okay.

Kim: Remember the old friends who'd lived right beside each other who met up that day? OMG, that was a miracle.

Theo: They both showed up individually, an older man and an older woman, and they recognized each other in the crowd after not seeing each other for like fifty years. Talking together, in that safe space, each shared with the other why it was that they came. Turned out they'd both suffered sexual abuse at the same time when they were living right beside each other growing up as kids. Neither had ever revealed it until that day.

Kim: If they would have had the ability or opportunity or coincidence much earlier in life, they might have been able to offer each other at least an ear, a lot earlier.

Theo: Walking those ten days was worth it to see that connection finally happen. I was really happy for them.

Kim: For me, I think joining the Victor Walk just those couple of days at the end is what really solidified for me the kind of impact you have on people personally. It was amazing.

Theo: Just like hockey players say in interviews when we're given CBC's *Hockey Night in Canada* towels, "It's all about team effort." It was and it is. Huge kudos to all those who walked, who came out and supported—to the daycare in a suburb along the way that had their kids all paint happy signs of encouragement for us as we walked by; to the major sponsors like Bill and Becky

Goodwin and their company, Terra-Sine Resources; Motor Home Travel for loaning us an awesome RV; and Subway who provided food along the trek. And the organizers in all the other towns who were holding similar events on that day across the country. We were reminded from how quickly it came together that there are a lot of committed, supportive people out there!

Kim: Aside from that gathering in Ottawa, I heard twenty-two other Victor Walks were held that day across the country!

Theo: There were; they were as far apart as St. John, New Brunswick and Vancouver, British Columbia. Six communities in British Columbia, seven in Alberta, two in Saskatchewan, one in Manitoba, five in Ontario, and one in New Brunswick. Everyone's talking the same way everywhere: we're not alone, we're getting help, and the cycle of abuse ends here.

Kim: This is like as grassroots as it's gonna get. Love it. Reminds me of that brilliant quote: "Never doubt that a small group of thoughtful, committed citizens can change the world; indeed, it's the only thing that ever has."

Theo: Hmm. Sounds true, eh. I've seen those words at the end of the YouTube video by Nickelback, "If Everyone Cared." Who was it that said them?

Kim: It was Margaret Mead. She was a cultural anthropologist who went around the world paying attention to different cultures. A neat thing about her is that it was her reports about the attitudes toward sex in South Pacific and Southeast Asian traditional cultures that helped shaped the 1960s sexual revolution.

Theo: Huh. (*smiling*) A revolution. That's what I'd like this to be. A revolution that says the cycle of abuse ends here. And the cycle of healings begins. I think it's time. And it's already a movement.

So many people have had enough and are finding a new way. The walk showed that.

Kim: How was it for you personally to spend that much time walking?

Theo: The whole walk affected me, changed my life. It kind of put an exclamation mark on the mission. As you know there was a core of seven of us who walked the full ten days. There was a lot of time for reflection on those long roads, and we all got in great shape. I started juicing on that trip! But the best part was we got super bonded in mutual support: Zoran, Dawn, Becky and Bill, Michael, Kim Charlebois, and me.

Kim: I saw that, and was personally struck by the amount of local people who'd join you briefly for parts of the walk and say, "Thanks." And the cars that would pull over—someone would get out, say, "Me, too," share a hug, and get back in their cars and be on their way, a little lighter.

Theo: I remember one day, I don't know where it was, we were walking and there was a little dog that ran out on the road. And by coincidence, the owner of that dog saw us and was freaking out that he was seeing me—Theo Fleury, hockey player—first and foremost (*laughing*). Then he asked what we were doing. When we told him, he broke down and told me his story. So if it weren't for that little dog, that healing moment wouldn't have happened. We spent about an hour there, just talking.

Kim: I heard lots of random spontaneous stories like that from the others who joined you. It's like it was a time when everything slowed down and made sense and people took time for one another.

Theo: It was very humbling for me to be a part of. It reinforced everything I know about people who are hurting: we're already a bit better when we stand up and walk together.

Kim: What will the Victor Walk look like going forward?

Theo: Whenever it's held next, there is a new plan. The principal walk won't be from Toronto to Ottawa this time, but Edmonton to Calgary. Beautiful Alberta!

Kim: Any idea when?

Theo: Maybe the summer of 2015; not sure. We'll make sure to post it on Twitter and Facebook. And we started a not-for-profit foundation, the Breaking Free Foundation. Its mission is to provide trauma survivors with the treatment and support needed to reclaim their lives. This will make sure that Victor Walks and these kinds of future events have some longer-term viability and continuity, and increased exposure.[xcvi]

Kim: Right on.

Theo: Another thing I've been doing is becoming a country music star! (*grinning*)

Kim: I bet not everyone knows you can carry a tune.

Theo: I started a band—Theo Fleury and The Death Valley Rebels— with a few friends in the industry who are really creative and supportive, and we have a blast!

Kim: What's your favourite part of it?

Theo: I love the creating. We sit around and put music to words, words to music, however it feels right, and pull out songs that we think people can relate to. They're about real life and sometimes about transformation. We wrote a song "Walk With Thousands" as the Victor Walk anthem and it was the opener at the Indspire Awards this year.

Kim: There has got to be some healing in that process!

Theo: For sure. But remember, I also like being on stage. It's really a lot of fun.

Kim: Have you always liked country music?

Theo: We're all products of our upbringing. (*acting like a cowboy*) Yes, Ma'am, I likes my country music just fine.

Kim: (*laughing*) You were great at the Saddledome! And you're about to release your album with your band the Death Valley Rebels![xcvii] You've been working so hard on that.

Theo: It's another way to spread the message. From struggle comes beautiful things and I think the album is that exactly. Yeah, we just finished recording it last week. (*smiling*)

Kim: What did you learn from going through that whole process?

Theo: Don't be afraid to try something that you're not so comfortable with, and it's okay to ask for help. And these lessons directly relate to healing. It's imperative that we find help, and it comes in all different sizes, shapes, and forms.

This reminds me about social media and the amazing way it allows us all to connect with one another. After Robin Williams' death a lot of people were triggered, you know, because of his suicide, and I saw so many people reach out to each other. Some of them who were in pain said, "I've tried to get help, but I've met people who just didn't care." And then many more offered these discouraged people beautiful encouragement. So it's important to remind people that there really are those who can help. They're everywhere! It's how badly do you want the help. Or say to yourself, "I never have to feel this way again. And it's up to me to choose which avenue or street or whatever, to go down."

Kim: I hear you.

Theo: Now that our album is done, we're planning to go on tour, and I'm really pumped about it. We're not looking to make millions of bucks, but it's something we love to do and it's also a great way to broaden the message. I've seen that music reaches people at different levels, and is a great connector. More healing conversations for sure.

Kim: What's the title of the album?

Theo: *Rattlesnake.*

Kim: Of course it is! (*smiling*) I know music is a big part of your life. I saw you singing a bunch of times with your five-year-old daughter, Skylah, at home.

Theo: When we jam together that's probably the most fun we have. (*big smile*) She's a ham like her Dad.

Kim: Two peas in a pod.

Theo: You know, my fondest memories of growing up are listening to my grandpa play the fiddle, looking out over the Assiniboine Valley. He worked for the railroad and was a hard working guy, but he married a difficult woman. Every Sunday growing up, we went to my uncle's farm, and even though my family was messed up, that one day a week everybody got along and danced and sang and it was normal, sort of. My cousins were all there and we played and it was an adventurous time. Those Sundays were something we looked forward to. And were a bit of routine. My dad was born on the farm. My great grandmother was a midwife. Here's a story: My uncle Pete weighed only one pound when he was born and they put him in a roasting pan in the oven as an incubator. He lived a long time! But died of alcoholism.

Kim: I can see where your love of music comes from.

Theo: I've got a song called "My Life's Been a Country Song" with the line "Like the path of life, your river flows." That's the river out back of my uncle's farm. The gist of the song is that we all want to go back in time to a place where we felt peaceful and happy, but life gets in the way.

Kim: Remember when we were first starting to think of writing a book together, the first working title was "As the Story Goes," as a nod to one of your most popular songs, but especially to the concept that the story always keeps going. There will always be stuff to work on, stuff to try not to react too badly about, and stuff that can benefit from reflection.

Theo: And stuff to clean up from when we make mistakes.

Kim: That song actually has a great tune, quite addictive really, but it's the words that are most powerful. I think we should share them as an example of working through things by expressing yourself creatively.

Theo: Sure, I'll sing it if you'd like.

Kim: Go for it! "As the Story Goes."

Theo: (*singing in perfect tune*)

> Now I've got a heart
> You gotta let me down slowly
> Can I at least take the memories
> Am I asking too much
> Like an old country song
> Like Conway Twitty
> Singin' only the make believe
> I'll be the man tryin' hard
> (*chorus*)
> As the story goes, as the story goes

I'm sleeping on couches
That I no longer own
Down dusty roads, down dusty roads
I guess I'll be walkin'
You get the truck I'm told
Just like an old time country song
If you play it backwards
We might all get along
(*verse*) Now I'm livin' life
and livin' on life's terms
I'm a comfortable passenger
You can go ahead and drive.
There aren't no straight lines
On my highway
From Calgary to Santa Fe
I'm gonna make things right.
(*he sings the chorus again*)
I got my heart back
I got my drive
I got my soul
I got my spirit back
I found a wife that made me whole
Then I got my kids back
I saw my face in my youngest boy
They got their father back
And with my story being told
(*giving a rousing fake guitar move, with kick*)
I got my life back.
(*singing last chorus*)
As the story goes, as the story goes
I'm sleeping on couches
That I no longer own
Down dusty roads, down dusty roads

> I guess I'll be walkin'
> You get the truck I'm told
> Ya. Just like an old time country song
> If you play it backwards
> We might all get along

Kim: That's pretty good!

Theo: (*laughing, exhausted*) Whew, I should do that more often! When I really connect to the words and emotions behind them like that, as long as there's some positivity somewhere in there, it's pretty empowering for me.

Kim: Ah. That's it! Maybe that's why I don't always adore country music. It seems the words are about their dogs dying and their girlfriends running away or their girlfriends dying and their dogs running away …

Theo: Kim, never make fun of a dog running away. The topics in country music are all to be taken very seriously. (*smiling*) But the songs we write and perform do all tell stories. You know it's the fastest way for tough cowboys to connect with their feelings without knowing it.

Kim: That's pretty snaky of you.

Theo: Any way to share and connect on this highway of life … that has "no straight lines" …

Kim: Well, it's good you find a way to have a lot of fun with it!

Theo: We absolutely do, and thank you.

Kim: So, how do you feel now that you're a doctor?

Theo: Man, what an honour! When the University of Guelph invited me this spring to get an Honorary Doctorate of Science for my "contribution to changing the face of Mental Health in Canada"—that's what they said—I was shocked and pumped at the same time. It all felt great until they told me I'd have to not just give a speech, but write it out ahead of time for all to see. My first lines were, "I've never written a speech before in my life." But I wasn't wearing underwear, so I was still able to feel comfortable with everyone in those fancy robes. Here's the speech that I pulled out of my socks.[xcviii]

"Honoured Graduates of the Faculties of Psychology and Business of the University of Guelph-Humber, Esteemed Faculty Members, Parents, and Distinguished Guests, I've never written a speech in my life. And I've certainly never spent years committing to the formal study of advanced anything, like you all obviously have. I've got a pretty good imagination, but never did I think I would be in an auditorium of scientists and academics honouring me for my work in spirituality and healing. Given where I've been, that this is happening is an example of a fuckin' miracle, and therefore, I hypothesize (and now that I'm a doctor I can hypothesize): it must be happening for a reason.

"I first of all want to congratulate, with all my spirit, the graduates who are sitting here, so ready to go out and take on the world. Well, on behalf of that crazy world out there, thank you for the efforts I know you're about to make. There is a lot of change needed.

"What can I leave you with that you might remember when the going gets tough? 'Cause it will. Two things. Very simple. Number One: work your asses off, don't expect anything from anybody. (Hey, I'm old school.) Number Two—providing you already got Number One in hand—is a concept that will ensure your success. This is not me making a hypothesis; this is science and experience, and it's making a difference everywhere if we just choose to pay attention. Here is the concept: we are all intricately connected and it's our relationships that matter for absolutely everything—for our brains to develop well, for us to treat each other with dignity and compassion, for us to create win-win outcomes in business, for us to win Stanley Cups as a team, and for us to heal when shit happens. Relationship. Build a better world no matter what you choose to do by being present, by listening, by tuning in, by sharing with honesty.

"After playing some hockey, revealing I'd lived through abuse, and working hard to deal with my own issues—hey, we never get perfect; we gotta keep working at it—I'm now dedicating my life to helping people get the help they need. And mental health is a big part of it. This Number Two concept of paying attention in relationships directly applies. It is healthy relationships that remind us not to carry shame and not to hurt each other to begin with.

"When I represent the one in three Canadians who have experienced childhood trauma, I feel like I have a clear purpose. My mission is to allow others to find their own voices through storytelling and healing conversations. Surrounding yourself with a strong team, whether that is personal, professional, or spiritual, creates a foundation for resilience and structure for the journey. Surround yourselves, consciously, with people who help bring out the best in you, and you in them. Trust me. We're really strong in our own ways, but better together.

"I remember what it's like to be young, and want everything to happen now. You want everything that you try, to succeed. All the technology we have today, it's about instant gratification, it's designed that way. But our spiritual sides know that it's important to know when to act and when to wait. Some of this technology is awesome, and keep going with it, but it's spirituality that will teach you patience and the importance of relationships. There's no relationship with an app. And there's no app, at least not yet, for relationships.

"I've got something to say about inspiration, or more to the point, the relative lack of it. Some of us here might recognize that when we get to be middle-aged, we sometimes just seem to be going through the motions. What I'm learning is that when you aren't finding it somewhere else, and you look for inspiration deep inside of yourself, guess what, it is always there. The deeper you dig, the more you will find. You can always dig deeper, longer, harder; and that extra effort—or call it connection with yourself, or spirituality, or whatever you call it that makes sense to you—that's what separates greatness from mediocrity. You know you can give yourself your own dopamine hits, just with your own brilliant thoughts! Honestly, who needs drugs?

"But seriously, all you graduating today, I bet you have amazing plans and hopes, but who knows where you'll end up? You know, there were certainly no straight lines on my highway. And this whole career thing, it's never an arrival, but a journey. It's not even so important which job or role you fill along the way. As the wise Kim Barthel always says, and I quote, 'It's not really *what* you do that matters, but *how* you do it.'

"So compete every day to be the best you can be. Work hard and put in the time needed to master your craft. But if you really want to be successful, and this applies to all areas of your life (believe me), pay attention to and nurture your relationships. This one will get you anywhere and everywhere.

"I want to say a big thank you to the University of Guelph-Humber for granting me this honour today. It means a lot, and I am humbled to be here with you.

"Thank you."

Kim: I was especially proud of you that day. You do know why they gave you that award, right? Because you are an example of someone who's learned, the hard way, that mental health really matters. And you are in a position to be helping thousands of others face their own demons and rally people to end this epidemic of abuse.

Theo: It was humbling. It felt good to be recognized for doing something I care so much about.

Kim: For me, seeing you receive that Honorary Doctorate was my version of seeing you being awarded a place in the Hockey Hall of Fame.

Theo: Hmm. I'm glad you were there with me.

Kim: You know, I saw a Facebook comment from one of your fans just before this year's Hockey Hall of Fame induction. Don't know if you saw it, but it struck a chord with me. It was in reference to the uncertainty in the induction process and it said, "Whatever happens with that, Theo would obviously make it into a worldwide HHF (healing hall of fame) if there were such a thing, and that's more important."

Theo: That was nice.

Kim: Do you see yourself in the Hockey Hall of Fame one day?

Theo: The guys that make it into that exclusive club are truly exceptional hockey players. If I ever got invited to join them, it would be the biggest hockey honour of my life. No question at all.

Kim: Except for maybe winning the Provincials with that team from Russell, Manitoba?

Theo: You know me. That team was outstanding! (*smiling*) But with the Hockey Hall of Fame, that's what exceeds the dreams of every little kid out there that's trying his hardest to break through. The Stanley Cup? That's the hill everyone's trying to climb. But the Hockey Hall of Fame? That's like the rainbow over the mountain. And there's nothing anybody—least of all I—can do to control decisions like that. Whether an honour of that magnitude ever comes or not, it's in someone else's hands. And either way, it isn't going to change what I choose to do every day. I know what path I'm on and I like it.

Kim: Hmm. (*smiling in agreement*) You are busy. Thinking of things coming up, going to London this August is going to be cool.

Theo: That "International Association for Group Psychotherapy" conference we'll be going to is another example of something I never thought I'd be attending, let alone co-presenting at, with you.[xcix]

Kim: It's at the London University in the UK and it'll be one of the largest conferences internationally for mental health practitioners and researchers. We'll be there a full week taking in all kinds of courses and presenting our model of healing that they seem to say is rather unique.

Theo: We'll just do what we do at our "Conversations with a Rattlesnake" Forums, only a little more condensed since the Forums are day-long events.

Kim: Right. In London, we'll introduce the format we use to a room full of PhDs and therapists, and demonstrate how it works.

Theo: Good thing I got my doctorate so I can fit right in. (*little laugh*)

Kim: It'll be fun. You'll be skating in my kind of arena for a change!

Theo: What's fun is all that learning, I'll be a kid in a candy store with all those healing ideas bouncing around.

Kim: Me, too! To someone who's never been to one of our "Conversations with a Rattlesnake" Forums, how would you describe what we do?

Theo: Well, we've had four so far: in Nanaimo, British Columbia; Winnipeg, Manitoba; Calgary, Alberta; and Barrie, Ontario. They are day-long events, like you say, in which the general public is invited to attend and participate in a day of information and healing. About half the people who come are therapists or teachers and the other half are people looking to feel better, or support their family and friends in the journey.

Kim: Each Forum's been a bit different, but the format has generally been that you tell your story, I then interpret it from a science and therapy point of view, we have a real-life (absolutely unscripted) therapeutic conversation, and end with a full-on interactive discussion with everyone.

Theo: Some people say it's the way we model healing conversations so honestly that helps them the most, but for the people who share and really engage at the end, I'm pretty sure that's the most memorable.

Kim: We're huge on the concept of emotional safety for everyone in the room, and wouldn't be able to share our own vulnerability if that weren't the case.

Theo: I think it's our vulnerability in the therapeutic conversation that gets everyone to open up at the end.

Kim: No question; we all affect one another. And we all come out feeling like our team's just got stronger.

Theo: Some testimonials that have come in afterwards have been over-whelming though.

Kim: That's an understatement. Dawn got a few phone calls and emails from people who were *so* thankful. A man from Winnipeg absolutely credits attending the Forum with *saving his life*. The amount of dopamine and oxytocin hits Dawn has got from that man's deep gratitude and love alone is enough to make her love her job more than anyone could imagine. He'd got a free ticket from the "Random Act of Kindness" program we offer with each Forum, for people who can't afford to go. Sometimes tickets get provided from people who just want to help and donate them for whoever needs them.

The concept came to us from a guy who'd seen us present together and thought of his grandma who'd kept a shameful family secret for over seventy years and only revealed it just before she died. His thinking was that if she'd had the information from our presentations back then, she could have avoided almost a whole lifetime of secrecy and pain. She's no longer around, so he anonymously offered to buy a ticket in her honour for anyone who would want it. No names mentioned at all.

Our Forums picked up on this, some sponsors got involved, and in the end, many people were able to attend who otherwise couldn't have. And those people who were able to come were so thankful.

This one guy I was speaking about who called Dawn to thank her, he revealed to her that he was on the verge of taking his own life that exact morning when Dawn called to offer him the ticket. He reluctantly came, with a pile of anxiety … and said he was blown away. He's since given us permission to share his story and emails. (*pulling a piece of paper out of her briefcase*)

Here are parts of a few emails he sent to Dawn and me recently. (*reading out loud*)

"Listening to Theo tell his story, then listening to you," meaning me, "connect the 'scientific dots' behind his story was an incredible experience for me. I'd like to think I'm a smart person, but it's always confounded me as to why I behaved the way I do. I have always felt powerless to change my angry, self-destructive destiny. What you two did for me at that conference was truly amazing—you have NO idea what you've done for this 'lost soul'…"

(*flipping to the next page*) He said he found it "so incredibly difficult accepting the fact that there are people out there that actually care about me, when even I don't care about me." And he talked about how he was completely overwhelmed by the outpouring of love in the room at one point when a young woman was struggling to tell her story and everyone held the space for her so respectfully …

And he said in another email to Dawn: (*reading*) "I always felt like no one understood me; I have always felt so incredibly alone … Now I know, thanks to you," (Dawn) "and Theo and Kim, that I am not alone, and there is light at the end of the tunnel, and that maybe—just maybe—there is hope for me yet, and someday I might actually be able to let myself be happy, and truly come to value myself for the kind, gentle, loving man that I am and want to be—and not some crazy, raging madman hell-bent on destroying myself and everyone else that has ever cared for me … And when I'm able to, I will give back … I will do my utmost to be a fellow advocate, walking alongside all of you, doing my best to help those unlucky enough to have experienced similar hells …"

Theo: I was so glad that guy was able to be there.

Kim: Another miracle is that the host agency in that case (who share in some of the proceeds if there are any) turned around and offered that man free counselling. He's been given unlimited free counselling for a year, and we just heard last week that he's going regularly and in his own words, "It is possible to shed one's skin ..." and "For the first time in my life ... I am happy ... Thank you so much."

Theo: That's why we do this. It's very powerful. I can't say how many people who've said it's the best workshop they've ever come to for information and healing. I know the Forums have transformed me. I have different major insights every time. With so many people in the room, there's a lot of material to work with and reflect upon. Helping others helps ourselves. And by being present, every one of us is helping others.

Kim: Going forward with these events, we're also planning visits to smaller communities. Sometimes, they invite us to lead a range of presentations and activities with different groups. Sometimes, we talk with youth separately; sometimes, you get to play some hockey; sometimes, we spend a lot of time with teachers and social workers of all kinds—community panels, sports teams, healing circles. We plan to spend a couple of days depending on what the community wants and needs.

Theo: I love it when there are community feasts and all the different generations come out. That's when we know our messaging is being endorsed and there is a real will to support change.

Kim: How many presentations, either together or on your own, would you say you did in 2014?

Theo: I could ask you the same. The truth is we're extremely busy and travel a lot. I know Bob was saying that for a stretch of about half a year, you were on the road three weeks out of every month. My schedule is similar. Maybe, too much sometimes, eh?

Kim: But if we're going to be addicted to something, I rationalize it that workaholism and trying to help others isn't the worst combination. And we'll balance it all out someday.

Theo: What I'd say is that while this work is often intense, it doesn't really feel like work. It's like when I played hockey. I've always been fortunate to be able to do what I love.

Kim: And this advocacy role is expanding, isn't it? You just spoke in Helsinki, Finland, at the 2014 IWG [International Working Group] World Conference on Women and Sport.

Theo: That was a step into the broader discussion for me. The kind of trauma I know about is a worldwide epidemic and it's only just beginning to get talked about openly. Remember when breast cancer wasn't talked about? Now, we're getting more info on it and we're all talking about it. And prostate cancer, that used to be something that made people too squeamish to talk about. When shame is attached to a subject, it's very difficult for people to come forward. But we are seeing that the veils of secrecy can be lifted. Child trauma and abuse is now on the cusp of being talked about too, everywhere.

Kim: I saw a video of your keynote address there in Helsinki.[c] I think it was some of the clearest messaging I've seen you present. I want to share a few parts of it with you so you can hear how clear it is yourself. Okay if I read it to you?

Theo: Sure, go ahead.

Kim: And listen to the level of conviction behind your message.

Theo: Okay, okay.

Kim: (*reading a transcript of part of Theo's Helsinki speech from the Internet*)

"I am one of the very few men in the world that speak openly about my experience with sexual abuse ...

"I got involved in addictions—alcohol, drugs, sex, gambling, food, workaholics—you name it. I'm a member of all the AA groups, twelve-step groups. And not only that, I had all kinds of problems in relationships, with family members, with former girlfriends, partners, wives, etcetera, etcetera, etcetera. So not only is sexual abuse detrimental, but it also manifests itself in so many other areas in our lives....

"I had a very difficult childhood. Both my parents suffered through their own addictions, and when this particular abuser came into my life, he showered me with all the things that I didn't get at the beginning of my life. He gave me attention, he gave me opportunity. I trusted him ... and because of that he took advantage. And he groomed me to the point where he could, you know, do his own addiction, which is pedophilia.

"For the first few years after my first book came out, I was all about justice, and putting these guys in jail, locking the door, and throwing away the key. And in Canada, we don't have a justice system. We have a system that coddles and protects pedophiles ... Did you know on average by the time a pedophile gets caught, they have 125 victims? And when we put them in jail and then they get out, 98 percent of those pedophiles reoffend, again. And so if we're gonna stop the cycle of abuse, going through my own process of healing, I don't care about justice, 'cause I'm healing....

"And so, I advocate hope, I advocate healing, and I advocate more conversation around this subject. Because more conversation allows others to get rid of their shame, come forward, tell their stories, and then start their journey of healing. And I realize that I'm in therapy for the rest of my life, and what a gift that is, for me. Because when I sit down and I bear down and I talk about my feelings and talk about the issues, my life gets better and better and better and better and better. And through my example, other people find that strength and that hope, and then they come forward and start their own healing journey. So, I think what we can all take from the conference, is that it's okay to talk about this subject....

"And because shame is obviously attached to this subject, it is very difficult for people to come forward. And you know what? I don't ever consider myself a victim. Because if I was a victim that would suggest that I played a part in what happened to me. So I'm a survivor and I'm a victor over child sexual abuse. I think using the word 'victim' shames, shames even more, so we need to get rid of that word, because it happened 'to' me and I wasn't responsible for it, and it certainly wasn't my fault....

"And so, the more we shame people around the subject, the more likely it is that we're going to stay silent, but, it's the biggest epidemic on the planet, so, I went through it, you went through it, let's work toward healing, 'cause healing is possible, and I'm living proof of that. You know, I have the greatest life you could possibly imagine, today, because I talk about it....

"We've got to make changes. And we've gotta allow people to tell us their deepest darkest secrets, without judgment, without ramifications, and just be human beings. And say, 'It's okay. It's okay. And where do you want to go from here? And how can I help you? And how can I help you get to where you need to go?'"

Theo: Not bad.

Kim: And then a lady asked you the question about what it was that made you speak up, to begin with. Remember how you answered that?

Theo: Not exactly, you have it here too, I bet?

Kim: The Internet is amazing. This is what you said: (*reading another piece of the transcript of Theo's panel discussion at the IWG World Conference on Women and Sport in Helsinki*)

> "Well, I knew I was gonna die if I kept going down the road that I was goin' on, and I didn't want to die. I played a very macho sport and I've always said, give me physical pain, I'll heal from physical pain. You know if I get my teeth knocked out, they can get replaced. If I break my nose, it'll heal; that kind of stuff. But emotional pain, I would never wish that on my worst enemy.
>
> "And for many, many years I was paralyzed by emotional pain from the scars that were left, not only from growing up in an addictive household, but also from the abuse that I suffered. And I knew that I wasn't showing the world the true me, the full potential of me. And, you know, I tried to commit suicide nine years ago, not because I wanted to die, but I wanted to just kill the pain that was inside of me that I could never get rid of…. Because I can't go to a doctor and say, 'You know what, Doc, I'm in a lot of pain. Not physical pain but emotional pain, and, can you write me a prescription for child sexual abuse? Can you give me a pill for that?' And he's gonna look at me and go, 'I don't have anything for that.'
>
> "And so I got to the point where I didn't care anymore about what anybody thought. It was my truth and my story and there

should be nothing wrong with that, and so I basically wrote my first book and told the world what happened to me, and you guys didn't run away, you didn't shame me. You know what you said? You told me I had courage, and you told me I had strength, and from that I became empowered ... so why can't we do that for everybody in the world who has gone through the exact same experience?"

Theo: I hope more survivors find safe people to get their conversations going with.

Kim: What I see from this kind of reception you're getting is that the world is waking up to the real kinds of heroes it needs. The humble, vulnerable, self-aware, and committed-to-helping ones.

Theo: (*jokingly*) You know Hollywood had asked me to play Iron Man instead of Robert Downey Jr. (*reflecting*) We have some other similarities come to think of it.

Kim: Very lovable, for being such shit disturbers from time to time.

Theo: Not what I was thinking, but I'll take it.

Kim: The coolest thing about all this messaging of hope is the ripple effect of healing—how it can transform one person at a time. A simple "Me, too" is so powerful.

Theo: What's motivating for me is the concept that everything I learn from you and everything we learn together are finding ways to get shared with a countless number of people down the road, and which specific roads we may never even know. Regardless of where and exactly how, the more I learn and heal, the more people I can potentially support. It is spirit at work, because even if the amount of support that eventually gets received is as small as a grain of sand, this idea makes me feel connected.

Kim: Which is the feeling we're all ultimately looking for. There's also a selfless quality to that thought.

Theo: Not entirely, because helping is healing. The cycle of abuse doesn't just stop here; the *Cycle of Healing* starts. Heal yourself first and change will follow.

Kim: (*smiling*) You know it, my friend.

i   Theo Fleury with Kirstie McLellan Day, *Playing With Fire*, 2009.

ii   www.reverbnation.com/theofleury.

iii   Alcoholics Anonymous.

iv   HBO Canada, *Theo Fleury: Playing with Fire*, 2011.

v   www.remigbiofeed.com.

vi   "Listening to Baby" is available at www.attachmentnetwork.ca, and "Still Face Experiment" can be viewed at www.youtube.com/watch?v=apzXGEbZht0.

vii   Dr. Nicole Letourneau, *Scientific Parenting: What Science Reveals About Parental Influence*.

viii   M.L. Knapp et al, *Nonverbal Communication in Human Interaction*, 2013.

ix   Lane Strathearn, et al, "Adult Attachment Predicts Maternal Brain and Oxytocin Response to Infant Cues," December 2009.

x   Allan N. Schore. *Affect Dysregulation and Disorders of the Self*, 2003.

xi   Linda Graham, *Bouncing Back*, 2013, p. 282.

xii   Attention Deficit Disorder.

xiii   Eye Movement Desensitization and Reprocessing.

xiv   *Assessing Adult Attachment: A Dynamic-Maturational Approach to Discourse Analysis*, 2011.

xv   Laurence Heller, PhD and Aline LaPierre PsyD, *Healing Developmental Trauma*, 2009, p. 154.

xvi   April 2014.

xvii   Laurence Heller, PhD and Aline LaPierre PsyD, *Healing Developmental Trauma*, p. 113.

xviii   Tricia Striano, Amrisha Vaish, and Joann P. Benigno, "The Meaning of Infants' Looks," 2006.

xix   Russell B. Lemle, PhD, "How Threat Emotions Cause Us To Misread Our Partner," www.psychologytoday.com/blog/me-first-we-first/201203/how-threat-emotions-cause-us-misread-our-partner-4

xx   Susan Gillis Chapman, *The Five Keys to Mindful Communication*, 2012, p. 51.

xxi   Don Miguel Ruiz and Janet Mills, *The Four Agreements*, 1997.

xxii   Jose Jose Ruiz and Tami Hudman, *My Good Friend the Rattlesnake*, 2014.

xxiii   Robert M. Sapolsky, *Why Zebras Don't Get Ulcers*, 2004.

xxiv   Robert M. Sapolsky, *Stress: Portrait of a Killer*, 2008.

xxv   www.drdansiegel.com.

xxvi Dr. Donald Hebb, *The Organization of Behaviour*, 1949.

xxvii *Outliers: The Story of Success*, 2008.

xxviii Dr. Brené Brown, *Daring Greatly*, 2012, p. 34.

xxix www.drgabormate.com.

xxx The childhood sexual abuse statue is at Glen Rhodes United Church, 1470 Gerard Street East, Toronto, Ontario.

xxxi www.winnipegfreepress.com/multimedia/video/local/theo-fleury-on-forgiving-the-offender-233645851.html.

xxxii Dr. Daniel Seigel, *Mindsight*, 2010.

xxxiii *The Fifth Estate*, Season 35, October 16, 2009, "The Fall and Rise of Theo Fleury."

xxxiv Dr. Daniel Siegel, *The Mindful Therapist*, 2010, p. 133.

xxxv Andrew Newberg, MD and Mark Robert Waldman, *How God Changes Your Brain*, 2009, p. 156.

xxxvi Ibid.

xxxvii Editors Paul Ekman and Erika L. Rosenberg, *What the Face Reveals*, 1997.

xxxviii Joe Navarro and Toni Sciarra Poynter, *Louder Than Words*, 2010.

xxxix David Grand, PhD, *Brainspotting*, 2013.

xl Crittendon, Patricia and Andrea Landini, *Assessing Adult Attachment*, 2011.

xli www.askdrsears.com/topics/parenting/child-rearing-and-development/sexuality/masturbation-six-ways-manage-it.

xlii Andrew Newberg, MD and Mark Robert Waldman, *How God Changes Your Brain*, 2009, p. 19.

xliii *When the Body Says No*, 2004.

xliv yellodyno.com/Statistics/statistics_child_molester.html and www.sex-offenders.us/child.molester.list.htm.

xlv D.M. Greenberg, J.M. Bradford, and S. Curry, "A comparison of sexual victimization in the childhoods of pedophiles and hebephiles," *Journal of Forensic Sciences* 38 (2) 1993 p. 434.

xlvi Dr. Norman Doidge, *The Brain That Changes Itself*, 2007.

xlvii Susan Gillis Chapman, *The Five Keys to Mindful Communication*, 2012, p. 6.

xlviii Kristen Neff, PhD, *Self-Compassion*, 2011.

xlix Rollin McCraty, PhD, Mike Atkinson, and Dana Tomasino, BA, "Modulation of DNA Conformation by Heart-Focused Intention," 2003.

l Rick Hanson, *Hardwiring Happiness*, 2013, p. 44.

li   Ibid, p. 24.

lii   Andrew Newberg, MD and Mark Robert Waldman, *Words Can Change Your Brain*, p. 23.

liii   Ibid, p. 29.

liv   Ibid.

lv   Dr. Joe Dispenza, *You Are the Placebo*, 2014.

lvi   Maureen Salaman, "Texting Doesn't Replace the Feel-Good Effects of Talking, Study Says," *Health Day*, consumer.healthday.com/mental-health-information-25/child-psychology-news-125/texting-doesn-t-replace-the-feel-good-effects-of-talking-study-says-672965.html

lvii   2014 Global Drug Survey, *Huffington Post*, www.huffingtonpost.com/2014/04/14/most-used-drug_n_5147042.html.

lviii   Alcoholism-statistics.com.

lix   CAMH—Centre for Addictions Mental Health, *Addiction*, March 2013.

lx   For FASD: H.E. Marroun, et al, "Maternal use of antidepressant or anxiolytic medication during pregnancy," May 2014, 1-20.
        For ADD: M.M. Iqbal, et al, "Effects of Commonly Used Benzodiazepines," January 2002.

lxi   Professor Heather Ashton, "Benzodiazepines: How they work and how they withdraw," 2002.

lxii   Volkow, N.D., et al, "Decreases in Dopamine Receptors but not in Dopamine Transporters in Alcoholics," 1996, and Seamans, J.K., et al, "Bidirectional Dopamine Modulation of GABAergic Inhibition," 2001.

lxiii   *Desert USA*, "Rattlesnakes," www.desertusa.com/reptiles/rattlesnakes.html.

lxiv   Hye Jeong Lee, et al, "Transgenerational effects of paternal alcohol exposure in mouse offspring," 2013.

lxv   Diane Malbin speaking at the International FASD conference, 2007.

lxvi   N. Makris, et al, "Decreased volume of the brain reward system in alcoholism," 2008.

lxvii   Frances A. Champagne, et al, "Variations in Nucleus Accumbens Dopamine," 2004, as referenced in Gabor Maté's *In the Realm of Hungry Ghosts* p. 189.

lxviii returntofood.com.

lxix   Andrew Newberg, MD and Mark Robert Waldman, *Words Can Change Your Brain*.

lxx   Ibid, p. 41 and 55.

lxxi   Ibid, p. 33.

lxxii   Ibid.

lxxiii   Faceoff.com, "Worshipping the Habs," www.faceoff.
         com/hockey/teams/montreal-canadiens/story.
         html?id=7f4006e6-a224-497c-a714-b4a5312062e0

lxxiv   Dr. Brené Brown, *Daring Greatly*, 2012, p. 226.

lxxv   www.ted.com/talks/brene_brown_on_vulnerability.

lxxvi   Ryan C. W. Hall, MD and Richard C. W. Hall, MD, P.A., "A profile of
         pedophilia," 2009, p. 457-71.

lxxvii   www.theofleury14.com/2014/03/08/compassion-for-offenders.

lxxviii Alan Fogel, *The Psychophysiology of Self-Awareness*, 2009, p. 111.

lxxix   www.greggbraden.com.

lxxx   HBO Canada, *Theo Fleury: Playing With Fire*, 2011.

lxxxi   by Karl Paul Reinhold Niebuhr, 1892-1971.

lxxxii   E.L. James, 2011.

lxxxiii Joseph Dispenza, *God on Your Own*, 2006.

lxxxiv   Benedict Carey, "Too Much Stress May Give Genes Gray Hair," www.
         nytimes.com/2004-11-30-health.

lxxxv   D. Ornish, et al, "Effect of comprehensive lifestyle changes on telomerase
         activity and telomere length," 2013.

lxxxvi   Stephen Post, "It's good to be good," 2009, p. 19.

lxxxvii Jennifer J. Baumgartner, PsyD, "This is Your Brain on Christmas:
         The Psychology of Altruism," www.psychologytoday.com/blog/the-
         psychology-dress/201112/is-your-brain-chritmas-the-psychology
         -altruism.

lxxxviii *Dartmouth Undergraduate Journal of Science*, "Is Altruism Good for the
         Altruistic Giver?" 2009. dujs.dartmouth.edu/spring-2009/is-altruism
         -good-for-the-altruistic-giver.

lxxxix   Sector Source, "Research About Volunteering in Canada,"
         www.sectorsource.ca/research-and-impact/sector-research/
         volunteering-research.

xc   Statistics Canada, "Caring Canadians, Involved Canadians: Tables
         Report," www.statcan.gc.ca/pub/89-649-x/89-649-x2011001-eng.htm.

xci   James Baraz and Shoshana Alexander, "The Helper's High," 2010,
         greatergood.berkeley.edu/article/item/the_helpers_high/

xcii   Jon Kabat-Zinn and Richard J. Davidson, Editors, The Mind's Own
         Physician, 2013.

xciii   Ibid.

xciv   Linda Graham, *Bouncing Back*, 2013 p. 277.

xcv   William Shakespeare, *Hamlet*, Act 1, Scene 5.

xcvi   www.victorwalk.com.

xcvii   www.reverbnation.com/theofleury.

xcviii   www.guelphhumber.ca/news/success-according-theo-fleury.

xcix   bpaconferences.files.wordpress.com/2014/07/final-programme-outline-
         bpa-and-iagp-international-conference-11-july-2014.pdf.

c   www.youtube.com/watch?v=hA1th_a3b8M.

Glossary

Aha Moment : When some insight—which is really helpful to your self-awareness—hits you. This word is interchangeable with "lightbulb moments," like when a lightbulb goes on over the head of a cartoon character. One of Theo's biggest aha moments was when he heard Kim talk about early childhood attachment theory and put together that the traumatic experiences he went through as a kid were not his fault. Shedding the shame from that belief was huge.

Attachment Theory : This theory teaches how early childhood relationships between kids and their parents shape children's relationship patterns throughout their lives. Theo's first relationships didn't fully support his emotional development through secure attachment, so he adopted strategies of behaviour (not all of them healthy) to adapt to his chaotic home environment.

Addiction : Someone is said to be addicted when the *need* to use or do something gets in the way of the life they want to lead. Theo has had many addictions, for example, to alcohol. His drinking got in the way of his key relationships, his career, his financial decisions, and his health. Addictions can be to anything that feels good, but may also hurt us: drugs, sex, gambling. Our addictions can also cause pain to our extended family, friends, and colleagues. With attention and assistance, addictions can be managed.

Amygdala : A part of the brain that plays a role in the processing of emotions. When the wolf spider crawled across Kim's face while she was camping, her amygdala registered the tickly sensation and processed the feeling as a threat. She immediately awoke and experienced fear, which resulted in a fight-flight stress response. The amygdala helps to signal potential threat in the environment and rapidly processes facial expressions.

Anterior Cingulate Cortex : A part of the brain that helps to regulate your emotions so that you don't hit your boss at a staff meeting, or cry in the middle of the grocery store when you think about your family pet that died many years ago. The anterior cingulate also allows you to feel compassion and empathy for others. Research shows that the anterior cingulate become active when we pray or meditate and is sometimes called the "seat of compassion."

Attunement : People are attuned to each other when they *tune in* to notice how the other is feeling during a conversation. An example of being attuned is the way Kim pauses deliberately when she and Theo are talking, whenever she sees from his body language that he needs time to think. When people are not attuned, they go on blabbing whether or not the listener is paying attention.

Boundaries : Boundaries are healthy safety limits that we set between ourselves and other people, both physically and emotionally. By not having clear boundaries at a young age, Theo was more vulnerable to the possibility of being taken advantage of.

Calgary Flames : Professional hockey team in Calgary, Alberta. Theo played for them from 1988 until 1999, and he's said many times that the biggest part of his heart is in Calgary and always will be.

Codependency : People are said to be codependent if they are controlled or manipulated by another. Codependents—often family members of alcoholics—grow up with the mindset that their own happiness is dependent on someone else's happiness. Codependents enable addictive behaviour as a protective measure for themselves, generally to avoid confrontation. Theo's mom was codependent on Theo's dad. When Theo was young, his mom enabled her husband's drinking and Theo remembers that as a youngster he was always doing whatever he could to keep the peace. Although understandable, the dynamic of codependency doesn't help either party to move beyond dysfunction.

Co-regulation : A form of interaction and communication where one person helps to regulate the other by being attuned and present. When one person gets upset, the other person can help him calm down with their facial expression, tone of voice, and words. This provides support during discomfort. Kim co-regulates Theo frequently, especially when he is triggered by an uncomfortable experience.

Crohn's Disease : A painful disease in which the stomach literally eats itself. It is an autoimmune disorder that is believed to be linked to people carrying high levels of stress. Not surprisingly, although this is not a cause, some studies have also linked Crohn's to people who have experienced sexual abuse. Theo is still living with Crohn's, but he is managing his stress levels and particularly his diet much better than he used to.

Coherent Narrative : A story that is clear and easy to understand, one that is integrated, succinct, and linked together in a logical sequence. After experiencing trauma, a person's stories are often not clear; with effort and time they often become more coherent, which is a sign that the storyteller is becoming more mentally healthy. At the beginning of Theo's conversations with Kim, he would often leave his sentences unfinished, use different verb tenses in the same sentence, and use distancing language like "you" and "they" instead of "I." As Theo became more comfortable with his feelings on various topics, his storytelling became easier to understand and more connected to his personal experience.

Compassion : A feeling of empathy toward a person who is suffering, and a desire to alleviate their suffering. When someone wrote a Facebook comment that was clearly an antagonistic projection, Theo—instead of reacting out of anger—was able to see that the comment said more about the writer than about himself. From his own sense of compassion for the emotional state of the writer, Theo was able to respond with mindfulness.

Conscious Friend Choosing : Selecting relationships with awareness, instead of automatic attraction based on old patterns of familiarity. Who we hang out with is reflective of where we are in our personal growth. At one time, Theo hung out with other people who had been hurt. Now he consciously chooses to spend time with friends and family who can nurture healthy relationships.

Connection : A relational bond. There are different types of connection, connection between parent and child, adult to adult, connection with God, and connection to self. You can also be connected to ideas or beliefs. Theo credits his connection to spirituality for helping him to stay the course in his sobriety.

Cortisol : A steroid hormone, cortisol is produced by the adrenal glands and released during many different normal bodily processes. In particular, cortisol is released during times of stress to provide an immediate supply of energy to enable a person to fight or flee—See *Fight or Flight Response*. When blood levels of cortisol remain high or become high too frequently, cortisol will interfere unfavourably in many bodily processes, causing faster aging, among other things. Cortisol is a killer of brain cells and when there is too much of it floating around in your brain while you are developing, it will interfere with brain growth. Kim explained to Theo when his mom was stressed out when she was pregnant, her body would have produced a lot of the stress chemical, cortisol. For him as a fetus, if there was a lot of cortisol hanging around while he was developing, it would have been like having a bath in toxic waste.

Depression : This is a mood disorder that can either be short-term and require no formal treatment or longer-term, requiring direct medical intervention. Depression negatively affects a person's emotional, mental, and physical well-being, leading to a weakened ability to create and maintain healthy relationships, to perform one's work productively, and to see an alternate way of living. Theo's mom experienced depression when he was a child. When children grow up with a parent who experiences chronic depression, the development of their brains may be seriously affected, with implications for their ability to learn, as well as for their own later physical and mental health.

Developmental Trauma : An experience of shame, separation, intense anxiety, or emotional pain at a young age. We all have some amount of developmental trauma in our past, but when it is severe it can negatively impact our capacity to have healthy relationships as we get older. Theo remembers that when he was little, all he heard at home was yelling and conflict. Having to constantly be on guard as a child contributed to his high levels of anxiety later in life.

Dissociation : This happens when your mind leaves your body. It happens unconsciously. If you are so terrified that your fight-or-flight response doesn't respond, dissociation is your only fallback survival strategy. Dissociating helped Theo to survive his sexual abuse. Also see *Fight or Flight Response*.

Distancing Language : When we say things like "People get sad when this happens" instead of "I got sad when this happened." Talking in the third person or in generalities is a form of protection, because it's one step further away from feeling the direct emotion.

But, from an emotional health perspective, it's not always helpful in the long run. Owning our feelings is a big part of working through them. Both Kim and Theo still use distancing language from time to time, however, either to emotionally protect themselves or the other in the moment of a conversation.

Dopamine : A neurochemical in the brain that provides us with the sense of pleasure and reward after completing some action, from winning a game to getting a smile or thinking a positive thought. Dopamine is what makes us feel good. Unfortunately, it can be created in the form of drugs, like cocaine, which is highly addictive. All forms of addiction have challenges with the dopamine system. Kim defines Theo as a dopamine seeker, given that he has had so many addictive patterns.

Dual Awareness : It is profoundly healing when you can be both in your trauma experience and in the present moment at the same time. When this happens you are rewiring the brain in positive ways! Dual awareness breaks apart old negative neural networks and creates new ones when you take a trauma memory and experience it in a new way. This is the power of healing conversations.

Enabling : An action that might look like helping, but it really only serves to keep an unhealthy dynamic in place. Examples are giving money to a drug addict, or never calling the police during a series of domestic disputes. Although enabling behaviour comes from the intent to protect and keep relative peace in the short term, it ends up keeping the dynamic unhealthy for everyone involved. When a family plans an intervention to help an addict, they have to remove all the enabling behaviours. It's hard to cut people off from old patterns, but it is what helps the growth and well-being of all the people involved, the addict perhaps most of all. When Theo stopped enabling members of his extended family with financial support, they went out and got more satisfying jobs, and seem to be doing much better now financially than when they were being more enabled.

Epigenetics : The study of how genes are affected by the environment— relationships, diet, toxins, rest. Theo's early childhood environment at home was not one of secure attachment. When his brain was laying down new DNA in early childhood development, the un-soothed stressors in his life would likely have resulted in chemical changes to his DNA affecting his long-term ability to handle stressors throughout his life.

Emotional Safety : A state in which a person feels emotionally safe from harm, whether from judgement, abuse, manipulation, or threat. Kim and Theo's healing conversations provide emotional safety for Theo to examine his emotional trauma experiences and rewire his brain in more positive ways.

Empowerment : In connection with these conversations, empowerment is the provision of greater emotional power. Healthy relationships, career success, and new dietary strategies are examples of empowering situations. In Theo's case, his decision to become healthier empowered his resolve to never abuse drugs and alcohol again.

Ephebophile : A person who sexually favours adolescents, specifically. Graham James seems to be an example of an ephebophile.

Expert : An expert can be a specialist in their field, or someone who has failed in thousands of ways and learned from it. Dr. Daniel Siegel is an expert in attachment theory, and Theo Fleury is quickly becoming an expert in helping others to heal from relationship trauma.

Fetal Alcohol Spectrum Disorder (FASD) : People who are diagnosed as having FASD were prenatally exposed to alcohol by their mom drinking during pregnancy. It can affect a child's memory, ability to learn, motor coordination, physical health, behaviour, and mental health. Prenatal exposure to alcohol has been shown to increase the prevalence of alcohol abuse later in life. Theo wasn't diagnosed with FASD himself, but many people are. It's a significant health challenge across Canada and is entirely preventable.

Fight or Flight Response : Part of the body's ability to respond to stress. The involuntary nervous system (also known as the autonomic nervous system) initially responds to what it perceives as threat in one of two ways: through either "fight" or "flight." Fight means we'll take immediate action to do what we can to combat the threat, and flight means we'll do whatever we can to get out of the situation immediately. If a threat is so intense that neither of these responses kick in, then the body resorts to a third "freeze" response. Also see *Freeze Response*.

Theo has lived much of his life experiencing high levels of stress and hypervigilance, so he would have a relatively highly activated fight or flight response. This may have helped him to function with intensity as a hockey player, but this also resulted in a state of chronic anxiety, which is not healthy for anyone.

Flashbacks : A traumatic event from your past that feels like it's actually happening in the present. Most flashbacks happen unexpectedly. They are personal experiences that pop into your awareness without any conscious attempt to search for them. Combat veterans often experience them when they hear explosions or sirens, or even when they watch war scenes on TV. For Theo, one way he prevents having flashbacks of his abuse today is by never sleeping in a completely dark room.

Forgiveness : Often misunderstood as accepting another's bad, hurtful, or even abhorrent behaviour, real forgiveness is a conscious process involving a decision that someone makes with their whole self after doing their own emotional work. It neither accepts nor excuses the other person's behaviour. Forgiveness of oneself is often harder work than forgiving someone else. Kim found that she could not forgive her boyfriend who dumped her on Christmas Day until she had allowed herself to experience the various emotional states connected with the trauma. Once she connected with her anger over the situation, she was able to forgive.

Forum : "Conversation With a Rattlesnake" Forums are day-long events hosted by Theo and Kim to promote healthy conversations about trauma and healing. To date, the local agencies that have helped organize these Forums include Footholds Therapy Center in Nanaimo, the Aulneau Renewal Centre in Winnipeg, and New Path Foundation in Barrie, Ontario. The title of "Forum" may be a nod to the old hockey shrine in Montreal where the fans were so highly engaged, but in this context the term really just describes a place for people to get together to learn, share, and collectively support one another.

Freeze Response : The third stress response that the human body adopts when the involuntary nervous system faces extreme threat. The more common responses are fight or flight. Freezing was Theo's response when he was sexually abused by Graham James. See *Fight or Flight Response*. When you are absolutely terrified, your body may freeze with immobilization; it is the last resort in the body's defense mechanisms when dealing with significant threat.

Genes : The template of information that is passed down in our DNA from one generation to the next. Genetics doesn't set your future in stone, because the environment around you matters a great deal, but it is of great importance. Of interest, Theo's genetics suggests he inherited some qualities of being a great hockey player from his dad.

Gleaming and Beaming : This is a term Kim first heard from psychologist Anita Remig to describe the positive emotional growth and connection that occurs between a parent and a baby. Gleaming and beaming is the dance of attunement visible in the form of smiles and non-verbal communication. This kind of caring attachment releases the love chemicals of oxytocin, dopamine, and endorphins helping the baby to feel loved and secure. In his childhood, Theo would not have experienced as much gleaming and beaming as a result of his mom's chronic depression and his dad's alcoholism. This relative lack of early connection would have contributed to his patterns of insecure attachment that were often evident in his future intimate relationships.

God of My Understanding, The : This is a term that permits someone to define for himself his own concept and relationship with whatever form of higher power he chooses. It is common for people struggling with spirituality to feel alone, and if none of the established religions are already working for them, defining their own God can help. Theo heard about this concept from Alcoholics Anonymous, and before that his models of God had come from his perceptions of his mom's Jehovah's Witness God of the apocalypse and his dad's Roman Catholic God who punishes sinners. Theo now has a strong connection with the God of his own understanding, and is feeling more regulated and connected as a result.

God Shot : An Alcoholics Anonymous term for a powerful aha moment that has a spiritual slant. Something that you can't explain, but it feels like it makes perfect sense. Theo says it was like a God shot when he walked into the room in Winnipeg and met Kim Barthel, as if he knew something was happening that was supposed to be happening. Kim describes a God shot as a moment of "grace" when everything is aligned and a new clarity, if only for a brief moment, is recognized.

Guilt : The feeling of responsibility for an action or behaviour that feels morally wrong or of which one is not proud. Guilt can be helpful as a motivator for change. It is unknown if, after years of self-reflection, Graham James feels guilty for having sexually abused a number of teenage boys. No one may ever know. But while feeling guilty is about feeling bad about a behaviour, it's different from feeling shame, which is about feeling bad as a person. Also see *Shame*.

Healing : Becoming in alignment with what is; it is not curing. Theo's healing from sexual abuse has had nothing to do with the justice system eventually putting Graham James behind bars. And it is not directly a result of his ability to stay away from alcohol and drugs. It has to do with Theo's self-awareness and understanding that what happened was not his fault, plus his commitment to helping others get to where they need to be.

Holding Space : Holding the space for others allows them to feel emotionally safe while they are dealing with something emotional, for as long as is needed. No rushing in to save them, no judgement of any kind, just allowing them to focus on their healing in our presence. When Kim and Theo and the rest of the audience at one of the "Conversations with a Rattlesnake" Forum consciously held the space for the man who had been abused as a child and later became involved in gangs and even became a gang leader, everyone felt connected and experienced healing at some level.

Implicit Memory : Implicit memory is available in our brains right from birth, and probably even before birth. It's the emotional memory for all of our experiences and it is encoded vastly throughout our brain, influencing much of how we think, act, and respond to other's actions. Although we remember these feelings, we can't recall the details. Theo's implicit memories from early childhood include feeling alone and unlovable; these memories continue to get triggered today.

Insight : A new awareness, perception, realization, or understanding that comes suddenly when we see a situation past or present in a new light. Insights can have a markedly new influence on our regular way of engaging with others. Through self-reflection, Theo is developing greater insight every day into why he feels and acts the way that he does.

Immune System : The body's complex and automatic mechanism for ensuring our survival from viruses, bacteria, parasites, and damage that can cause infections and diseases. The system comprises specific organs and cells, and the substances they create. Science is demonstrating through research that children who experience chronic stress and insecure attachment often have vulnerable immune systems. This state can lead to the child developing autoimmune diseases later in life. Theo believes his Crohn's disease may be due to his chronic stress, from both early childhood development trauma and his sexual abuse trauma and subsequent life traumas. It's being increasingly proven that our immune systems can become healthier by thinking positively, having healthy relationships, eating healthier, exercising, helping other people, and even by giving hugs.

Making Amends : In the Twelve Steps of Alcoholics Anonymous, Steps Eight and Nine relate to making amends. Step Eight requires a person who wants to heal themselves to make a list of all the people they feel they have wronged during their whole life. AA then suggests sorting the list into three types of relationships—safe ones that they can approach directly; ones in which they must use more caution; and ones that they should leave as is, for fear of causing more trauma. Step Nine has the person making amends with people in the first two types of relationship. Making amends is different from simply apologizing, because aside from saying sorry it's also about restoring some level of justice to the situation—such as by paying back money that was borrowed a long time ago. A "living amends" is an even more meaningful concept that is encouraged, which involves the demonstration, day in and day out, of living with more integrity. It's an evolved state of apology as it shows a genuine change in behaviour patterns day by day. It requires constant attention and reflection on how a relationship plays out in the future. Theo is focussing on making consistent living amends with his children, and it's a meaningful part of his life.

Meditation : An internal effort to self-regulate the mind through training and practice with the intent to relax, focus attention, develop compassion and loving kindness, and/or improve your mental health. This is achieved by concentrating on breathing, repeating a mantra, or by being led through a shared visualization exercise. Theo says that he would never be able to meditate in a traditional sense because he has what he calls "squirrel brain." Kim suggests that golf provides Theo with a form of meditation that suits him, and also describes some relatively simple forms of meditation that anyone can try, such as the Sanskrit "sa ta na ma" finger mantra exercise and the *Journey to Wild Divine* video game.

Mental Illness : A wide range of disordered mental and behavioural patterns that result in suffering, impeding a person's ability to function and participate in daily life. Kim and Theo talk about many forms of mental illness, including depression, addiction, anxiety, sociopathy, pedophilia, and psychopathology.

Mindfulness : An intentional accepting and nonjudgmental focus on your thoughts, emotions, and body sensations in the present moment. Being mindful helps a person to stay present in a stressful or triggering moment. It takes a high level of self-awareness and awareness of others to avoid reacting in a hurtful or non-productive manner. Theo is mindful when he's being interviewed by the media, because in the past he's sometimes been asked questions designed to get him to react with emotion. Encouragingly, at the same time as Theo is becoming more mindful and capable of self-regulation, many people who work in media are also becoming more trauma-informed and therefore more respectful.

Mirror Neurons : Mirror neurons are nerve cells in the brain that fire both when we act and when we observe the same actions performed by another. These neurons "mirror" the behaviour of others, and we feel those behaviours as if we were doing them ourselves. In a baby, mirror neurons enable the baby's sharing of their parent's emotions such as happiness and sadness. Current research says that these neurons help us to empathize with each other. Kim and Theo got into a spell of yawning through a discussion on the topic of the benefits of yawning and the involvement of mirror neurons in spreading yawns from one person to the next. Understanding mirror neurons reminds us of how much we are all influencing one another all the time.

Montreal Canadiens : The most successful hockey team in the history of the NHL. Theo was part of the 1989 Calgary Flames team that managed to beat the Montreal Canadiens for the Stanley Cup.

Neglect : A failure to do something or to give full care, attention, or time to someone. Neglecting a child can lead to that child developing poorly physically, emotionally, and mentally. Kim suggests that when a parent is emotionally or physically unavailable, their child can feel abandoned, rejected, and unlovable. Theo recognizes that his feelings of abandonment, rejection, and being unlovable are his core emotional issues, underlying much of his later trauma and addictions.

Neurobiology : As a branch of biology, neurobiology is the scientific study of the anatomy, physiology, pathology, and biochemistry of the human nervous system. Basically, it's the study of the brain. Kim has thirty years of experience integrating occupational therapy with the science of neurobiology to help people understand why we do what we do. As a teacher of therapists, Kim presents worldwide on the subject of neurobiology and how it affects behaviour. She believes that an understanding of the brain helps therapists, teachers, social workers, parents, and all caregivers to have a more compassionate understanding of the people they support, each other, and themselves.

Out of interest, at the time of the printing of this book, Kim and Theo are preparing to travel to co-present their healing conversation model used in their "Conversations with a Rattlesnake" Forums at the International Association for Group Psychotherapy Conference at London University in the UK in late August 2014.

Nonverbal Communication : Also known as body language, nonverbal communication is considered to supply more than 65 percent of human messaging in interpersonal communication. Included in nonverbals are facial expressions, arm gestures, body positions, and movements. When Theo and Kim discussed an unpleasant memory of the side effects Theo experienced from a prescribed drug clonazepam, Kim noticed that his body was curling up into a ball as a sign of distress. In that instance, by tracking Theo's nonverbal communication, Kim knew Theo needed some help regulating himself while he was talking about a distressing event. Through attuned interaction, Theo was able to share his emotional pain around the situation and begin to feel a sense of relief.

Oxytocin : A hormone that is known as the chemical of love. We all get hits of oxytocin every time we hug someone, think about a specific person whom we love, when we volunteer, and even when we yawn. Oxytocin is a significant stress reliever. Babies and parents receive oxytocin when they are gleaming and beaming, which helps develop the feelings of secure attachment between them.

Pedophile : Someone who is sexually attracted to children who have not entered puberty. Pedophilia is technically identified as a mental illness. Some pedophiles have pedophilia combined with being a sociopath or a psychopath. Not all pedophiles abuse children, as the description defines the urges, not the actions. Of people who do sexually abuse children, some are true pedophiles (only attracted to children) and some are "non-exclusive" pedophiles who can also be attracted to adults. There is evidence that a significant percentage of child molesters of all types are people who were sexually abused themselves as children.

Post-Traumatic Growth : The emotional growth and self-awareness that can occur after any emotional trauma, including such events as childhood neglect, sexual abuse, and experiences like war, fire, and natural disaster. Theo continues his own post-traumatic growth by defining himself as a victor rather than a victim. Currently, both he and Kim actively advocate for those who have survived trauma and are doing what they can to help these people get the information and support they need.

Post–Traumatic Stress Disorder (PTSD) : A collection of problematic behaviours that develops after experiencing emotional trauma—such events as childhood neglect, sexual abuse, and traumatic experiences like war, fire, and natural disaster—is sometimes diagnosed as Post-Traumatic Stress Disorder. Whereas everyone requires a recovery period from any type of trauma, if the event feels life-threatening, its accompanying stress goes on for far longer than is normal, and the ongoing symptoms are complex. Those who experience childhood sexual abuse, for example, sometimes exhibit signs of PTSD, such as dissociating or checking out from events and discussions, being excessively fearful, emotionally numb, and occasionally showing hostile and aggressive behaviour. When Theo describes his difficulties with sleeping because he was abused in a dark room, this is an example of a PTSD symptom.

Projecting : This psychological theory states that humans defend against the stumbling blocks in their own behaviour by denying their existence in themselves and attributing the behaviour to those around them. Theo says that when he gets triggered by another person's questions or actions, he used to react by projecting his own issues on to the other person. This tendency didn't help any of his early adult romantic relationships. Today, he is more mindful and self-reflective of his projections, which has improved the quality of his interactions and is helping his relationships be less unnecessarily dramatic. What helps to be mindful about our own projections is the quote by Anaïs Nin: "We don't see things as they are, we see things as we are."

Quantum Physics : Quantum physics says that all life and matter and the space between them exist as energy in a single system called the quantum field, and that our thoughts influence and affect this quantum field such that it yields different results in response to our thoughts. Kim and Theo talk about how everything we do, think, and feel affects everything else around us. Quantum physics explores and begins to explain how we are all connected to everything in the universe. Some people would say that this thought alone helps make us all be a little nicer to one another.

Relationship : An association or connection between anything. Generally refers to the bonds between people: whether the people are connected through blood ties, friendship, business, community, or romantic liaisons. The relationships that are of greatest importance in the healing conversations between Theo and Kim are three-fold: between individuals (the kind we are used to hearing about), between a person and themselves (in this case mostly Theo's sense of self), and between individuals and the Gods of their Understanding. In discussing Theo's relationships with other people, over the past years he has been increasingly surrounding himself with people he can trust and enjoy so that he can build strong relationships supported by healthy boundaries.

The relationship that Theo and Kim share between them is admittedly not your average one; theirs is an example of a healthy friendship that came together out of their common goal to support others. Their conversations are just naturally therapeutic given their experiences around trauma and healing, and shared passion in promoting emotional well-being.

Relentless Positivity : This is a mindset of consistent positive regard for another person that does not ask for anything in return. It has no ulterior motive other than to hold the space and to provide unconditional love so that the receiver of the relentless positivity may see him- or herself in a new and positive light. Over the course of their two years of conversing with one another, Kim's relentless positivity toward Theo has allowed him to begin to see his real self and to reduce the prevalence of his negative self-talk. As a comparison, the opposite of relentless positivity would be consistent verbal and emotional abuse. There is a world of difference between the two.

Repair : Reconnecting after there's been a disruption in closeness. It may be in the form of an apology, a forgiveness, or something else, but whatever form repair takes, it's about restoring a bond. It only happens when both people want it, but Kim says it's never too late for repair.

Reveal : To reveal something is to make something known, to bring it into view, such as disclosing a secret for the first time ever, or for the first time in a particular setting. When Theo wrote *Playing With Fire* with Kirstie McLellan Day in 2009, his book became a very public reveal of the very private circumstances around having been sexually abused by his former Junior hockey coach, Graham James.

Script : Having a prepared set of words in your mind that you can recall from memory quickly when faced with an emotionally challenging situation. Kim commonly uses her script of "This is hard for me" when she can't think of what else to say in the moment. It helps her regulate her own state of distress, buys her some time to think, and invites the person she's talking with to reflect a little bit themselves. We can all use scripts for many different kinds of potentially sensitive moments, as tools that can make our lives a little less stressful.

Secure Attachment Figure : Parents usually fill the role of secure attachment figures in a person's life. When Theo watched the videotapes of babies and their different kinds of parents, he was able to recognize that he did not experience the gleaming and beaming of a secure attachment. For people who do not have secure attachment experiences as children, they can still develop this later on with other people in their lives. Whether they are family, friends, relatives, teachers, therapists, coaches—anyone trusted, caring, and consistent can become a secure attachment figure. When a relationship is unsafe or unpredictable, insecure attachment will occur.

Self-Abuse : Inappropriate behaviour toward oneself to express emotional pain. The behaviour includes self-mutilation, bulimia, anorexia, and addictions to drugs and alcohol. It can range from subtle but consistent negative self-talk to the final act of self-abuse, which is suicide. Theo was often self-abusive both in his thoughts about himself and in his addictive self-destructive behaviours.

Self-Awareness : The ability of a human to be aware of how she feels and how she acts within the context of her environment. Getting to know yourself is a lifelong process. The counsellor who had Theo speak to his anger as though it were a separate entity allowed him to become far more self-aware about the reasons why he would become so angry. As one upside, increasing our self-awareness helps every one of us to be on guard for things that could trigger us, thereby reducing the odds that we might someday lash out unnecessarily against someone we care about.

Self-Medication : The process of taking alcohol, unprescribed medications, recreational drugs, or other harmful substances to deal with the symptoms of stress and emotional pain. It can also extend to taking prescription drugs in higher doses than have been prescribed or taking dangerous substances in any number of combinations. When Theo was at rock bottom in his addictions, as an attempt to cope with his shame and emotional pain, he was self-medicating to excessive amounts with vodka and cocaine. As the millions of people who attend self-help groups and their friends and families know, self-medication is a form of self-abuse and it does not solve anyone's long-term issues.

Self-Reflection : A personal method of throwing light on one's behaviour in order to examine it for personal growth. Self-reflection is a process that contributes to self-awareness and self-understanding. It becomes a method of integrating one's inside feelings with one's outside actions and communication. Kim finds that driving on long highways is a useful time for self-reflection where she can think about how and why she might have responded in a particular interaction, and what would be her most appropriate course of action next time. Only a small percent of us are capable of self-reflecting in the middle of our conversations, but it is helpful for all kinds of relationships when this skill can be developed and practised.

Self-Regulation : The ability to increase one's level of stimulation or calm oneself down in response to the demands of any situation. If we want to be able to function, we don't want to be either too high or too low, so we need to find ways to help ourselves stay calm, alert, and focused. Theo's increasing ability to self-regulate allowed him to stay present during a difficult trigger he experienced in Winnipeg when the woman from the Forum shared her sexual addiction that reminded him of his own. Theo was able to catch himself checking out and he self-regulated enough to stay connected to the interaction so there could be a more positive outcome for both of them.

Self-Soothing Behaviour : A way for people to specifically calm themselves during a stressful thought or encounter. These actions are often done unconsciously, such as by rubbing our face, crossing and recrossing our legs, clutching our hands or our genitals, picking our nose, playing with our hair, chewing a finger nail, smoking, eating, and drinking. Kim explains that the midline structures of our body are supersensitive and therefore provide more soothing than peripheral parts of our body. Theo often rubs his face when he is agitated. Kim explains the science is clear in describing that the fastest way for anyone to feel soothed is through the body, rather from listening to words.

Sexual Abuse : Sexual abuse is a form of trauma that happens when a person is forced to have sexual interaction without consent. While the term is broad in definition and is often interpreted in different ways, sexual abuse is tragically harmful on many different levels and illegal throughout the world. It's never okay. But it happens, in numbers that are hard to quantify given the instances that are not reported, but conservatively estimated at one in four people across Canada. The good news is that there is enough growing awareness of its damaging effects that hope is emerging—it's through enough healthy conversations that perhaps the cycle of sexual abuse will be stopped. As Theo knows, "We're only as sick as our secrets."

Shame : Different from guilt, shame is the intensely painful feeling we have when we believe that we are inherently flawed and therefore unworthy of love and belonging. Theo grew up unconsciously believing he was unworthy of being loved and accepted, and this belief didn't help him at all. From understanding that everything wasn't his fault, on both a scientific and deeply personal level, he was able to consciously reduce his feelings of shame. The self-awareness journey goes on, but Theo says that the release of this specific emotional weight is what's now allowing him to enjoy his life more than he ever has before. See also *Guilt*.

Shift : In hockey, it's when you go on to the ice and play your heart out for forty-five seconds, then get back on the bench. In therapy, a shift is when we have a change in consciousness from one way of being to another way of being. An example of a great shift is an awareness that stops us from feeling sorry for ourselves, and starts us taking control of our lives. Theo experienced a subtle shift recently when he realized that in just over a week, over 361,600 people on Facebook checked out a simple photo of him with a sign that said "Bring Back Common Sense." The shift was that since so many people are paying attention to his actions, even the small ones, his responsibility to speak clearly and with compassion is that much more pronounced.

Sideways Approach : A strategy that helps people come to awareness and conclusions about themselves, without being pushed for explanations they are not ready to investigate. It's like asking a nonjudgmental question that plants a seed, and then waiting. Kim often uses the sideways approach with Theo when she knows there's a hot topic for him and that direct confrontation wouldn't be helpful.

Sliding Off : A comment that minimizes or dismisses what the other person just said. It typically means what the person said was emotionally hard for the listener to hear. When Kim couldn't take in a compliment, she slid off it because she didn't truly believe it about herself yet. We can also slide off accusations when we find them uncomfortable.

Somatic Mindfulness : When you begin to connect to sensations in your body in response to what's going on around you, you are experiencing somatic mindfulness. It helps you to learn to trust the feedback from your body. When Theo catches himself rubbing his face during a conversation, he knows it's a self-soothing behaviour so he can check in and ask himself where the stress might be coming from in that moment.

Spirituality : An attempt to seek meaning, purpose, and direction for one's life in relation to a higher power. Theo believes it's often the piece that is missing when we are trying to heal from addiction and trauma. Kim says a big part of it is finding a way to feel connected with everything around us.

Stress Response : How stressed the body gets from a particular event or feeling. We all experience stress responses all day long, to varying degrees. A combat vet with PTSD can still have flashbacks and feel huge stress responses in his body years later, even from minor events that aren't really threatening. It is the "perceived" threat that registers in the brain and produces the chemical stress response. Theo lived through intense anxiety for a long time after his trauma events, and it still takes a lot of self-awareness to regulate those anxious moments.

Survivor : A person who's lived through trauma and has internalized that it wasn't her fault. Theo doesn't ever call himself a victim, because that would suggest he's feeling sorry for himself and that he's still stuck in that debilitating belief. Referring to himself as a survivor honours the emotional work he's done to move forward, and empowers him to keep moving forward.

Sweat Lodge : Used in many First Nations healing practices, a sweat lodge is a place (a dome-shaped structure about the size of a big round tent with a low ceiling) and a process, where healing takes place. It is heated by rocks brought inside from a fire just outside, and represents cleansing and spiritual connection; it is where personal stories may be shared in emotional safety. For Theo, the sweat lodge is a spiritual practice that is very helpful.

Subconscious Mind : The subconscious is the storage room of everything that is not in your conscious mind, including thoughts that are yours without you knowing about them. The subconscious highly influences your current behaviour. As soon as we bring our subconscious thoughts to consciousness, they have less influence on us. Subconsciously, Theo used to believe that everyone was out to screw him. Knowing that he used to think that way, with awareness, overtly distrusting people is not as much of an issue for him.

Team : Working toward a common goal with other people who have your back exemplifies being part of a team. This is the most important concept for Theo, in sports and in life.

Telomeres : Often referred to as "shoelace tips" on the end of the DNA strands to protect the DNA from fraying down over time and degenerating. Chronic, unremitting stress is known to damage telomeres resulting in premature aging and disease. Science has shown that helping and compassion help to grow these shoelace tips back, counteracting the damaging forces of stress. Kim and Theo believe that helping is healing and research is helping to prove it.

Therapy : A process or treatment designed to bring about physical, mental, or emotional healing either in oneself or in another person. The healing conversations that Kim and Theo have together are therapeutic for both of them, but they are not considered therapy in the traditional sense as there is no formal client/therapist relationship involved. The "Conversations With a Rattlesnake" Forums that Kim and Theo co-host are definitely therapeutic for those who attend, but again, they are not a replacement for formal therapy, which is specifically designed to help a person with a specific matter.

Transgenerational Trauma : Trauma that is passed on from generation to generation through the attachment interaction styles of those involved. First Nations families whose beliefs and heritage were undermined by the residential school system in Canada are an example of peoples who suffer transgenerational trauma; as did the Jewish descendants of survivors of the Holocaust; as did the descendants of the Africans who were brought to America as slaves.

Trigger : A trigger is anything from a word to an action, from a smell to an image, from the name of a city to a face of a person in the crowd who just looks like someone who did something bad to you. It is anything that launches a person who has suffered some form of trauma back into a defensive style of self-protection and/or reaction. The switch happens so quickly that the participant(s) often do not realize what has happened. Moving beyond such reactivity requires a person to be mindful and to behave with dual awareness, recognizing that they have been triggered back into the emotions that accompany their trauma while also observing their emotions. Such awareness rewires the brain positively along new neural pathways. Theo recognizes many of his triggers, particularly those around rejection and abandonment, and the more he recognizes them, the easier they are to deal with.

Trauma : Trauma is a physical, emotional, or mental shock or injury to a person. The resulting wound may or may not be visible, but its repercussions might be long-lasting. Sexual abuse is a type of trauma that can leave scars of shame, anger, sadness, revulsion, and confusion. Because sexual abuse is still something of a taboo topic, the secretiveness adds another layer of wounding to the event. Theo and Kim's "Conversations With a Rattlesnake" Forums are expanding the platform for discussing all forms of trauma. Their aim is to bring the topic into a more everyday exchange of information and ideas to ultimately help people on their paths to regain whatever health and happiness they are looking for.

Victim : A person who has been hurt by another person or situation, and hasn't yet been able to see their experience any other way.

Theo felt like a victim for years, and it didn't help him either to label himself in that way or keep his pain bottled up. If you have been sexually abused, Theo recommends you reframe your story, so that you can see yourself as a survivor, because you are. The idea of being a survivor provides a much better platform from which to heal.

Victor Walk : In May 2013, Theo Fleury and six others decided to walk the 450 kilometres from the child sexual abuse statue in Toronto to the Parliament Buildings in Ottawa to raise awareness of the widespread nature of childhood trauma and the damage it causes. It took the seven people ten days to reach Canada's Parliament Buildings, and on the day they arrived, twelve hundred people stood with them, either saying, "Me, too," or supporting someone who was saying, "Me, too." Each person claimed himself and herself to be a victor for participating. Across Canada, another twenty-two Victor Walks took place in various communities, involving many hundreds more people.

Organized by the new Breaking Free Foundation—which Theo and Kim as well as others are involved in—the next Victor Walk is slated to happen in 2015, with the principal walk being from Edmonton to Calgary. For information leading up the next event, see www.victorwalk.com.

Vulnerability : The ability to be vulnerable suggests a willingness to be open to what is happening in the moment. Theo was very vulnerable in the conversation about his experience of sexual abuse.

Recommended Resources

Examples of Resilience for People Who Are in Pain

A House in the Sky is a memoir book by Amanda Lindhout about surviving abduction in Somalia and her subsequent efforts at finding compassion for her own well-being.

Daring Greatly: How the Courage to Be Vulnerable Transforms the Way We Live, Love, Parent and Lead is a book by Dr. Brené Brown inspiring others to dare to be vulnerable in order to grow and heal.

Mindful Recovery: A Spiritual Path to Healing from Addiction is a book by Thomas Bien, PhD and Beverly Bien, MEd.

My Name is Shield Woman: A hard road to healing, vision, and leadership is a book by Ruth Scalp Lock (Theo's Grandma Ruth) about her spiritual awakening.

Thanks for Sharing is a movie written by Stuart Blumberg and Matt Winston about sex addiction.

For Those Helping Others

The Conscious Parent: Transforming Ourselves, Empowering Our Children is a book by Shefali Tsabary, PhD that helps parents become attuned to their children through their own self-awareness.

The Five Keys to Mindful Communication: Using Deep Listening and Mindful Speech to Strengthen Relationships, Heal Conflicts, and Accomplish Your Goals is a book by Susan Gillis Chapman explaining skills that will strengthen relationships.

Healing Developmental Trauma: How Early Trauma Affects Self-Regulation, Self-Image, and the Capacity for Relationship by Laurence Heller PhD and Aline LaPierre PsyD describes how early trauma affects self-regulation, self-image, and the capacity for relationship.

How God Changes the Brain: Breakthrough Findings from a Leading Neuroscientist is a book by Dr. Andrew Newberg, MD and Mark Robert Waldman explaining how spirituality affects our brains.

Words Can Change Your Brain: 12 Conversation Strategies to Build Trust, Resolve Conflict, and Increase Intimacy is a book by Dr. Andrew Newberg, MD and Mark Robert Waldman describing the impact of our words and thoughts on our well-being.

For Insight Into Research on the Brain

William Arntz, Betsy Chasse, and Mark Vicente's movie *What the Bleep do we Know!?* describes the brain and some of the emerging science that explains and theorizes how we're all interconnected.

Norman Doidge, MD is one of the leading authorities on neuroplasticity and cutting-edge developments in neuroscience. He wrote *The Brain that Changes Itself: Stories of Personal Triumph From the Frontiers of Brain Science*.

Rick Hanson, PhD is the author of *Hardwiring Happiness: the New Brain Science of Contentment, Calm and Confidence* and *Buddha's Brain: The Practical Neuroscience of Happiness, Love, and Wisdom*

Nicole Letourneau, RN, PhD is a Canadian leader in research and education on parent-infant mental health. She's authored *Scientific Parenting: What Science Reveals About Parental Influence*.

Stephen Porges, PhD is the developer of Polyvagal Theory, which helps us to understand our autonomic nervous system. He is a Director of the Brain-Body Center in the College of Medicine at the University of Illinois at Chicago.

Dan Siegel, MD is one of the pioneers in bringing brain science into clinical practice. He has authored *The Mindful Therapist* and other books.

For Advocacy and Support in Connection With Childhood Sexual Abuse

www.littlewarriors.ca is a website that is about helping protect children from sexual abuse.

www.victorwalk.com is a website that promotes advocacy and healing from trauma.

www.1in6.ca is a website providing Canadian information about male sexual trauma and recovery.

www.sacqd.com is a website providing confidential, non-judgemental support for survivors of sexual abuse (Sexual Assault Centre for Quinte and District in Ontario).

www.themensproject.ca is a website dedicated to helping male survivors and their families build better lives.

Theo's Personal Favourites

Return to Food is a book-in-progress by food philosopher Sherry Strong. Theo and Kim are both working to improve their relationships with the foods they choose to eat, and Sherry's information and insights into everything to do with food are so basic that they are revolutionary.

Fat, Sick & Nearly Dead is a documentary movie by Joe Cross about juicing to regain health.

Good Will Hunting is a movie written by Matt Damon and Ben Affleck, features neglect, abuse, and the importance of therapeutic relationship.

Playing With Fire: The Highest Highs and Lowest Lows of Theo Fleury is a book by Theo Fleury and Kirsty McLellan Day. This was Theo's first book.

Sleepers is a movie by Barry Levinson. This is the first movie Theo saw about institutional abuse and the amount of pain that it causes.

The Big Book aka *Alcoholics Anonymous: The Story of How Many Thousands of Men and Women Have Recovered from Alcoholism* is a book that helped Theo significantly with his recovery from alcoholism.

The Outliers: The Story of Success is a book by Malcolm Gladwell about intelligence and ambition in which he includes the concept that ten thousand hours of doing anything will make you a master at it.

The Power of Now is a book by Eckhart Tolle about the importance of living in the present moment.

Kim's Personal Favourites

Fifty Shades of Grey by E. L. James is a book illustrating how early childhood trauma can impact the potential for healthy loving relationships.

The Girl with the Dragon Tattoo Series are books and movies that show how a person can come through devastating trauma and abuse with such amazing resilience.

Lie to Me is a crime drama television series about the science and understanding of what nonverbal communication says.

Louder Than Words is a book by Joe Navarro and Toni Sciarra Poynter that reveals the hidden power of nonverbal intelligence.

Saving Grace is a television series created by Nancy Miller. Following sexual abuse and addiction, Grace Hanadarko reluctantly accepts a non-traditional spiritual path.

Scattered Minds and *In the Realm of Hungry Ghosts* are two books by Dr. Gabor Maté that woke Kim up to how early infant relationships leave a legacy in brain development, addiction, and relationships.

Stress, Portrait of a Killer is a *National Geographic* documentary by Robert M. Sapolsky, PhD, which shows how stress affects our health, and how healthy relationships restore our physical health.

Suits is a television series created by Aaron Korsh displaying high intelligence, and the balance between integrity and manipulation.

Bibliography

Books

Brown, Dr. Brené. *Daring Greatly: How the Courage to Be Vulnerable Transforms the Way We Live, Love, Parent, and Lead*. Penguin Group, 2012.

Chapman, Susan Gillis. *The Five Keys to Mindful Communication*. Shambhala, 2012.

Crittenden, Patricia and Andrea Landini. *Assessing Adult Attachment: A Dynamic-Maturational Approach to Discourse Analysis*. W. W. Norton & Company, 2011.

Dispenza, Dr. Joe. *You Are the Placebo: Making Your Mind Matter*. Hay House, 2014.

Dispenza, Joseph. *God on Your Own: Finding a Spiritual Path Outside Religion*. San Francisco, Jossey-Bass, a Wiley Imprint, 2006

Doidge, Dr. Norman. *The Brain That Changes Itself: Stories of Personal Triumph From the Frontiers of Brain Science*. Penguin Books, 2007.

Ekman, Paul and Erika L. Rosenberg, Editors. *What the Face Reveals: Basic and Applied Studies of Spontaneous Expression Using the Facial Action Coding System (FACS)*.Oxford University Press, 1997.

Fleury, Theo with Kirstie McLellan Day. *Playing With Fire: The Highest Highs And Lowest Lows Of Theo Fleury*. Toronto: HarperCollins Publishers Ltd., 2009.

Fogel, Alan. *The Psychophysiology of Self-Awareness: Rediscovering the Lost Art of Body Sense*. W. W. Norton & Company, New York, 2009.

Gladwell, Malcolm. *Outliers: The Story of Success*. Little, Brown and Company, 2008.

Graham, Linda. Bouncing Back: *Rewiring Your Brain for Maximum Resilience and Well-Being*. Novato, CA, New World Library, 2013.

Grand, David PhD. *Brainspotting: The Revolutionary New Therapy for Rapid and Effective Change*. Sounds True, 2013.

Hanson, Rick. *Hardwiring Happiness: The New Brain Science of Contentment, Calm, and Confidence*. Harmony Books, 2013.

Hebb, Dr. Donald. *The Organization of Behaviour*. New York, Wiley & Sons, 1949.

Heller, Laurence PhD and Aline LaPierre PsyD. *Healing Developmental Trauma: How Early Trauma Affects Self-Regulation, Self-Image, and the Capacity for Relationship*. Berkeley: North Atlantic Books, 2009.

James, E.L. *Fifty Shades of Grey*. Vintage Books, a Division of Random House, 2011.

Kabat-Zinn Jon and Richard J. Davidson, Editors. *The Mind's Own Physician: A Scientific Dialogue with the Dalai Lama on the Healing Power of Meditation*. New Harbinger Publications, 2013.

Knapp, M.L., J.A. Hall, and T.G. Horgan. *Nonverbal Communication in Human Interaction*. Wadsworth Publishing, 2013, 8th Edition.

Letourneau, Dr. Nicole. *Scientific Parenting: What Science Reveals About Parental Influence*. Dundurn, 2013.

Lindhout, Amanda and Sara Corbett, *A House in the Sky*, Scribner, 2013.

Maté, Gabor. *In the Realm of Hungry Ghosts: Close Encounters with Addiction*. North Atlantic Books, 2010.

Maté, Gabor. *When the Body Says No: The Cost of Hidden Stress*. Random House, 2004.

Navarro, Joe and Toni Sciarra Poynter. *Louder Than Words: Take Your Career from Average to Exceptional with the Hidden Power of Nonverbal Intelligence*. Harper Collins, 2010.

Neff, Kristen, PhD. Self-Compassion: *Stop Beating Yourself Up and Leave Insecurity Behind*. HarperCollins Publishers Ltd, 2011.

Newberg, Andrew, MD and Mark Robert Waldman. *How God Changes Your Brain: Breakthrough Findings from a Leading Neuroscientist*. Ballantine Books, 2009.

Schore, Allan N. *Affect Dysregulation and Disorders of the Self*. New York, NY, W. W. Norton & Company, 2003.

Rogers, Carol, *On Becoming a Person: A Therapist's View of Psychotherapy*, Mariner Books, 1995.

Ruiz, Don Miguel and Janet Mills. *The Four Agreements: A Practical Guide to Personal Freedom*. A Toltec Wisdom Book, Amber-Allen Publishing, 2011.

Ruiz, Jose Jose and Tami Hudman. *My Good Friend the Rattlesnake: Stories of Loss, Truth, and Transformation*. Plain Sight Publisher, 2014.

Sapolsky, Robert M. *Why Zebras Don't Get Ulcers: The Acclaimed Guide to Stress, Stress-Related Diseases and Coping*. Holt Paperbacks, McMillan, CA, 2004.

Shakespeare, William. *Hamlet*, Act 1, Scene 5.

Siegel, Dr. Daniel. *Mindsight: The New Science of Personal Transformation.* Random House, 2010.

Siegel, Dr. Daniel. *The Mindful Therapist.* W. W. Norton & Company, 2010.

Articles In Print and Online

Ashton, Professor Heather. "Benzodiazepines: How they work and how they withdraw." www.benzo.org.uk. 2002.

Baraz, James and Shoshana Alexander. "The Helper's High." *Greater Good: The Science of a Meaningful Life.* 2010 greatergood.berkeley.edu/article/item/the_helpers_high.

Baumgartner, Jennifer J., PsyD. "This is Your Brain on Christmas: The Psychology of Altruism." www.psychologytoday.com/blog/the-psychology-dress/201112/is-your-brain-christmas-the-psychology-altruism.

Carey, Benedict. "Too Much Stress May Give Genes Gray Hair." www.nytimes.com/2004-11-30-health.

Champagne, Frances A., Pablo Chretien, Carl W. Stevenson, Tie Yuan Zhang, Alain Gratton, and Michael J. Meaney. "Variations in Nucleus Accumbens Dopamine Associated with Individual Differences in Maternal Behavior in the Rat." *The Journal of Neuroscience*, April 28, 2004, 24(17):4113–23.

Dartmouth Undergraduate Journal of Science. "Is Altruism Good for the Altruistic Giver?" dujs.dartmouth.edu/spring-2009/is-altruism-good-for-the-altruistic-giver.

Greenberg, D.M., J.M. Bradford, and S. Curry. "A Comparison of Sexual Victimization in the Childhoods of Pedophiles and Hebephiles." *Journal of Forensic Sciences*, 1993, 38 (2):432-36.

Hall, Ryan C. W., MD, and Richard C. W. Hall, MD, P.A. "A profile of pedophilia: definition, characteristics of offenders, recidivism, treatment outcomes, and forensic issues." Mayo Clinic proceedings 2007, 82 (4):457-71.

Iqbal, M.M, T. Sobhan, and T. Rylas. "Effects of Commonly Used Benzodiazepines on the Fetus, the Neonate, and the Nursing Infant." *Psychiatric Services*, January 2002, 53 (1).

Lee, Hye Jeong, Jae-Sung Ryu, Na Young Choi, Yo Seph Park, Yong Il Kim, Dong Wook Han, Kisung Ko, Chan Young Shin, Han Sung Hwang, Kyung-Sun Kang, and Kinarm Ko. "Transgenerational effects of paternal alcohol exposure in mouse offspring." *Animal Cells and Systems*, 2013, 17 (6).

Lemle, Russell B., PhD. "How Threat Emotions Cause Us To Misread Our Partner." *Psychology Today*. www.psychologytoday.com/blog/me-first-we-first/201203/ how-threat-emotions-cause-us-misread-our-partner-4

Makris, N., M. Oscar-Berman, S.K. Jaffin, S.M. Hodge, D.N. Kennedy, V.S. Caviness, and G.J. Harris. "Decreased volume of the brain reward system in alcoholism." *Biological Psychiatry*, 2008, 64(3):192-202.

Marroun, H.E., T. White, F.C. Verhulst, and H. Tiemeier. "Maternal use of antidepressant or anxiolytic medication during pregnancy and childhood neurodevelopment outcomes: a systematic review." *European Child and Adolescent Psychiatry*, May 2014:1-20.

McCraty, Rollin, PhD, Mike Atkinson, and Dana Tomasino, BA. "Modulation of DNA Conformation by Heart-Focused Intention." *The Institute of HeartMath Research Center*, Boulder, Colorado, 2003.

Ornish, D., Lin, J., Chan, J.M., et al. "Effect of comprehensive lifestyle changes on telomerase activity and telomere length in men with biopsy-proven low-risk prostate cancer: 5-year follow-up of a descriptive pilot study" *Lancet Oncology*, 2013, 14 (11):1112-20.

Post, Stephen. "It's good to be good: Science says it's so." *Health Progress*, July-August, 2009.

Salaman, Maureen. "Texting Doesn't Replace the Feel-Good Effects of Talking, Study Says." *Health Day*, consumer.healthday.com/mental-health-information-25/child-psychology-news-125/texting-doesn-t-replace-the-feel-good-effects-of-talking-study-says-672965.html.

Seamans, Jeremy K., Natalia Gorelova, Daniel Durstewitz, and Charles R. Yang. "Bidirectional Dopamine Modulation of GABAergic Inhibition in Prefrontal Cortical Pyramidal Neurons." *The Journal of Neuroscience*, May 15, 2001, 21 (10).

Sector Source. "Research About Volunteering in Canada." www.sectorsource.ca/research-and-impact/sector-research/volunteering-research.

Statistics Canada. "Caring Canadians, Involved Canadians: Tables Report." www.statcan.gc.ca/pub/89-649-x/89-649-x2011001-eng.htm.

Strathearn, L., P. Fonagy, J. Amico, and P. Read Montague. "Adult Attachment Predicts Maternal Brain and Oxytocin Response to Infant Cues." *Neuropsychopharmacology*, December 2009, 34 (13):2655-66.

Striano, Tricia, Amrisha Vaish, and Joann P. Benigno. "The Meaning of Infants' Looks: Information Seeking and Comfort Seeking?" *British Journal of Developmental Psychology*, 2006, 24:615-30.

Volkow, N.D., G.J. Wang, J.S. Fowler, J. Logan, R. Hitzemann, Y.S. Ding, N. Pappis, C. Shea, and K. Piscani. "Decreases in Dopamine Receptors but not in Dopamine Transporters in Alcoholics." *Alcoholism: Clinical & Experimental Research*. 1996, 20 (9):1594-98.

DVDs and Movies

Arntz, William, Matthew Hoffman, Betsy Chasse, and Mark Vicente. *What the Bleep do We Know!?* 2004.

Fletcher, Geoffrey S., adaptor of the 1996 novel *Push* by Sapphire. *Precious*. 2009.

HBO Canada. *Theo Fleury: Playing with Fire.* 2011.

Johnston, Conroy and Becky adaptors of *Prince of Tides*, novel by Pat Conroy. *Prince of Tides*.1991.

Sapolsky, Robert M. Stress: *Portrait of a Killer. National Geographic,* 2008.

Shadyac, Tom, Director. *Patch Adams*. Film based on *Gesundheit: Good Health is a Laughing Matter* by Adams and Maureen Mylander. 1998.

The Fifth Estate. "The Fall and Rise of Theo Fleury." Season 36, Episode 6, Oct 29, 2010.

Winston, Blumberg and Matt. *Thanks for Sharing*. 2012.

Zwick, Edward. *Love & Other Drugs*. 2010.

Biography for Theo

Theo Fleury's passion for understanding relationship trauma and healing is as outstanding as was his passion and talent when he put on a pair of skates. At every level—Stanley Cup, Olympics, World Juniors—he did everything in his power to help great teams be even better. His desire to help is very much the biggest part of his life today, only the focus is now decidedly off the ice. In 2009, his best-selling autobiography *Playing With Fire* exposed the world to the shock of his childhood trauma and the emotional pain that surrounded his every move.

Now Theo's mission has evolved. He aims to understand himself, and to translate and share his healing experiences in ways that everyone can understand. As a dynamic motivational speaker, Theo is brutally honest, vulnerable, and engaging. Although he's recently won many awards for his contributions to improving the mental health of Canadians, this work is just beginning. Theo will tell you it really is okay to be having these conversations and that, as human beings, we're all on the same team.

Biography for Kim

Kim Barthel is a one-of-a-kind, highly sought-after speaker and therapist, and solver of unique mental health mysteries. She actively teaches around the world in the fields of relational trauma, attachment theory, and sensory processing. As an occupational therapist, she blends her own brand of intuitive inquiry with cutting-edge developments in neuroscience to help people develop awareness, compassion, and healthy relationships. In Winnipeg, Kim pioneered the first private pediatric multidisciplinary therapy clinic in Western Canada. She's worked in the trenches with high-risk youth, developed mental health services for children in Canada's Arctic, and provided trauma fieldwork training in Eastern Europe, New Orleans, and the Middle East.

For Kim, this collaboration with Theo is not a traditional therapist/client relationship; it's encouraging a level of healthy conversation previously unheard of in her career.

Authors' Contact Information

For media and speaking engagement enquiries please contact:
For Theo Fleury and Kim Barthel - dawn@theofleury14.com

Website
www.ConversationsWithARattleSnake.ca
www.ConversationsWithARattleSnake.com

Twitter
#CWAR

Theo Fleury
Website: www.theofleury14.com
Twitter: @TheoFleury14
Facebook: /TheoFleury14

Kim Barthel
Website: www.kimbarthel.ca
Twitter: @laby66
Facebook: /Kimberly.Barthel1

Notes

Notes

Notes

Notes

Notes